Write or Be Written

Early modern women poets and cultural constraints

Edited by

Barbara Smith and Ursula Appelt

D0088368

Ashgate

Aldershot • Burlington USA • Singapore • Sydney

Published by
Ashgate Publishing Limited
Gower House
Croft Road
Aldershot
Hants GU11 3HR
England

Ashgate Publishing Company
131 Main Street
Burlington, Vermont 05401-5600
USA

Ashgate website: http://www.ashgate.com

British Library Cataloguing-in-Publication Data

Write or Be Written: early modern women poets and cultural constraints
(Women and gender in early modern England, 1500–1750)
1. English poetry – Early modern, 1500–1700 – History and criticism
2. English poetry – Women authors – History and criticism
3. Women in literature
I. Smith, Barbara   II. Appelt, Ursula
821'009'9287

Library of Congress Card Number: 00-48475

ISBN 1 84014 288 X

Printed on acid-free paper

Printed and bound by Athenaeum Press, Ltd.,
Gateshead, Tyne & Wear.

Contents

Acknowledgments

We should like to thank our contributors who produced manuscripts that were a joy to read, participated in stimulating conversations about the topic, and cheerfully met all deadlines. Erika Gaffney and Rachel Lynch, our editors at Ashgate, supported and nurtured the project. We are indebted to Jill Cherveney-Keough for her flexibility and expertise in formatting the volume. Finally, we wish to thank our spouses, Nick Baechle and Ira Berger for their encouragement, sacrifice, and general good nature during the many months in which our attentions were directed at the compilation of this book.

Introduction

Ursula Appelt

> Although we know we love, yet while our soule
> Is thus imprison'd by the flesh we wear,
> There's no way left that bondage to controul,
> But to convey transactions through the Ear.
> Katherine Philips, 'To my Lucasia, in
> Defense' (154)

> I am obnoxious to each carping tongue,
> Who sayes, my hand a needle better fits,
> A Poets Pen, all scorne, I should thus wrong;
> For such despight they cast on female wits:
> If what I doe prove well, it wo'nt advance,
> They'l say its stolne, or else, it was by chance.
> Anne Bradstreet, 'The Prologue' (B2v)

> Alas, a woman that attempts the pen,
> Such an intruder on the rights of men,
> Such a presumptuous creature is esteemed,
> The fault can by no virtue be redeemed.
> Anne Finch, 'The Introduction' (336)

The polemical title of this collection, 'Write or Be Written,' delimits rhetorically a spectrum of possibilities. While the imperative might have elicited affirmative responses from many women writers of the early modern period, others might have paused and considered the fact that inevitably they would be written, regardless of what they did or wrote. There can be no assurance that writing can hold at bay or stave off the attempts of others to script our identities, our selves, our lives. Moreover, the impulse to write certainly does not have to stem from a need for self-defense. For instance, Katherine Philips's image of 'transactions through the Ear' (154) figures poetry as an exchange that suspends speech while employing it; channeling words not through the mouth, the suspect organ of female speech, but through the ear, the receiving organ of speech, enables women to communicate through poetry as a form of female speech, while simultaneously acknowledging its transgressive and evasive nature. She claims, as the alliterative and syntactical link between 'controul' and 'convey' emphasizes, that women can overcome bondage through auditory exchanges. Such 'conveyances' are this book's concern.

This collection addresses the meaning of poetry in the lives of early modern women and the importance of writing as an act of cultural engagement and commentary. By dedicating a whole collection of essays to women poets, we want to emphasize the rich and varied body of poetry by women, explore the different kinds of cultural work this poetry performs, and develop our understanding of poetry by women in a period well known for both its traditional and innovative poetic forms. In particular, the essays investigate the multiple interactions between poetry and cultural constraints. We have long been aware of the formidable restrictions women faced in the early modern period; 'chaste, silent and obedient' has become an all-too familiar refrain. Women had limited access to education and employment; emerging bourgeois ideology relegated them to the domestic sphere and its attendant obligations; sexual anxieties produced prejudices that demonized female sexuality; and religion preached the inadequacy and weakness of women's intellects and souls. But the historical record quite clearly shows that oppression and patriarchy do not tell the whole story. In spite of these seemingly insurmountable obstacles, women read and wrote, ruled, worked, studied, preached, practiced professions, had affairs, displayed themselves in public, and challenged rules and norms. On the other hand, an easy and uncritical pride in their achievements would obscure historical and ideological realities. More importantly, these two polarized ways of reading early modern women writers do not allow us to ask new and different questions, to break free from the hermeneutic either/or, and become more self-aware of our own presuppositions.

Our subtitle points to the multiple connections and mutual implications between poetry *and* culture, women *and* constraint. Rather than either bewailing the reality of patriarchal oppression or lauding valiant efforts at resistance, the authors consider women poets' efforts to engage, respond to, and problematize cultural injunctions. They are interested in teasing out early modern women's relations to, and interactions with, their cultural environments, and in historicizing how we approach the meaning of social and ideological restrictions. Thus the essays in this volume register and chart some of the many ways in which women participated in their culture and its literary productions. Reading them teaches us to pay more careful attention to early modern, and twentieth-century, politics and modes of literary production.

We are at a critical juncture in our ongoing conversation with early modern women writers: while there is still much archival work that needs to be done, we can look back on a formative body of criticism. We are witnessing increased publication of women's writings and of anthologies relating to women and gender, as well as a flourishing critical debate on women, gender, sexuality, and culture. Theory and archival research should not be separated or opposed methodologically; nor should this potential conflict endanger our critical and historical projects. Margaret Ezell has warned us that interpretative assumptions and ideologies can predetermine in adverse ways which women writers we analyze, how we analyze them, and what we think they say (*Writing*). Yet compared with the attention given to other genres or forms, or to more general issues such as gender and sexuality, the attention paid to *poetry* by women has been focused primarily on a few exemplars such as Aemilia Lanyer or Aphra Behn.

The poets discussed in this volume are all highly aware of the workings of their socio-cultural context and its impact on their lives. Though many of them were not overtly political or even revolutionary, and though most of them were of privileged rank, they nevertheless explored the meanings that writing, and poetry in particular, can have for women's lives, their identities, and their stance vis à vis their culture. Writing itself was a disreputable cultural activity for women, deplored by humanists and religious leaders as leading to temptation or, worse, lasciviousness. As Anne Finch put it, 'The fault can by no virtue be redeemed' (336). The women who dared to speak (up) ran the risk of incurring not only censure, but condemnation and ridicule from men, as well as from friends and relatives (male and female alike). Various constraints determined suitable choices for subject matter and genre: religious and moral issues and child-rearing were deemed appropriate subjects for female pens. But these constraints also became thematic concerns, the object and target of women's writings. As the title of Elaine Hobby's book indicates, early modern women writers 'made a virtue of necessity' by transforming these 'proscriptions into a kind of permission' (7). It is obvious that these women's lives were circumscribed. But what did they do in response?

A central problem in dealing with women's literary production lies in assessing their education as the ground for their ability to engage with and produce literary works. Evaluating women's literacy and educational backgrounds has been one of the most challenging areas of historical research. Historical records are not always easy to come by nor are they easy to interpret.[1] In 1701, Lady Mary Chudleigh complained that women are 'Debarr'd from Knowledge, banished from the Schools, / And with the utmost Industry bred Fools' (30). While in principle humanist ideas would have allowed women an equal right to education, cultural practice lagged far behind such lofty ideals. To begin with, they were often couched in rather restrictive terms. Vives's grudging plan for educating women transforms the learning process, and hence literacy itself, into a means of indoctrination. He wanted women to avoid poetry in particular, when they were learning to write: 'And whan she shall lerne to wryte, let nat her example be voyde verses, nor wanton or trylfynge songes, but some sad sentence, prudent and chaste, taken out of holy scripture, or the sayenges of philosophers, which by often wrytyng she maye fasten better in her memory' (Trill 25). Given such copy texts, learning to write becomes a literal, almost physical, inscription of norms onto the woman's mind. Given such restrictive thinking, it is no surprise that we do not find many classically educated women.

Yet there were many women who could read and even write. In the wake of the Reformation and the further upheavals of the seventeenth century, not only humanist principles but also religious reform allowed women an entry into education, even if it was mainly to equip them to read the Bible. Protestantism demanded that its followers read and study the Bible for themselves, often with surprising results for women's literacy and literary production. Yet Protestantism also emphasized woman's essential inferiority to man and sought to control women's voices (Jones 25-27). As Chudleigh observed, society invested its 'industry' in prohibiting women's education so that it could then claim 'we are incapable of Wit, / And only for the meanest Drudgeries fit' (30).

Not only was women's education carefully monitored and a source for masculine anxiety, but writing threatened to subvert women's inferior status and circumscribed identity; it violated the injunction to be 'chaste, silent, and obedient.' A woman who writes is not silent and therefore neither chaste nor obedient. And, as Wendy Wall has extensively argued in *The Imprint of*

Gender, writing and especially publishing were gender-coded activities which had overtones of licentiousness and unruliness. Thus writing is doubly scripted against women: by writing, women undermine their identity and reputation as women and writing itself is troped in feminized and sexualized terms. Print is an already suspect realm that solidifies the worst prejudices against women. What Wall has called the 'social and sexual stigma of print' (340) forces women writers to devise and fashion new kinds of authorization and authorial identity. Poetry, albeit an elite mode, provided both the most challenging and the most innovative genre.

The poetry considered in this volume spans the sixteenth to the early eighteenth century. During this period poetry was probably the richest and most varied of genres, both formally and thematically. Poetry was both imitative and innovative. It encompassed many subgenres (for example, pastoral, elegy, satire, epigram, country house poetry, and the love lyric.) It addressed definitions of the self, the nature of God, and the politics of the state. It was both read and heard, in public and in private. It was printed and it circulated in manuscript. In other words, the range of its forms, themes, modes of production, and varieties of reception was probably wider than that of any other kind of literature.

However, the subject matter and production of poetry were also culturally regulated. That is, there were not only cultural and social constraints, but also constraints in the form of literary conventions and institutions. Thus women were forced to find ways in which they could justify their participation. One method was translation, which was considered a literary activity appropriate to women's meekness. Yet it too could be appropriated by women for their own purposes (Krontiris, Goldberg 75-131). For example, in the first stanza of 'The Prologue,' Anne Bradstreet shuns the epic as the mode most suitable to men and their abilities. The poem continues to position her poetic abilities carefully vis à vis male and classical writers. Her disclaimer echoes, for instance, Ovid in his *Amores* and Catullus in his dedicatory poem. In her reworking of classical precedents, Bradstreet transposes the hierarchy of genre onto a hierarchy of gender. In this commentary on men and writing poetry, Bradstreet ironically marshalls cultural knowledge and ideological presuppositions to craft an admission of unworthiness and lack of skill – a consummate performance of what Ann Jones (*pace* Christine Gledhill and Stuart Hall) has termed 'negotiation' (2-6).

An age that celebrated and conceptualized poetry as the fountain of culture also witnessed poetry's popularization and its invasion of the marketplace. The cultural practice of writing verse itself changed in this period, as did its cultural value. Graham Parry has described seventeenth century poetry as 'a serviceable social art' which bound and solidified social groups (10). Less elite writers begin to participate in its production, consumption, and distribution. (Broadsides and ballads are exceptional in that they were already popular forms.) In particular, 'the English Revolution was more thoroughgoing in the extension of the possession and use of words than it was in the property redistribution' and thus helped to democratize writing (Smith 6). The cultural work poetry performs makes it an at once contested and contestatory mode. The seventeenth century saw an intensified reconceptualization of the relationships between poetry and politics, reader and author, manuscript and print, authority and community (Barash 17-24). In other words, changes in politics called for changed poetic practices and aesthetics. Interpretations of women's participation in 'an ongoing process of political, generic, and ideological transformation' (23) have reshaped our understanding of literary production, poetic authority, and political intervention for the early modern period as a whole.

For poetry's formal and thematic variety, its status and marketability offered women a unique entry into any number of cultural and political debates. And women made extensive use of available forms and modes (Hageman 190-208). Moreover, as a highly coded form of writing, drawing on other modes and genres, poetry allowed for the simultaneous use of multiple ways of producing meaning, and incorporated various methods of signification. What does it mean for an early modern woman to write poetry in an age that was acutely attuned to these multiple ways of encoding and signifying? It enabled them, for example, to inscribe counter-discourses into their verse; paradoxically, exclusionary tendencies opened avenues for women to enter into writing, precisely because they could put them to their own uses.

Early modern poetry has also been considered the locus for the development of interiority, for the creation and representation of individuated and psychologized selves.[2] While poetic self-figurations are most familiar from the Petrarchan love lyric, they can be found in religious and devotional poetry as well. Of course, such a 'poetic self' is never simply biographical. Rather it can result from the orchestration of a plurality of voices and references, or it can consist of an amalgamation of identities for contingent manifestations of the self. Or, it can be represented as a composite created from a poetic and discursive repertoire. Citationality necessarily troubles and complicates not only the notion of a 'poetic self' but also the strategies for writing such a 'poetic self.' Poetry's generic and rhetorical markers, its invocations and imitations, provide a further layering of reference that can bring the speaker's 'identity' to light or obfuscate it. By using all these methods for poetic self-figuration, women poets open up further possibilities for interiority and identity, and for reading and writing.

The Essays

Though we have grouped the essays in thematic sections, we invite our readers to explore different connections, to let the essays engage in dialogue with each other and generate further questions. For example, Pamela Hammons ('Strategies and Contexts'), Margaret Hannay ('Poetic Conventions and Traditions'), Joan Pong Linton ('Negotiating Power and Politics') and Helen Wilcox ('Writing the Female Poet') all discuss authorial self-figuration and the creation of a poetic voice, but their authors inhabit different writerly, generic, and political contexts. The essays in the first section, 'Strategies and Contexts,' focus on individual writerly strategies that women used to cope with or to change their cultural contexts. They explore in detail the deployment of poetry by individual writers to negotiate social positioning, to intervene in and reshape existing literary practices, and to register the tensions between obligation and desire in a woman's life.

In 'Widow, Prophet, and Poet: Lyrical Self-Figurations in Katherine Austen's "Book M" (1664),' Pamela Hammons studies the manuscript miscellany of a widowed gentlewoman and traces the strategies through which Austen crafts and contextualizes her identity. Because Austen was ambitious and wanted to rise in rank, she was acutely aware of social conventions and painstakingly defended and asserted her perceived identity. She works against the cultural prejudice that widows are licentious, devious, and uncontrollable by presenting herself as helpless and defenseless, though, in fact, she was quite successful in preserving her wealth and position. Austen's prophetic aspirations do not contradict her politics and her concern with rank, but rather aid her in 'negotiating the incompatibilities between her socioeconomic ambitions and gender' (12). For Austen, reading, writing, and revising poetry are inextricably linked with social life.

Anne Russell investigates a crucial yet neglected role that Aphra Behn played in the literary marketplace, as editor and publisher of two poetic miscellanies, *Miscellany* (1685) and *Lycidus* (1688), in which women predominate as either writers or addressees. As the first female compiler of such miscellanies, Behn was instrumental in making 'public' what had previously circulated in coteries. '"Public" and "Private" in Aphra Behn's Miscellanies: Women Writers, Print, and Manuscript' traces the circulation history of the poems by the only two named female contributors. The effect of these identifications differs: by printing three poems by 'Mrs Taylor' Behn enhances the poet's reputation, while the oblique identification of Anne Wharton signals Behn's own affiliation with a more aristocratic coterie and writers of higher rank. By contextualizing these activities in Restoration practices, Russell shows that Behn is significantly involved in bridging, as well as exploiting, the differences between these two modes of literary production.

Margaret Ezell's '"Household Affaires are the Opium of the Soul"' argues that readings of Damaris Masham's life have subjected it to conventional ideological and sociological constructions. Contemporary and subsequent readers have read her in the shadow of the powerful men surrounding her (the Cambridge Platonists, led by her father, Dr Ralph Cudworth, and John Locke). Masham herself, however, called into question the codes for constructing gender and was aware of the coerciveness of the material circumstances of women's lives. Ezell chronicles Masham's struggle to create a physical and intellectual space for herself, and her reading and writing, which are to function as an antidote to the numbing domestic world. But Masham also views domestic responsibilities as an integral part of life. Her poetry envisions 'a life of "converse"' (51), while simultaneously laying bare the processes by which a person's identity and socio-sexual role are shaped and performed.

The second group of essays, 'Poetic Conventions and Traditions,' addresses the association of women poets with established and emerging poetic forms. The essays by Clare Kinney and Jacqueline Pearson investigate female interventions in male-dominated or patriarchal genres (Petrarchan love poetry and country house poetry), while Margaret Hannay's essay discusses the Psalms as a particular and productive venue for women's writing. In their engagements with poetic traditions, women poets employ a number of strategies to write themselves, and women's lives, into established discourses.

Female appropriations of conventions invest them with new, gendered meanings and exploit these conventions' norms to achieve enabling, subversive, or revisionary results.

In 'Mary Wroth's Guilty "secrett art",' Clare Kinney analyzes the productive workings of jealousy in Wroth's *Pamphilia to Amphilanthus*. The essay revises our understanding of Wroth's lyrics by revealing a counter-discourse to the speaker's protestations of constancy. Writing to and about a faithless, male beloved forces the speaker to invent an aesthetic alternative to the Petrarchan model, one which at once celebrates love and critiques the lover's motives. Kinney finds located in the ambiguities of Wroth's syntax imaginings and jealousies that threaten to oust the constancy of her love and become the sole source of poetic production. Wroth's poetics of jealousy problematizes the poetic project of making love present through verse; love could turn out to be nothing but 'idle phant'sie' fueled by jealousy. Significantly, the speaker's ultimate re-investment in constancy, a final exorcism of jealousy, silences the poet.

Jacqueline Pearson's '"An Emblem of themselves, in plum or pear": Poetry, the Female Body and the Country House' focuses on a paradox: the female body at once guarantees and threatens the political and patriarchal project of these poems, and therefore 'poetic representation itself may be seen as contingent upon the female body' (89). Against this ethos, most notably enshrined in Ben Jonson's 'To Penshurst,' Aemilia Lanyer writes the female body into the matriarchal yet lost world of 'The Description of Cooke-ham.' Through the poem's performance of memory, its images, and particularly through its rhyme schemes, Lanyer inscribes the feminine onto and into the poem and its world. Lanyer employs these poetic devices to construct a female language for her 'radical sexual politics' (98). Like Lanyer, Anne Finch structures her anti-country house poem, 'A Nocturnal Reverie,' so as to undercut the genre's class and gender hierarchies. In Finch's poem, the female speaker has no place in the constricting domestic sphere, but roams the nocturnal landscape, which becomes 'a feminized sphere of the free soul' (102).

In '"So may I with the *Psalmist* truly say": Early Modern Englishwomen's Psalm Discourse,' Margaret Hannay investigates why so many women poets resorted to the Psalms for their own poetic productions. Psalm discourses were ubiquitous in the lives of early modern people; they spanned all religious and political divides, 'rivaled the Petrarchan lyric' (105) in popularity, and could be used for multiple purposes. Paradoxically, following the scripted text of the Psalms gave women an opportunity to express their own interiority. Hannay argues that the Psalms' 'sanctioned' and 'foundational discourse' (106, 107) provided an ideal medium for women, not only for religious meditation and dialogue but also for life-writing, for exploring their inner selves, for participating in both a literary and a religious community, for instructing other women in devotional practices, and for circumventing social restrictions. Psalm writing could take many forms; the resulting texts experiment with various poetic and stanzaic forms and, more importantly, radically unsettle our notion of 'voice' and 'self' by weaving together the voices of the Psalmist and the woman writer.

The essays in the section 'Negotiating Power and Politics' deal with poems by women whose situations range from persecuted to privileged. Central to all three essays is the question of poetic voice, its location, origin, and identity. The martyr Anne Askew creates a plurality of voices, which enables her at once to attempt to evade her prosecutors and to enter into her chosen community of faith. By reconfiguring patronage conventions, Mary Sidney propagates a Protestant poetics and invents the figure of the 'female courtier' (156). And in the political climate of the mid-seventeenth century, Katherine Philips introduces a contestatory dimension to friendship.

Joan Pong Linton argues in 'The Plural Voices of Anne Askew' that the three poems written by or attributed to the Protestant martyr Anne Askew present a 'plural voice and self' (138). There is a complicated interplay between Askew and martyrologists, as well as between texts and textual histories. As an amalgamation of oral and written sources, her composite texts create a 'voice' that is both exemplary and participatory. It figures forth Askew's own case and her connection to a community of believers. Part of the martyr's strategy for evading her interlocutors was to respond to them by invoking other voices and texts. Yet the resulting multi-vocality also bespeaks Askew's desire for and participation in a larger community. Through this interplay of self and community, then, her 'personal agency [becomes] socially transforming' (138): it also lets the audience take part in her story. As a result, 'Askew' is located between the oral and the written, between speaking and being spoken. And through these interstices we can keep listening to Askew's story – and retell it.

Shannon Miller's 'Mary Sidney and Gendered Strategies for Writing Poetry' demonstrates that Mary Sidney's four original poems challenge the divide between 'public' and 'private,' restructure the patron/client relationship, and fashion a national Protestant poetics. Far from being isolated, private productions, these poems were written for specific occasions, 'produce a receptive audience in the Queen herself' (157), and devise strategies through which Sidney becomes a female courtier and enters into a number of political debates. Mary Sidney audaciously reminds Elizabeth of her troubled relationship with Philip Sidney and uses the image of Philip to displace the Queen as the ultimate fountain of reward. As a consequence of these conceptual innovations, she can posit a spiritual rather than material system of exchange and can call on Elizabeth to protect national Protestant poetry.

Andrew Shifflett's '"Subdu'd by You": States of Friendship and Friends of the State in Katherine Philips's Poetry' offers a re-reading of Philips's friendship poetry which deepens and complicates our understanding of these poems. As Shifflett shows, Philips invokes a philosophy of friendship that posits the friends as equals – just as monarchs are equals. Such sovereignty and equality among friends become problematic when sovereigns turn out to be poor friends. Drawing on Cicero and Hobbes, Shifflett argues that Philips uses images of sovereignty when friendship turns sour, or even turns to war. For friendship is the result of historical, political, and ideological contingencies, which can, obviously, change. The politics of friendship, then, rescript consent as coercion.

The last group of essays focuses on women's strategies for 'writing a female identity.' These essays concentrate on the particulars of, and possibilities for, a specifically female, gendered identity in authorial, sexualized, and biographical contexts. Women poets resort to a variety of strategies to fashion a gendered, writerly persona. As Helen Wilcox shows, they evince highly complex understandings of the concept of the 'author' and her actions. Concerns about the propriety of female writing can also be used to unsettle the perceived affiliation between speech and sexuality, as Bronwen Price argues for Katherine Philips's notion of 'innocence.' Yet, as Jeslyn Medoff argues about Aphra Behn, not even a writer who plays in sophisticated and complex ways with identity politics can escape the scripting of later readers and critics.

Helen Wilcox's '"First Fruits of a Woman's Wit": Authorial Self-Construction in English Renaissance Poets' analyzes the tropes and strategies through which women poets present authorial identities. Because of the ideological injunctions against women's writing and publishing, prefaces are a crucial textual space for the fashioning of a speaking position and an authorial persona. Wilcox finds surprisingly forthright and proud, as well as carefully contrived, entrances, into women's poetry. Yet the concern of women to justify their activities as writers inevitably genders their self-representations as well as their notions of literary production. Their gendered concepts of authorship allow them to exploit the stigma of writing, to expose gender as a cultural category, and to feminize 'the hitherto patriarchal term "author"' (214).

In 'A Rhetoric of Innocence: The Poetry of Katherine Philips "The Matchless Orinda,"' Bronwen Price argues that Philips deflects the sexual resonances of entering print by presenting herself as a passive, debilitated, and exploited object. Yet underneath the cover of innocence, the poems produce a set of codes in which the conventional alignment between feminine identity and the female body is problematized. Instead, the feminine 'innocence' of Philips's verse offers an alternative type of erotics to that found in much heterosexual poetry of the period, as well as becoming a means of critiquing the 'masculine' world and its politics. In her readings of the poems, Price maintains that Philips argues against the convention that figures a sexual relationship as a representation of male desire; she argues for expression and affirmation of the women's own desires.

The last essay in this collection chronicles a very different fate for a woman poet. Jeslyn Medoff's '"Very Like a Fiction": Some Early Biographies of Aphra Behn' reassesses the making of Behn's reputation and biography by tracing how early biographers constructed Behn's life by conflating it with her writings, particularly with *Oroonoko*. In Behn's case, an early modern woman writer was most certainly written. The standard versions of Behn's life came about when early biographers took rumors as facts and began speculating about a supposed real-life relationship between Behn and Oroonoko. Behn has never been disentangled from this involvement in her own fiction. Though Behn herself was most adept at sophisticated identity politics, early biographers were blind to the distinction between author and persona, because the demands of their fledgling genre forced them to presume scholarly information in texts that merely flirted with historical accuracy.

These essays are a tribute to the diversity of female poetic invention and intervention, the complexity of poetry's work, and the self-conscious manipulation of cultural norms and prejudices by women poets. In their interrogations of writerly and poetic strategies the contributors at once enhance and complicate our understanding of early modern culture, its poetry, and its constructions of gender and the woman writer.

Notes

I should like to thank Katharine Maus, Thomas Maresca, Clifford Huffman, and Nicholas Baechle for reading and commenting on the introduction.

[1] On education and literacy see, Rebecca Bushnell, David Cressy, Betty Travitsky (4-9), and Margaret Ferguson (143-152); for a discussion of the fluctuating ideals and practices of Renaissance education of women, see Hilda L. Smith 9-29; for an analysis of the historical record, see Merry E. Wiesner 117-145. Although education for boys was equally restrictive, Rebecca Bushnell has argued that 'arguments about the education of girls, as well as of the poor, thus tended to orient themselves doubly – to the nature inherent in gender and rank and to social function' (111).

[2] For this now familiar, yet also problematized, point see Braden and Kerrigan, as well as Greenblatt. The New Critics' heritage is probably still most strongly felt in our approaches to poetry, which proves resistant to newer methodologies and ideologies, perhaps because it has become so entrenched in the realms of the personal and private, while still being perceived as universal and transcendental. For studies of seventeenth-century poetry which apply new historicist strategies to texts central to new criticism, see Elizabeth D. Harvey and Katharine E. Maus, eds. *Soliciting Interpretation.*

Works Cited

Barash, Carol. *English Women's Poetry, 1649-1714. Politics, Community, and Linguistic Authority*. Oxford: Clarendon P, 1996.

Bradstreet, Anne. *The Tenth Muse*. ed. Josephine K. Piercy. Gainesville: Scholars' Facsimiles & Reprints, 1965.

Bushnell, Rebecca W. *A Culture of Teaching. Early Modern Humanism in Theory and Practice*. Ithaca: Cornell UP, 1996.

Chudleigh, Mary, Lady. *The Poems and Prose of Mary, Lady Chudleigh*. ed. Margaret J. M. Ezell. New York: Oxford UP, 1993.

Cressy, David. *Literacy and the Social Order: Reading and Writing in Tudor England*. Cambridge: Cambridge UP, 1980.

Ezell, Margaret J. M. *Writing Women's Literary History*. Baltimore: Johns Hopkins UP, 1993.

Ferguson, Margaret. 'Renaissance Concepts of the "Woman Writer".' Wilcox, ed. 143-68.

Finch, Anne, Countess of Winchelsea. "The Introduction." *Major Women Writers of Seventeenth-Century England*. eds. James Fitzmaurice, Josephine A. Roberts, Carol L. Barash, Eugene R. Cunnar, and Nancy A. Gutierrez. Ann Arbor: U of Michigan P, 1997. 335-336.

Goldberg, Jonathan. *Desiring Women Writing. English Renaissance Examples*. Stanford: Stanford UP, 1997.

Greenblatt, Stephen. *Renaissance Self-Fashioning*. Chicago: U of Chicago P, 1980.

Hageman, Elizabeth. 'Women's poetry in early modern Britain.' Wilcox, ed. 190-208.

Harvey, Elizabeth D. and Katharine Eisaman Maus, eds *Soliciting Interpretation. Literary Theory and Seventeenth-Century English Poetry*. Chicago: U of Chicago P, 1990.

Hobby, Elaine. *Virtue of Necessity. English Women's Writing 1649-88*. Ann Arbor: U of Michigan P, 1989.

Jones, Ann Rosalind. *The Currency of Eros: Women's Love Lyric in Europe 1540-1620*. Bloomington: Indiana UP, 1990.

Kerrigan, William and Gordon Braden. *The Idea of the Renaissance*. Baltimore: Johns Hopkins UP, 1989.

Krontiris, Tina. *Oppositional Voices. Women as Writers and Translators of Literature in the English Renaissance*. London: Routledge, 1992.

Parry, Graham. *Seventeenth-Century Poetry. The Social Context*. London: Hutchinson, 1985.

Philips, Katherine. *The Collected Works of Katherine Philips, the Matchless Orinda*. ed. Patrick Thomas. Vol. 1. Stump Cross: Stump Cross Books, 1990.

Smith, Hilda. 'Humanist Education and the Renaissance Concept of Woman.' Wilcox, ed. 9-29.

Smith, Nigel. *Literature & Revolution in England, 1640-1660*. New Haven: Yale UP, 1994.

Travitsky, Betty, ed. *The Paradise of Women. Writings by Englishwomen of the Renaissance*. New York: Columbia UP, 1989.

Trill, Suzanne, Kate Chedgzoy and Melanie Osborne, eds. *Lay by your needles Ladies, take the Pen. Writing Women in England, 1500-1700.* London: Arnold, 1997.

Wall, Wendy.   *The Imprint of Gender. Authorship and Publication in the English Renaissance.* Ithaca: Cornell UP, 1993.

Wiesner, Merry E.   *Women and Gender in Early Modern Europe.* Cambridge: Cambridge UP, 1993.

Wilcox, Helen, ed.   *Women and Literature in Britain 1500-1700.* Cambridge: Cambridge UP, 1996.

PART I

Strategies and Contexts

Widow, Prophet, and Poet: Lyrical Self-Figurations in Katherine Austen's 'Book M' (1664)

Pamela Hammons

The poems of Katherine Austen, a relatively unknown seventeenth-century widow, illustrate how an early modern woman used lyrics to reconceptualize her social position.[1] Austen includes her lyrics – which illuminate the range of poetic practices available for a woman's participation in a manuscript environment in early modern England – in her miscellany 'Book M' (1664). As we will see, for Austen, writing lyrics was shot through with social implications: her engagement with the formal and thematic conventions associated with the composition and preservation of verse in manuscript is intertwined with her sensitivity to the social conventions corresponding to the role of a woman of rank.

Austen (d. 1683) grew up in a wealthy mercantile family and lived in London. She married Thomas Austen, who had similar riches and status. He died in 1658, leaving their children and property under her management, which included hiring lawyers and attending hearings at Parliament to fight for possession of an estate, building houses as investment properties, and investing in the East India Company. Thomas's will restricted her ability to remarry for seven years – a detail which gave 'seven' a special significance for Katherine.[2]

Austen was very concerned with status and social propriety; 'Book M' suggests that she was anxious to display the proper appearances associated with having a high rank and that her anxieties about her rank were compounded by her status as a widow.[3] When she became a widow, she became aware of her gender as a liability, because she discovered how it rendered her less capable of protecting her material holdings than her husband

was.   While I do not claim that Austen became actively conscious of the
conflicts between her status (and her ambitions for ever higher rank) and her
gender, I show that the inconsistencies engendered by this conflict underpin
Austen's complicated, discontinuous self-representations, which she often
presents in the form of lyrics.[4] Austen represents herself, for example, both as
a helpless, persecuted widow and as a prophet with divine gifts.   These roles
can seem incompatible with each other: in one case, Austen represents herself
as abjectly weak, while in the other, she fantasizes about accessing divine
power.   However, both help Austen to negotiate between her gender and rank,
and both advance her ambitions for increased social status and personal
power.[5]
        As a Royalist and Anglican writing at the beginning of the Restoration,
Austen's investment in increasing her status compels her to avoid revisionary
political and religious ideas, especially those that disrupt social decorum.
Hence, in some cases, she makes her verse as socially acceptable as possible:
she composes uncontroversial religious meditations and occasional poems
about relatives.   Nevertheless, she also writes lyrics that experiment with
reconceptualizing her position in society to advance her social status and
personal power. Attention to these poems reveals Austen's appropriations of
particular conventions and practices: they show, for instance, how Austen
capitalizes upon the malleability of manuscript verse and how she shapes
metrical paraphrases of biblical texts so that they criticize English society in
the 1660s.   Before examining her poems, however, it will be helpful to
become more familiar with her manuscript.

'Book M'

'Book M' includes Austen's spiritual meditations, sermon notes, economic
records, family correspondence, and about thirty-five poems.   Austen cites
sources for enough of the contents of 'Book M' to suggest that when she
leaves a text uncited, it is likely that she wrote it herself.   For instance, her
sermon notes usually include the name of the author in the title, e.g., 'Sermon:
Doc: ffeatlyes' (17r). Austen cites an author for only one poem in 'Book M':
'Out of a poeme of Doc Corbets: to his ffriend when she might be a Widow:'
(71v). Austen's inclusion of this excerpt is as significant as her own verse on
widowhood insofar as 'Book M' provides a specialized context for

interpreting it. While some of Austen's poems are so generic that anyone could have written them, many refer so specifically to autobiographical events that her authorship seems clear.

Her revisionary marks also suggest that she composed much of 'Book M.'[6] She wrote in it primarily between 1664 and 1666, and edited and amended it, until 1682.[7] In fact, she explicitly comments on reviewing her writings:

> When I view over the assurances and hopes I have had in this book of my meditations As Sometimes I am puting on wreathes of Victory, I have overcome my Enemies and my feares But such is the Unsurenes of Every ground in this World to Anchor on as I Soone come to wade in deep places againe. The Moone hath not more Variations then the affaires of this life. Then the Ebes and flowes of ffortune. (Austen 112v)

Writing and reading her life are thus ongoing organizational and analytical practices for Austen.

Using such writing to organize one's life conceptually, especially to isolate the providential workings of God, was typical of seventeenth-century spiritual meditations.[8] Many of Austen's poems entitled 'Meditation' discover a divine hand in seemingly bad events. In the above passage in which Austen reflects on 'Book M' as a whole, however, providence is strangely absent, and Austen faces the stark changeability of life (figured as the sea and moon). Her revisionary examination of her writing exposes the fluctuating emendations of her life, in which she discerns not the hidden yet ultimately straightforward trajectory delineated by providence but 'the Ebes and flowes of ffortune.' That Austen sees her compilation of texts in 'Book M' as representing her life is essential to my argument about the different roles that she constructs for herself to negotiate the contradictions inherent in her position as a socially and economically ambitious widow.

Austen's composition of occasional poems not only represents a specialized effort at documenting, organizing, and analyzing her life, but it also reflects the tradition of circulating lyrics in manuscript in courtly and satellite-courtly environments – such as the universities and Inns of Court – and within the household.[9] Although Austen could not attend a university, her accounts in 'Book M' indicate payments towards her son Thomas's education at Oxford. Moreover, a letter to Thomas (43-44v) and her entries about her

Scottish suitor reveal her awareness of university and court affairs (e.g., 97r). While Austen was neither student nor courtier, she observed such men as they moved within their respective, overlapping public spheres, and 'Book M' suggests that she knew about the practices associated with circulating lyrics in manuscript in those spheres, as well as within the family.

Many scholars have recently highlighted how examining lyrics produced and circulated in manuscript environments allows us to rethink lyrical production during the early modern period. Of particular importance to understanding Austen's verse is the idea that lyrics in manuscript were not conceptualized as stable, author-centered artifacts detached from specific historical and social circumstances.[10] As Marotti writes,

> In the system of manuscript transmission, it was normal for lyrics to elicit revisions, corrections, supplements, and answers, for they were part of an ongoing social discourse. In this environment texts were inherently malleable, escaping authorial control to enter a social world in which recipients both consciously and unconsciously altered what they received. . . . In the manuscript environment the roles of author, scribe and reader overlapped . . . (135)

Austen does not appear to have been a coterie poet like John Donne or Katherine Philips; however, her verse still reflects the practices and values of seventeenth-century manuscript culture. As Todd observes, in 'Book M' Austen composed 'drafts of important letters and other personal records' ('A Young Widow of London' 207), which she presumably copied and shared with their intended audiences. It remains unclear whether Austen circulated her poetry by copying it or allowing others to do so. However, certain of her poems appear to have had an intended audience as surely as her letters did. Austen might have shown her sister Lady Mary Ashe the poem that she wrote about Lady Mary's daughter's death. Likewise, she might have wanted her children to read her poem, 'Meditation on my death.' Finally, as I discuss below, she circulates lines from one of her poems within the pages of 'Book M' and transcribes lines from a poem by Richard Corbett that speak to her concerns as a widow, suggesting her awareness of the acceptability of editing lyrics within a manuscript context.

In addition to indicating that she read some of Corbett's verse, Austen reveals that she read Donne's writings (certainly his sermons, possibly his poetry) and knew about events concerning Donne and Sir Henry Wotton.[11]

Her child loss and country-house poems perhaps best reveal her knowledge of the conventions associated with particular kinds of lyrics.[12] Austen's verse meditations suggest that she studied David's Psalms; she also may have learned about religious verse through hearing lyrics interspersed with sermons.[13] As a literate woman living in London, Austen had many opportunities to encounter lyrics in different settings.

The titles and themes of Austen's poems further reveal her awareness of the conventions associated with the composition of lyrics in manuscript. Marotti indicates that it was common for scribes and poets to '[attempt] to preserve the information that enabled [any given lyric] to be read in its social contexts' (15). Likewise, '[t]he manuscript environment was especially receptive to occasional poetry, especially to elegies and epitaphs about members of one's own family or social circle' (Marotti 173-4). The precise title of her child loss poem, 'Dec[ember] 5: 1664 Upon Robin Austens recovery of the Smal Pox and Coronal Pop[oins?] Son John diing of them: a Youth of a very forward growth their ages the Same Popoins: 3 yeares for growth more,' indicates, for example, her knowledge of the practice of providing contextualizing information for lyrics in manuscript. The inclusion of a title page for 'Book M' and the numbering of the poems, after the first few, also reveal her awareness of the formal conventions associated with verse miscellanies. Not only did Austen know the conventions associated with the transmission and preservation of verse in manuscript, but as I discuss below, her desire to rise in rank also made her sensitive to the social conventions corresponding to the role of the high status widow.

The Gentle Widow

> Men never think their wifes may be Neccesitate by Missery (Austen 60r)
>
> For commonly widows are so froward, so waspish, and so stubborn that thou canst not wrest them from their wills. (Swetnam 214)

A variety of early modern English writing represented widows of high social status as seductively wealthy, sexually voracious, and absolutely uncontrollable.[14] The widow's ability to remarry and to redistribute property thereby underpins this stereotype of the widow as unruly and lustful.[15] According to masculinist representations, a widow might be 'gentle' in the sense of having elevated status, but she was unlikely to be 'gentle' in the sense of being docile and obedient. Instead, the high status widow was likely to be among the most 'froward . . . waspish . . . stubborn' of women (Swetnam 214). Yet other texts suggest that despite whatever resources for personal power a woman might have as a widow, remarriage could instantly dissipate those resources.[16] Austen, in implicitly justifying her continued independence as a widow, inverts the stereotypical demonization of the powerful, lustful widow through figuring herself as an exaggeratedly helpless one.

Sara Heller Mendelson observes that 'Austen continually bemoaned the sad state of her financial affairs since her widowhood . . . ' (199). While accurate in that Austen does complain about finances, this characterization of Austen's representation of her economic status simplifies its significance within the contexts of 'Book M' and of contemporary depictions of widows. Many well-known masculinist representations of widows could lead today's reader to believe that widows were powerful women who had escaped the bonds of patriarchy.[17] Austen's self-figuring, however, in which she tries to hide the power that she has whenever she explicitly writes about her widowed state, suggests how much the notion of a woman having any recourse to self-empowerment was threatening to patriarchy. Austen thus downplays her personal resources, including intellectual agency and material possessions, lest they attract envious or punitive attention.[18] The disparity in her manuscript between the glimpses we receive of her actual property and her self-representation as a poor, helpless widow that I discuss below reveals that her self-figuration was strategic both as a refutation of her culture's pervasive stereotyping of widows and as a deflection of attention away from her economic and social ambitions.

'Book M' suggests that Austen was self-conscious about her widowed state and its implications.[19] She was well aware that, for bachelors, she represented an opportunity for economic advancement.[20] However, in her ruminations about her widowhood, Austen generalizes the threat to widows as potentially coming from any man, not just from suitors. The question of remarriage aside, Austen characterizes the widow as helpless, harmless, and persecuted. 'I am in the hands of potent men,' she writes, 'Men skilful to distroy, of subtil men, who lay traines to ruine y^e [the] widow and ffatherles' (Austen 65r).[21] Although Austen portrays herself as the potential victim of any man, she does not represent men as aggressors only. She connects her vulnerability to men at large to her lack of immediate, adult male relatives. The 'subtil men' who are 'skilful to distroy' specifically 'lay traines to ruine y^e [the] widow and ffatherles' (Austen 65r), women and children lacking a private patriarch. Part of Austen's self-figuration as a gentle widow relies on her implied wish for patriarchal protection against her male aggressors. After all, a gentle widow would not be so critical of the patriarchy as to oppose it altogether. Implying her need for male protection, Austen relates dreams in which her late husband, his father, and his brother protect her from hostile men (e.g., 64r, 65), and she consoles herself with the idea that, if her husband's male relatives cannot aid her, she can rely upon the supreme patriarch – God – to oppose the men who conspire against her (65r).

A poetic fragment that Austen copied into her manuscript centers on the notion of male protection from beyond the grave. This fragment is significant because it provides insight into how Austen participated in manuscript culture. Although she did not compose it, she shapes its possible meanings. She selects lines relevant to her situation as a widow, and her manuscript provides a context for those lines, suggesting a specialized interpretation. This instance of transcription exemplifies how attending to lyrics transmitted through manuscript helps us to refine our understanding of early modern authorship (and readership). Austen's transcription represents a collaboration between herself and Corbett and shows her playing several roles related to textual transmission. She is a reader of other poets' work; she is an editor who decides which lines to borrow for her own book; she is a scribe who copies those lines; and she is an author insofar as her own writing ('Book M') participates in how the transcribed lines create meaning.

She includes these lines 'Out of a poeme of Doc Corbets: to his ffriend when she might be a Widow' (Austen 71v):

> And as the paphian Queen by her griefs show'r (1)
> Brought up her dead Loves Spirit in a fflow'r
> So by those precious drops rain'd from thine Eyes
> Out of my dust, O may some Vertue rise:
> And like thy better Genius thee attend, (5)
> Till thou in my dark period shalt end.

In a rare engagement with a Renaissance tradition of love lyrics, Austen transcribes this fragment containing a conceit in which Corbett's poetic speaker compares himself to the slain Adonis and his wife to the mourning Venus. Austen presumably includes these lines to reflect on her own situation: her husband, like Corbett's poetic speaker, is like Adonis, and she herself is like 'the paphian Queen' (1). Her inclusion of this fragment is consistent both with her self-figuration as an especially 'gentle' widow and with her tendency towards social conventionality or conservatism. While her poems indicate her familiarity with the conventions associated with the manuscript transmission of lyrics and with specific poetic traditions, Austen's lyrics tend to avoid direct engagement with any tradition of amorous verse.[22] It is not surprising that Austen would limit her experimentations with literary forms that could associate her with the derogatory stereotype of the lustful widow. Hence, she transcribes, instead of composing, lines from a love lyric that has widowhood as its theme.

The implicit self-comparison to Venus in Austen's transcription allows the widow the compliment of being like the goddess of love but attempts to define the terms of that comparison very strictly. Venus, for instance, is never explicitly named as such in the fragment; instead she is the grieving 'paphian Queen' (1), a high-ranking woman who properly mourns her dead husband. In the context of Austen's accounts of her dreams implying her wish for her husband's spirit to protect her, the erotic subtext underpinning Corbett's figure of the dead lover as a 'better Genius' who 'attend[s]' his beloved diminishes in significance (5). In the context of Renaissance love poetry, it is difficult to avoid the bawdy connotation of Venus's 'dead Loves Spirit' (2); likewise, even a mournful 'paphian Queen' seems only slightly less licentious than Venus in hot pursuit of the classical paragon of male beauty.[23] Further, when considered within the tradition of Ovidian erotic verse, the 'Vertue' that 'rise[s]' like a Phoenix from its own ashes in line four suggests a speedy post-coital phallic recovery. In the context of 'Book M,' however, one can interpret the figure of the ghostly husband's 'Genius' so that it not only offers protection, but also ensures the beloved's continued chastity. Neither the beloved, nor a suitor could escape the watchfulness of such an attending spirit, and the implication that Austen wishes for such an attendant protects her from the stereotype of the insubordinate, lustful widow. The environment of Austen's miscellany also highlights how this fragment domesticates the female agency behind the central transformation in the Ovidian account of Venus and Adonis. While the primary metamorphosis in Ovid's story is Venus's transformation of Adonis into a flower memorializing her passion and sorrow,[24] here the female agent behind the teardrops (3) that engender 'Vertue' out of dust (4) falls under the surveillance of that resurrected aspect of the dead male lover. The metamorphosed synecdochical figure for the male lover accompanies the female beloved to the end of her life, which is circumscribed by the male poet's sentence: the 'better Genius' will attend her 'Till [she] in [his] dark period shalt end' (5, 6). Austen's inclusion of this fragment thus contributes to her self-representation as a gentle widow who eschews personal agency and power to the extent that she wishes to be subjected to patriarchal control in the form of her dead husband's ghostly attendance.

While Austen dramatizes her vulnerability in her poem 'Upon Courtiers at the Committee of Parliament Striving for Highbury,' she simultaneously critiques male power. This poem shows how she represents her abject weakness as a widow and reveals her awareness of traditional poetic practices. In the first six lines, for example, she participates in the widespread practice of translating biblical passages into metrical verse[25]:

> Wise Sollomen he tells me true (1)
> There is a time for all thinges due
> A Time to Spare, a time to spend
> A Time to Borrow time to lend
> A time of Trouble time of rest (5)
> A time there is to be opprest. (Austen 59v)

Austen's rendering of Ecclesiastes in the tetrameter typical of such metrical translations focuses on issues relevant to her embattled economic situation.[26] The first couplet corresponds to Eccles. 3:1; the second paraphrases Eccles. 3:6; and the last is Austen's variation on Eccles. 3:8. While Austen's imitation of the repetition and syntactical balance characteristic of the third chapter of Ecclesiastes makes her brief metrical paraphrase seem a more straightforward translation than it is, a comparison of Austen's verse with the biblical text reveals that she adapts it to fit her circumstances. Most significantly, Eccles. 3:6 ('A time to get, and a time to lose; a time to keep, and a time to cast away') becomes more explicitly economic in Austen's translation. 'Get' and 'lose' become 'spare' and 'spend'; 'keep' and 'cast away' become 'borrow' and 'lend.'

Austen's paraphrase of Ecclesiastes appears twice in 'Book M.' It first appears early in the manuscript in a version that seems an initial effort at an

extended metrical translation of or meditation on the biblical passage. Yet
Austen stops her attempt after the seventh line: 'A time of ffolly. Time to be'
(40v). She circulates these verses, however, between the pages of 'Book M':
they reappear in the opening lines to her critique of the courtiers at parliament
– with a significant revision. She replaces the seventh line from her first
version ('A time of ffolly. Time to be') with a new one ('Such is this time
now men of power'), which enables her to move beyond the limitations of
metrical paraphrasing to incorporate the biblical passage into a more explicitly
autobiographical lyric. Austen's new seventh line becomes a point of
transition:

> Wise Sollomen he tells me true (1)
> There is a time for all thinges due
> A Time to Spare, a time to spend
> A Time to Borrow. time to lend
> A time of Trouble time of rest (5)
> A time there is to be opprest.
> Such is this time now men of power
> Doe seeke our well faire to devoure
> Confederated in a League
> By an ["oppresive" struck out] <unjust and> Dire intrege . . . (59v)

Austen makes a supremely patriarchal text – Solomon's legendary wisdom can
be thoroughly misogynist[27] – into the authority prefacing her critique of 'men
of power,' whom she represents as united against her. Here Austen
dramatizes her helplessness both by attaching references to her particular,
personal circumstances to an ancient, sacred exposition on the universal
effects of time and by using especially forceful, vivid diction. The legal
contest over the Highbury estate to which the poem's title refers becomes
tantamount to political conspiracy at court.

　　　Austen's self-representation as an innocuous, vulnerable widow is her
answer to the stereotype of the widow as a woman who had, at best,
humorous, and at worst, horrifying power over men. Although Austen
strategically represents herself as a proper widow who knows that frailty's
name is woman, her stern independence becomes evident nonetheless.
Austen's 'gentle' widow is only one aspect of her multi-faceted, discontinuous
self-figuration, through which she negotiates the incompatibilities between her
socioeconomic ambitions and gender. As a woman interested in securing

social and economic power for herself, she also mobilizes the role of the prophet to her advantage.

The Ambivalent Visionary

> If men doe listen to Wispers of fear, and have not reason, and observation Enough to confute trifles Every old woman shal be a prophetes. (Austen 25r)

> Was not one of my Dreames the presaigement of blesing to the Nation As the Dream of a poor Stranger did confirme Gedion to goe on with the more confidence to his Victory? (Austen 15r)

In 1664, when Austen began writing 'Book M,' there were increased restrictions against radical religious sects – Quakers, Fifth Monarchists, Ranters, etc. – which had proliferated during the revolutionary period.[28] As many scholars have noted, an unprecedented number of women involved themselves publicly in political and religious debates in the 1640s and 1650s. Women petitioned Parliament; they helped found new religious sects; and they acted as missionaries.[29] Prophetic activity flourished during this period. Being a prophet in seventeenth-century England did not simply involve predicting the future. As Elaine Hobby explains, many of the women who wrote prophecies between 1649 and 1688 'present[ed] themselves as divinely inspired counterparts of the Old Testament prophets, whose role was to report and interpret God's messages to His people. Women prophets were possessed by the Lord, burdened with the duty to speak' (26). Such women prophets were not simply seers; they were divine messengers. A prophet's messages could be complex and could derive from multiple traditions, as Keith Thomas explains: 'The real boost to ancient prophecy . . . came with the Civil War, when Galfridian prophecies joined astrological prognostication and religious revelation to place an unprecedented amount of prophetic advice before the lay public. Although the three genres were distinct, their separate identity was not always preserved' (409). Austen's ambivalent engagement with prophecy suggests her familiarity not only with the role of female prophets from radical religious groups during the civil wars but also with this generic mixing of prophetic traditions.

While her self-fashioning as a prophet in 'Book M' contrasts with her self-portrait as an especially weak widow, both roles represent strategies for negotiating the incompatibilities between her gender and her socioeconomic desires. She simultaneously dissociates herself from a figure of exaggerated female power (the widow) and experiments with underwriting her ambitions with divine power. Both roles allow her to hide her personal agency, and therefore, to distract attention away from her financial and intellectual resources and her aspirations for social and economic advancement. Prophecy, like poetry, becomes a specialized means through which Austen organizes and ascribes meaning to her life in 'Book M.'[30] While her participation in manuscript culture associates her with elite social groups, her claims to prophetic insights align her with rebellious low-ranking urbanites during the revolutionary period.[31] Hence, her occasional verse that touches upon prophetic matters and requests divine revelations represents an odd hybridization: Austen flirts with a discourse which, in the wake of the revolutionary period, is marked as low class, but she inscribes that discourse into a conservative, elitist form.[32]

Austen's account of her 'Dreame on 2[d]: of Jan: 1668' highlights her concerns about how her gender impacts her economic status and suggests that she can assert a sense of interpretive authority through her claims to prophetic abilities.[33] She dreams of leaving her mother when she goes to a wedding where she sees her late husband talking to another man in a room with a long table. Her later experience at Parliament seems to confirm the visionary quality of her dream. The room in which she conducts her business concerning her estate is the one that she saw in her dream, and the man whom she saw with her husband looks like a person at Parliament, 'S[r] John Birkenhead.' Retrospectively, she concludes that 'This busines was a Weeding: for it was a Contract, a Confederacy to take away our Estate. And I shal noe more be of that opinion generally observed in Dreames that a Weeding foretels a burning and a burning a Weeding. But that it is danger of Conspiracy against one – as This was to us' (Austen 60v-61).[34] Austen's vacillation between plural and singular pronouns provides a starting point for unraveling her overlapping concerns about her gender, financial status, and prophetic authority. First, Austen conceptualizes the contested estate as the property of herself and her dead husband, who appears at the negotiating table in her dream. She specifies that there is 'a Confederacy to take away our

Estate.' She switches to the first person singular, however, in asserting that her accurate prediction in the case of this dream gives her the authority to question the notion that dreaming about a wedding 'foretels a burning' to claim instead that such a dream signifies 'danger of Conspiracy against one.' In claiming a right to interpretation, Austen acknowledges that on the most immediate, material level she – not her husband (except insofar as his heirs represent him) – is the one who might lose the estate. Yet when she moves away from the significance of the dream – 'it is danger of Conspiracy against one' – and back to her account of what transpired at Parliament, she again uses a plural pronoun: 'as This was to us.' Austen's prophetic dream thus allows her to assert interpretive, organizational authority over her experiences, even if she does not conceptualize herself as an economic agent absolutely independent of her husband.

Ultimately, Austen interprets her difficulties with Parliament as signifying at the national level. When she makes her personal grievance against Parliament tantamount to a general, public concern and suggests that Parliament's behavior will doom the nation to a recurrence of the upheaval of the previous decades, Austen sounds like the radical female prophets of the revolutionary period. In an essay entitled 'On report at Parliament,' Austen writes:

> ffor this Complaint of oppression, God hath punishet the Land fformerly, in the great Callamities wch fell upon the times, And Surely if they pursue, and commit the same Crimes, of Unjistice, and Injuries to poore men. And Especially to acte violence on Widdowes and orphanes, how will their cries and greviances perce the Eares of Heaven, who will hear and Judge their cause, against an Unjust Nation. (67v)

In a fleeting instant of solidarity with the lower classes, Austen threatens that Parliament's unjust handling of her estate will bring down God's wrath on England – again.

Austen's self-figuration as a prophet is fissured and inconsistent due to her ambivalence both towards exposing her socioeconomic ambitions and towards the potential association of prophetic activity with disreputable persons: the urban rabble and outspoken women. The association of prophetic activity with the lower classes during the revolutionary period made asserting oneself as a prophet of questionable, but tempting, value to Austen.[35] As

Mack explains, the tensions related to social rank and gender among the prophets were such that the radical sects, despite 'champion[ing] the poor and deprived,' did not pursue women's concerns, while 'those women who were most conscious of their authority as females, Quaker and non-Quaker, were also those middle and upper class women who had the least affinity with the plight of the laboring classes' (4). While laying claim to uninstitutionalized knowledge and divine power might have been attractive options for Austen, her aspiration to rise in rank must have made any seeming similarity to low-ranking prophets an uncomfortable proposition for her.

Not only does Austen's elitism inflect her attitude towards prophetic activity, but so does her awareness of her gender as a threat to her rank.[36] Mack observes that '*all* enemies of the propertied classes and of the religious establishment, both male and female, were portrayed symbolically as women . . . while actual female visionaries were portrayed as tramps, in both the sexual and economic sense' (57). As the first epigraph to this section suggests, Austen appears to have known about the derogatory association of prophetic activity with women: 'If men doe listen to Wispers of fear, and have not reason, and observation Enough to confute trifles . . . Every old woman shal be a prophetes' (25r). Given Austen's essay about being called an 'old goat' by an anonymous male pedestrian (see note 3), it is clear that she is sensitive to the implication that she qualifies as such an 'old woman.' '. . . I should be unwilling to call a woman of foure score old,' Austen writes, 'Ancient is honourable: old is despicable. Old belongs to Old Shooes. Old clothes. Not to my self' (22v). Given her understanding of 'old woman' as disparaging, her comment about how superstitiousness leads men to think 'Every old woman . . . a prophetes' reveals her bitter sense of the ridicule associated with woman prophets.

Her gender aside, Austen had significantly different views from the radical sectarian prophets of the previous decades. As a landowner and a parent with a son at Oxford, she was invested in a national church and a mandatory church tithe.[37] It is not surprising that she disapprovingly refers to 'the beginning of the troubles [in] 1643 When Ministers was put out of their liveings' (10r). She opposed the beliefs of women prophets like Anna Trapnel, who argued vehemently against the tithe. Hence, Austen remains ambivalent towards prophetic activity for much of her manuscript, as is evident in how she occasionally converts her boldest claims of having spiritual gifts into the conventional attributes of meditative verse.[38] Austen's poem, 'Upon My

Dreame the 20th Oct 1664 When I Dreamet I Saw 4 Moones in a Clear Sky: Meditation,' highlights the tentative role of prophetic claims with respect to her writing:

> Will ffoure Moones more my ffate declare?
> Waight I in hope? or in Dispaire?
> Dus life or Death my date Unfold?
> I know not Lord thou are my hold.
> Which state is fittest Lord for thee (5)
> To that most willingly agree
> If through the pavement of y^e [the] grave
> Heavens providence more beauty have
> My God I doe Submit and know
> More glory unto me will Show   (10)
> Then this fraile life can contribute
> When pleasures to our hearts most Suite
> The mean time Lord prepare my heart
> ffor what thy ["purposes" struck out] <goodnes shal> impart
> ffor what thy purposes intend   (15)
> In Embassaige of life, or end.
> Addorne my Soule and beautify
> That chiefest part, I may comply
> O fit me Lord, to dye or live
> To doe my Duty while I breath.   (20)
> Then weelcome life or death Each one
> If thou Entitle me thy one
> If thou convert this litle Sand
> To Stand the Shoke of thy Command. (63v-64r)

Austen integrates her interest in the possibility that her dreams have prophetic significance with her concern for writing an 'appropriate' kind of verse – verse befitting the manuscript miscellany of a woman of rank. Thus, she turns her questioning of her dream's meaning into a commonplace articulation of her submission to God's will. I include the entire poem to demonstrate, first, the degree to which Austen compensates through generalized, unobjectionable entreaties to God for the opening lines in which she explicitly wonders about the meaning of her dream, and second, the coherence of the poem despite this shift from prophetic interrogation to humble prayer. Austen converts her potentially controversial effort to determine whether her dream foretells further life or imminent death for her into a prayer accepting whatever God dictates.[39]   Although the poem strays from the topic of prophetic dream interpretation, it is still tightly constructed around the problem of an uncertain future.   (Austen's repetition and reversal of the phrase 'life and death' contribute to this thematic coherence; see esp. lines 3, 16, 19, and 21.)

That Austen periodically displays less ambivalence about her own prophetic claims is evident in the poem she numbers her twenty-first. While 'Has Conduct Carried me through Seaven great yeares' retains the commonplace features – such as the acceptance of affliction and desire for contrition (e.g., lines 14 and 17-18 below) – of some of Austen's verse spiritual meditations, it integrates Austen's prophetic concerns more thoroughly with those thematic conventions:

> Has Conduct Carried me through seaven great yeares
> Great in perplexities, and great in feares
> Great Griefes with Job: could hardly be Exprest
> Neither by Sighings or by teares redrest
> Six folded trials and a seaventh as great   (5)
> By a perticular and genneral waight
> Hard knot Negotiates by oppresion knit
> A Dread consumeing Sickenes came, And Yet
> Mercy out Shined all those dark Eyed Clouds
> Design'd to me, in Seaven yeares ruged folds (10)
> The Wise Egiptianes deemed six compleate
> The Divine Scriptures dus the same repeate
> Six hardest trials, and to give renowne
> There comes a Seaventh. This is afflictions Crowne
> My Gracious Lord, Wilt Thou admit to me   (15)
> Thy Dearest <speciall [inserted below the line]> favours Soe much
>   glory See
> O that Upon thy Alter I may lay
> A Contrite heart and perfectly obay
> That Every day and minute be Confind
> Thy bright Memorials to bear in minde   (20)
> And to the future generations tell
> How high, how Excellent, Thy glories swell. (102v-103)

In 'Upon My Dreame the 20th Oct 1664 When I Dreamet I Saw 4 Moones in a Clear Sky: Meditation,' the ninth poem that Austen numbers in 'Book M,' she incorporates her brief initial prophetic interrogation into a conventional spiritual meditation.   In this much later poem, however, she maintains her interest in prophetic interpretation throughout. The first fourteen lines not only meditate on the numerological significance of the seven years Austen interprets as her allotted period of suffering before she gains some great reward (which corresponds to the stipulation in her husband's will that she not remarry for seven years), but they also justify that meditation through biblical and legendary references. Hence, Austen cites Job as the scriptural model of endurance (3-4); she borrows from the ancient authority of 'The Wise Egiptianes' who, like her, see six as a symbol of 'compleate[ness]' (11); and she confirms the sacred significance of six and seven by alluding to the six days of creation and the seventh day of rest in Genesis (12-14). Rather than diminishing the implications of her numerological meditation by retreating into a purely conventional prayer after line fourteen, Austen incorporates an explicit plea for extraordinary gifts into her address to God. In line sixteen, Austen changes her request for God's 'Dearest favours' into a request for '<speciall> favours.' Austen's revision alters the rest of the prayer such that it suggests that her ability to 'lay / A Contrite heart' upon God's 'Alter' and 'perfectly obay' depends upon God's granting her those '<speciall> favours' (17-18). Austen thus combines prophetic discourse with the conventions of meditative verse.

The last two couplets similarly merge these discourses. Lines nineteen and twenty continue the series of conditional results of God's bestowal of '<speciall> favours' upon the poetic speaker; this divine gift will enable the poet 'Every day and minute' to 'be Confined / Thy bright Memorials to bear in minde.' The gift of '<speciall> favours' here appears to assist the speaker's meditative self-discipline, but it does not seem to give her access to anything particularly extraordinary. The image of constant 'Confine[ment]' suggests that the poet will simply engage in the most private – and therefore the most appropriate for a seventeenth-century woman – of religious exercises. The final couplet, however, questions the privacy of that 'Confine[ment].' The '<speciall[y]> favour[ed]' poet will 'the future generations tell / How high, how Excellent, Thy glories swell' (21-22). The implication connecting these last two couplets as a logical sequence of thought is the act not only of writing, but of textual transmission, of 'publishing' in the sense of making public.[40] The fruits of contemplation in an isolated, private space will transform into a public declaration across generations.[41] The ambivalent prophet seeks to go public – on behalf of the gentle widow and the unpublished poet.

Notes

[1]   In transcribing Austen's text, I balance preserving its characteristics with making it accessible to today's reader. I have added punctuation for clarity, expanded abbreviated words (using brackets), and placed '< >' marks around Austen's revisions. For excerpts from 'Book M,' see Todd, 'A Young Widow of London' 215-37.

[2]   Sources for this biographical information include 'Book M' and Todd, 'A Young Widow of London' (207-211) and 'The Remarrying Widow' (76-77). Todd specifies that her most important sources are 'the Orphans Finding Book and Account Book of Money Received for Orphans (Corporation of London Record Office Mss. 93C and 94A) and the wills of Thomas and Katherine Austen in the Public Record Office, PROB 11/285/338 and PROB 11/PROB 11/ 375/1' ('A Young Widow of London' 214n1). Other scholarship on Austen includes Heller Mendelson and Hammons. Houlbrooke includes a transcription from 'Book M' (79). Marotti lists Austen as owning a manscript containing verse (50). Mendelson and Crawford refer to Austen's resistance to remarriage and her comments on household management (184, 308).

[3]   Austen's status seems difficult to define. Mendelson categorizes her as a gentlewoman (183 and 205n13), while Todd indicates that she aspired to join the gentry. Nonetheless, it is clear that 'she was well-to-do by contemporary standards' (Todd, 'A Young Widow of London' 209) and that she was ambitious to attain the highest rank possible. See Heal and Holmes 6-19, on the complications involved in defining the 'gentry.' An episode that Austen relates in which a male pedestrian calls her an 'old goat' illustrates her frustration when the outward signs of her wealth – her coach, for instance – do not guarantee respect: 'Surely I have not deserved in my conversation among men his most abusive and Scandalous Speech. I ride in my coach while I dare to let the way be so bad for them to walke./. old goat. The rudest Speech not proceeding from a gentleman as he pretends but from a Hinde, a Soughter' (22v). She responds to the pedestrian's insult by denying his gentle status, a gesture suggesting her awareness of the ideal correspondence between decorous behavior and rank.

[4]   On the incompatibility between the notion that men and women can have equal rank and the ideology of gender hierarchy, see Jordan, 'Renaissance Women and the Question of Class' 94.

[5]   On Austen's ambition, also see Todd, 'A Young Widow of London' 209,

212, 215.

[6] Todd claims that Austen's poems 'were carefully transcribed from other notebooks [of Austen's]' ('A Young Widow of London' 207).

[7] Austen indicates 1664 as the starting date for her entries in 'Book M' in its prefatory pages. Most of the dates that she mentions range between 1664 and 1666. On folio 10v, however, she heads one entry, '1682 Sr Edward Thurland.'

[8] On references to providence in spiritual diaries, see Mendelson 186-7. On recording successful prayers, see Thomas 115. Also see Todd, 'A Young Widow of London' 212-13.

[9] On the manuscript transmission of lyrics in these locations and on women's participation in the circulation of lyrics, see Marotti 30-61. On women and scribal publication, see Love 54-58. On women exchanging lyrics in manuscript coteries and on the limiting assumptions that have led scholars to overlook early modern women's manuscript writings, see Ezell 39-65.

[10] On rethinking early modern lyrics in light of manuscript culture, see especially Ezell, Marotti, and Wall. On the notion that lyrics produced and transmitted in manuscript were not conceptualized as author-centered, textually stable, or universalizing, see Marotti 135. Also see Wall on the social construction of 'the "closed" printed work and the "open" manuscript' (8).

[11] She refers to 'all the workes of Doc: Dun' and relates an anecdote about 'When D^c: Dun was in ffrance, with Sr Henery Wotten' (91v, 11r). In addition to noting Austen's familiarity with Donne's sermons, Todd indicates that Austen refers to 'Ralegh's *History of England* and Isaak Walton's *Lives*; [and] Thomas Fuller's account of Hildegarde of Bingen' ('A Young Widow of London' 212).

[12] On Austen's awareness of child loss poetry conventions, see Hammons, 'Despised Creatures: The Illusion of Maternal Self-Effacement in Seventeenth-Century Child Loss Poetry.' On her knowledge of the commonplaces of country-house poetry, see Hammons, 'Katherine Austen's Country House Innovations.'

[13] For more on preachers' use of lyrics, see Wenzel *passim*.

[14] Two well-known masculinist treatments of widows that follow this stereotype are Shakespeare's *The Taming of the Shrew* and Joseph Swetnam's *The Arraignment of Lewd, idle, forward, and unconstant Women*. Also see Overbury's contrasting characterizations of 'A Virtuous Widow' and 'An

Ordinary Widow' (253-4). Representations of low status/poor widows often portrayed them as witches, rather than shrews (see Willis 6n6). On the stereotype of the widow, see Todd, 'The Remarrying Widow' 54-55. On the connection between representations of high-ranking widows' lustfulness and inappropriate remarriages in *The Duchess of Malfi* and *Hamlet*, see Jardine esp. 70-72. On the status of Renaissance widows, see Jordan, *Renaissance Feminism* esp. 46, 71-2 and Keeble 252.

[15] See Todd, 'The Remarrying Widow' 74, on a seventeenth-century trend towards testators limiting their widows' ability to control inherited land and money.

[16] See Jane Owen's *An antidote against purgatory* for the assumption that remarriage could financially destroy a widow. Also see Heal and Holmes 75.

[17] Jardine observes that early modern women seemed to have 'become frighteningly strong and independent' in 'the area of inheritance and property, and Land Law' but that 'actually they remain[ed] in thrall' (Jardine 77-78, 88).

[18] In 'Book M,' it is clear that Austen had enough wealth to make several loans (e.g., 52r). She also lists expenses, such as money spent on property maintenance; funds that she lost through being cheated; and loans or financial gifts to a few cousins (99v). Austen's economic transactions suggest that she was not imminently at risk of becoming destitute. See Todd, 'A Young Widow of London' esp. 209-10, 211, 229.

[19] While Todd's study of remarriage focuses on Abingdonian widows, she refers to 'Book M' because Austen, unlike the Abingdoninan widows, writes extensively about remarriage ('The Remarrying Widow' 76).

[20] She asks God to help her avoid 'giv[ing] so great a Satisfaction as the reward of my Selfe, and all my Estate, ffor that which I am in a Capacity Civilly to requite by a lesser reward' (Austen 91r). She also tells her suitor that 'he was mistaken' when he 'protested if I was a very begger women if I wud have him he wud have me' (Austen 96r). Also see Austen 50r, 94v, 95r.

[21] She writes, 'Surely My God is prepairing for me Halcione daies, for daies of trouble and Molestation I have found from men Who considers not afflicted widows. They take advantage of them, who has little help and gives frequent occasion of more disturbance' (Austen 35v). Also see Austen 69r.

[22] See Marotti 75-133, on controversial sexual and political themes – with which Austen does not engage – in manuscript verse miscellanies.

Austen's poem, 'On Vollantines Day this 14 ffeb: 1665/ My Jewel'– which answers back to lyrics such as Donne's 'A Jet Ring Sent' and 'The

Funeral,' Carew's 'Upon a Ribbon,' Shirley's 'To a Lady Upon a Looking-Glass Sent,' and Waller's 'Upon a Girdle' – represents her most direct engagement with any tradition of love poetry (108v-109r).

[23] For the bawdy connotation of 'spirit,' see Shakespeare's sonnet 129 and Stephen Booth's discussion of it (441-443). The commonplace resonance of 'dying' with orgasm increases the potential for reading 'spirit' as a sexual pun. On the poetic speaker's meditation on his own death in amorous complaints, see Donne's 'The Apparition,' 'The Damp,' 'The Funeral,' and 'The Relic' and Shakespeare's sonnets 71-74.

[24] See Ovid 10.708-739.

[25] On metrical paraphrases of biblical texts, see Christopher Hill, *The English Bible and the Seventeenth Century Revolution* esp. 338.

[26] On Austen's struggles concerning the Highbury estate, see Todd, 'A Young Widow of London' esp. 211, 229-30.

[27] See Proverbs esp. 11:22, 12:4, 21:9, 21:19, 22:14, 23:27, 27:15.

[28] See Hill, *The Century of Revolution* 211.

[29] For an introduction to the issues involved in women's participation in the religious and political events of this period, see Phyllis Mack, *Visionary Women*; Elaine Hobby, *Virtue of Necessity* esp. 26-75; and Margaret Ezell's *Writing Women's Literary History* esp. 132-60.

[30] On Austen's prophecies, also see Todd, 'A Young Widow of London' 211.

[31] On the association of manuscript culture with elite status, see Marotti 34. On the association of prophecy and radical sectaries with the lower ranks, see Hill, *The World Turned Upside Down* 80 and Capp 82, 85, 93.

[32] For examples of Austen's prophetic interpretations of her dreams, see 38v, 54r, and 70v. She is similar to the female prophets of the revolutionary period in her tendency to compare herself to biblical figures (21r, 56r, 85v, 75r, 155r). On radical prophets and biblical figures, see Mack 105 and Hobby 26.

[33] Austen's ambivalence about the possibility that dreams have prophetic significance is visible in the juxtaposition of two titles: 'How ill to desier to know our ffortune,' followed by 'Some Dreames not to be Slighted: of S: of Serpent.' She both acknowledges that it is inappropriate to guess what providence has in store and intimates that this restriction does not always apply. In an essay entitled 'Of the ffeare of God,' Austen records the spectrum of arguments against interpreting dreams. For example, she writes, 'Dreams are without rule, and without reason. They proceed very much from the temper of the body and trouble of the minde. Tho Sometimes from Some

Daemon good or bad' (25r). Whether she composed such assertions or simply recorded them, they indicate her awareness of warnings against reading meaning into one's dreams (despite her many efforts to interpret her dreams).
[34] Todd reads 'burning' as 'burying' ('A Young Widow of London' 233).
[35] Lady Eleanor Davies might seem a possible model for Austen of the high status female prophet. However, Davies' notoriety and her disregard for propriety might have made Austen even more ambivalent towards pursuing a prophetic role had she known about Davies (Spencer 51-3).
[36] Austen's letter to her son Thomas reveals her awareness of how nonconformist beliefs could become socially disruptive, challenging the conventions of civility dear to the elite classes; see 44r.
[37] On the tithe, see Hill, *The World Turned Upside Down* 79.
[38] Austen's conflicted opinions about prophecy are evident in her collection of arguments against particular prophetic claims and against the possibility of contemporary prophecy altogether; see 12v, 14-16.
[39] On Austen's awareness of the controversial nature of dream interpretation, see note 33 above.
[40] Wilcox notes that 'The obligation to use the gifts of God and display the works of providence compromises the notion that women's devotional lives can be inviolably private' (57).
[41] The final lines (12-20) of Austen's nineteenth numbered poem include a similar linkage of a plea for an extraordinary gift from God with her promise to make a public declaration of God's greatness in return (101v).

Austen's preface to 'Book M' assumes a reader: 'Whoso Ever shal look in these papers and shal take notice of these personal occurrences wil Easily discerne it concerned none but my self and was a private Exercise directed to my self. The Singularity of these conceptions doth not advantaige any' (4v). (For a different reading of the preface, see Mendelson 183-4). Austen addresses her reader to construct her writing as perfectly acceptable: she rhetorically circumscribes herself as a writing woman strictly within the bounds of the private sphere. (Also see Todd, 'A Young Widow' 213.) However, Austen did not restrict her writing to private concerns; see esp. 73v and 86r. Furthermore, Austen's interest in Hildegard of Bingen (34r) – who could serve as a more socially acceptable model of the female prophet than Austen's more immediate, revolutionary prophesying sisters – leads one to wonder if Austen hoped for a posthumous discovery of her own manuscript, since post-Reformation legends concerning Hildegard suggested that her fame increased after the posthumous discovery of her prophecies in manuscript (*The Nunns Prophesie* 1-3).

Works Cited

Austen, Katherine. 'Book M.' British Library, Add. MS 4454, 1664.

Capp, B. S. *The Fifth Monarchy Men: A Study in Seventeenth-Century English Millenarianism.* London: Faber and Faber, 1972.

Ezell, Margaret J. M. *Writing Women's Literary History.* Baltimore: Johns Hopkins UP, 1993.

Hammons, Pamela. "Despised Creatures: The Illusion of Maternal Self-Effacement in Seventeenth-Century Child Loss Poetry." *ELH* 66 (1999): 25-49.

_____. Katherine Austen's Country House Innovations." *SEL 40* (2000): 123-137.

Heal, Felicity, and Clive Holmes. *The Gentry in England and Wales, 1500-1700.* Stanford: Stanford UP, 1994.

Hill, Christopher. *The Century of Revolution.* New York: Norton, 1980.

_____. *The English Bible and the Seventeenth-Century Revolution.* New York: Penguin P, 1993.

_____. *The World Turned Upside Down: Radical Ideas during the English Revolution.* New York: Viking P, 1972.

Hobby, Elaine. *Virtue of Necessity: English Women's Writing: 1649-88.* Ann Arbor: U of Michigan P, 1989.

The Holy Bible. King James Version. New York: Ballantine Books, 1991.

Houlbrooke, Ralph. *English Family Life, 1576-1716: An Anthology from Diaries.* New York: Basil Blackwell, 1989.

Jardine, Lisa. *Still Harping on Daughters: Women and Drama in the Age of Shakespeare.* New York: Columbia UP, 1989.

Jordan, Constance. *Renaissance Feminism: Literary Texts and Political Models.* Ithaca: Cornell UP, 1990.

_____. 'Renaissance Women and the Question of Class.' *Sexuality & Gender in Early Modern Europe: Institutions, Texts, Images.* ed. James Grantham Turner. New York: Cambridge UP, 1995. 90-106.

Keeble, N. H., ed. *The Cultural Identity of Seventeenth-Century Woman: A Reader.* New York: Routledge, 1994.

Love, Harold. *Scribal Publication in Seventeenth-Century England.* Oxford: Clarendon P, 1993.

Mack, Phyllis. *Visionary Women: Ecstatic Prophecy in Seventeenth-Century England.* Berkeley: U of California P, 1992.

Marotti, Arthur. *Manuscript, Print, and the English Renaissance Lyric.* Ithaca: Cornell UP, 1995.

Mendelson, Sara Heller. 'Stuart Women's Diaries and Occasional Memoirs.' *Women in English Society, 1500-1800.* ed. Mary Prior. New York: Methuen, 1985. 181-210.

Mendelson, Sara and Patricia Crawford. *Women in Early Modern England 1550-1720.* NewYork: Oxford UP, 1998.

The Nunns Prophesie: OR the True, Wonderful, and Remarkable PROPHESIE of St. Heldegard, First NUNN, and then ABESS: CONCERNING The Rise and Downfall f those Fire-Brands of EUROPE, the whole Order of JESUITS. London, 1680.

Overbury, Sir Thomas. *A Wife.* Keeble, ed. 253-54.

Ovid. *Metamorphoses.* Trans. Rolfe Humphries. Bloomington: Indiana UP, 1955.

Owen, Jane. *An antidote against purgatory. Renaissance Woman: Constructions of Femininity in England.* ed. Kate Aughterson. New York: Routledge, 1995. 279-280.

Shakespeare, William. *Shakespeare's Sonnets.* ed. Stephen Booth. New Haven: Yale UP, 1977.

Spencer, Theodore. 'The History of an Unfortunate Lady.' *Harvard Studies and Notes in Philology and Literature* 20 (1938): 43-59.

Swetnam, Joseph. *The Arraignment of Lewd, idle, froward, and unconstant women. Half Humankind.* eds. Katherine Usher Henderson and Barbara F. McManus. Urbana: U of Illinois P, 1985. 189-216.

Thomas, Keith. *Religion and the Decline of Magic.* New York: Scribner's, 1971.

Todd, Barbara J. '"I Do No Injury by not Loving": Katherine Austen, A Young Widow of London.' *Women & History: Voices of Early Modern England.* ed. Valerie Firth. Toronto: Coach House Press, 1995. 207-237.

_____. 'The Remarrying Widow: A Stereotype Reconsidered.' *Women in English Society, 1500-1800.* ed. Mary Prior. New York: Methuen, 1985. 54-92.

Wall, Wendy. *The Imprint of Gender: Authorship and Publication in the English Renaissance.* Ithaca: Cornell UP, 1993.

Wenzel, Siegfried. *Preachers, Poets, and the Early English Lyric.* Princeton: Princeton UP, 1986.

Wilcox, Helen. 'Private Writing and Public Function: Autobiographical Texts by Renaissance Englishwomen.' *Gloriana's Face: Women, Public and Private, in the English Renaissance.* eds. S. P. Cerasano and Marion Wynne-Davies. Detroit: Wayne State UP, 1992. 47-62.

Willis, Deborah. *Malevolent Nurture: Witch-Hunting and Maternal Power in Early Modern England.* Ithaca: Cornell UP, 1995.

2

'Public' and 'Private' in Aphra Behn's Miscellanies:
Women Writers, Print, and Manuscript

Anne Russell

In 1678, in the address 'To the Reader' that precedes *Sir Patient Fancy*, Aphra Behn described herself as 'forced to write for Bread and not ashamed to owne it' (Todd 6:5). Behn also hoped for fame, as a passage added to her translation of Cowley's 'Sylva' makes clear. A marginal note, 'The Translatress in her own Person speaks' directs the reader's attention to Behn's appeal, 'Let me with *Sappho* and *Orinda* be / Oh ever sacred Nymph adorned by thee; / And give my Verses Immortality' (Todd 1:325). Behn is among the first women writers in England to cultivate a public persona; Catherine Gallagher in particular has argued that in the prefaces to her plays and novels Behn deliberately and self-consciously exploited her place as a 'public woman' in the literary marketplace.[1] But in addition to publishing plays, poetry, and novels, Behn participated in a number of coterie literary circles in which manuscript works were exchanged. These 'private' circles included not only court poets, Oxford students, and academics, but also a considerable number of women. When Behn edited two poetic miscellanies in the 1680s, *Miscellany, Being A Collection of Poems by Several Hands. Together with Reflections on Morality, or Seneca Unmasqued* (1685) and *Lycidus: or the Lover in Fashion. . . . Together with a Miscellany of New Poems by Several Hands* (1688),[2] she brought into print not only works by 'public,' print-oriented or 'professional' writers, but also a number of poems by women and men which had been circulating in manuscript.

Behn is, as far as I know, the first woman to compile and publish a poetic miscellany, and her miscellanies include more works by women than are found in other print collections of the period. Yet only two of the women whose works are published in Behn's miscellanies are identified; the others are attributed to anonymous 'ladies.' Behn's miscellanies indicate some of the ways women's poetry moved from manuscript to print, and from print to manuscript – two systems that engaged each other in complicated ways. Although different themes and arrangements were often associated with poetry made 'public' in print, as opposed to poetry which circulated 'privately' in manuscript, in her collections of the 1680s Behn combined some of the conventions of the two systems of poetry circulation. In the process, she brought a number of women poets into print without seriously compromising the 'privacy' that was sought, or was assumed to be sought, by the many women writers who circulated their work in manuscript and who made no efforts to have their works printed.

In addition to compiling printed miscellanies, Behn was also involved in the production and circulation of poetry in manuscript. Behn's poetry, and poetry ascribed to her, is found in a number of surviving seventeenth-century manuscripts (Beal 2:1-6). Mary Ann O'Donnell makes a strong argument that a manuscript miscellany entitled 'Astrea's Booke for Songs & Satyrs' is partially in Behn's hand ('Bodleian MS Firth c.16' 189-222).[3] (Astrea was Behn's literary sobriquet.) And significantly, Behn included poetry in her print miscellanies that had been circulating in manuscript, thus taking editorial control over texts produced by others.

Behn's miscellanies include significantly more women as both writers and addressees than do other contemporary print miscellanies. A number of pieces are addressed to Behn as 'Astrea,' though several employ the more prosaic 'Mrs B.' Poems address women by pastoral pseudonyms such as 'the famed Antonia,' 'Laurinda,' and 'Gloriana.' Poems written by women in Behn's miscellanies are ascribed 'By a Lady' or 'By a Lady of Quality,' the latter presumably signalling the high rank of the unnamed writer(s).

Behn's inclusion of three poems by 'Mrs Taylor' in *Miscellany* and a poem by Anne Wharton in *Lycidus* demonstrates some of the ways women's poetry was presented in manuscript and print, 'private' and 'public' spheres. Taylor and Wharton are the only women contributors whom Behn identifies – one explicitly, the other obliquely. Behn promoted the 'public' poetic reputation of 'Mrs Taylor' by printing signed works that also appeared anonymously in other print and manuscript sources. On the other hand, without naming her directly, Behn discreetly drew attention to her own 'private' exchanges of poetry in manuscript with Anne Wharton, a woman of high rank. *Miscellany* prints a poem addressed to 'Mrs W.,' and *Lycidus* includes a piece in which Wharton is identified even more indirectly. Differences in the ways Behn presents and contextualizes Taylor's and Wharton's works in her print miscellanies suggest that a consideration of poetic themes and the writers' ranks might have determined some of Behn's strategies for bringing works by women into print. In the process, Behn drew attention to her participation in 'private' poetic correspondence, as well as to her roles as 'public' poet and editor.

In the seventeenth century, printed poetry circulated in broadsheet and in single-author and miscellany volumes; poetry was also disseminated in many manuscript forms, including single sheets of paper, letters, commonplace books, and miscellanies. There was considerable overlap between print and manuscript circles, as poetry moved from one system to the other, often without the knowledge or volition of the writer. In recent years, the once-firm critical distinctions between 'public' writing for the press and 'private' material that circulated in manuscript have been queried by a number of critics. Harold Love's use of the term 'scribal publication,' for example, emphasizes the social and 'public' aspects of manuscript circulation (35-45). In considering the complex ways in which manuscripts could become 'public' as a result of uncontrolled copying and circulation, Helen Hackett comments that 'the privacy of courtly writings can consist largely in their textual assertions of their own privacy' (171). Carol Barash notes that many women 'published (or were published) in both privately circulated manuscripts and printed books,' and suggests the importance of noting the tensions between what are conceptualized as 'private meanings' and 'public self-constructions' (8).

In spite of the many intersections of public and private, print and manuscript, there were nevertheless some significant differences between the ways poetry was produced, and circulated, in print and manuscript form. Although women's poetry in print was relatively rare and considered exceptional, women had important roles in the composition and transmission of poetry that circulated in manuscript. As poetry passed from hand to hand among a group of friends and acquaintances, both women and men wrote poems in response to others' work. Mary Hobbs lists a number of examples of early seventeenth-century women who 'wrote and copied poetry and songbooks' (2), and in mid-century, Katherine Philips was the center of a circle of male and female correspondents who shared poetry with each other.

Harold Love's study of manuscript culture briefly notes 'those women poets who either through preference or lack of access eschewed the press' (58), and Arthur Marotti documents a number of manuscript collections of poetry that women owned, compiled, and/or wrote (38-40; 48-61). Victoria Burke's study of women and manuscript culture examines manuscript collections written or compiled by women of different ranks and ages in England and Scotland, including songbooks, elegies, and many other kinds of poetry. The particular contribution of women to late seventeenth-century manuscript culture is emphasized by Margaret Ezell, who notes many texts by women in a wide range of genres (*Patriarch's Wife* 64-83), and who stresses the extent to which writing anonymously or pseudonymously, and writing 'privately' in manuscripts with limited circulation, involved a 'thriving female literary network' ('Revisioning the Restoration' 146-7).

In the early modern period, the miscellany was a popular and influential form in both print and manuscript. Miscellanies could include works of almost any genre, such as poems, epigraphs, riddles, and translations. Although there were changing styles in miscellanies, recent critical accounts argue that print miscellanies compiled in different periods often functioned to make links between 'private' coterie circulation and 'public' printed texts. Wendy Wall, for example, emphasizes the complex relationships between social status and authorship, manuscript and print, that are negotiated by *Tottel's Miscellany* (1557) and its imitators and successors of the last half of the sixteenth century (23-9). In the 1650s, poetic miscellanies known as drolleries focussed on songs and satires attacking parliamentary figures and policies (Raylor 202-207; Geduld 89). After 1660, drolleries which collected a wider range of comic poems and songs continued to be popular, reaching a peak of popularity in the early 1670s. Behn may have been the 'A.B.' who compiled *Covent Garden Drolery* (1672),[4] a volume of poetry and songs associated with the theater which Harry M. Geduld has argued was influential in establishing the conventions of the Restoration miscellany (88-9). Barbara Benedict, discussing the role of the Restoration print miscellany in the development of a poetic canon, makes a similar claim for the Dryden-Tonson *Miscellany Poems* (1684). Benedict describes that volume as a 'court anthology' (85-6) bridging a gap between court and middle class, between 'private' coterie manuscript circulation and 'public' print publication.

Behn's print miscellanies of the 1680s, I would suggest, draw considerably more varied 'private' poetry into the 'public' mode than do

Dryden's. Behn brings together a network of poets, both men and women, 'public' and 'private,' with different relations to Behn and to each other. In *Lycidus* in particular, Behn begins to develop a mode that is both 'public' and 'private.' The 'public' elements emphasize, among other things, Behn's own role in professional literary production as an editor and political poet. At the same time, Behn brings informal, more 'personal' or 'private' poetry written by both men and women, into print.

Dryden's influential *Miscellany Poems* emphasizes translations of classical texts into English verse by 'eminent hands,' all of them male. Dryden juxtaposed these courtly and aristocratic contributors' translations with his own 'public' and political verse, including 'Absolom and Achitophel' and 'Mac Flecknoe.' Although Behn's *Miscellany* also includes translations from the classics, there is a wider range of topics and contributors, more theatrical and political poetry, and works by women writers. Of the women contributors, only Behn and 'Mrs Taylor' are named. Two poems are by 'A Lady of Quality,' but they are not printed together and the text does not indicate if they are written by the same 'Lady.'

One classical text in Behn's volume is 'Verses made by Sappho, done from the Greek by Boileau, and from the French by a Lady of Quality' (212-13). Behn also includes her own long translation from the French of Rochefoucauld's *Maximes*, under the title *Reflections on Morality, or Seneca Unmasqued*. Both titles allude to the fact that most women knew classical texts only indirectly, through modern-language translations or adaptations. In her commendatory poem to Thomas Creech's English translation of Lucretius, Behn, who did not read Latin, thanks Creech for helping women repair the gaps in their educations: 'So thou by this Translation doth advance / Our Knowledg from the State of Ignorance, / And equals us to Man' (*Poems Upon Several Occasions* 52).[5] In the course of her career, Behn published several poetic translations, or 'imitations,' of passages from Latin texts; presumably she did so by working from prose translations in modern languages.[6]

The only signed poems in *Miscellany* by a woman other than Behn are three songs by 'Mrs Taylor.' In spite of the ascription, information about 'Mrs Taylor' is difficult to find and document. Reference works compiled in the 1980s differ in their approach. In 1987 Janet Todd suggested that 'Mrs Taylor' might be Behn herself (*A Dictionary of British and American Women Writers* 301),[7] and Todd's *British Women Writers: A Critical Reference Guide* (1989) does not include an entry for Mrs Taylor. In 1987, Margaret Ezell noted that a contemporary manuscript miscellany includes poems by 'Mrs Taylor', who 'may, or may not be' the same Mrs Taylor as Behn's (*Patriarch's Wife* 71). Ezell suggests that 'Mrs Taylor,' like many other women whose works are in manuscript, is 'probably untraceable' (69). In 1988 the editors of *Kissing the Rod* made a tentative identification of Behn's Mrs Taylor as the Elizabeth Taylor who married Francis Wythens or Withens in 1685,[8] a suggestion that has been incorporated into several later reference works.[9]

Behn prints the three pieces by 'Mrs Taylor' in sequence. 'Song, Made by Mrs Taylor,' begins 'Ye Virgin Pow'rs defend my heart/ From Amorous looks and smiles' (69-70). It is followed by 'To Mertill who desired her to speak to Chlorinda of his Love. By Mrs Taylor' ('Mertill though my heart should break / In granting thy desire' [71-2]) and 'Song, By Mrs Taylor,' ('Strephon has Fashion, Wit and Youth, / With all things else that please' [72-3]). The speaker of 'Ye Virgin Pow'rs' hopes 'Honour' will defend her 'if through Passion I grow blind' (70). The speaker of 'Mertill' agrees to speak to 'cold Chlorinda' on his behalf. The speaker of the third poem is wary of Strephon's power over her: 'But he is flint, and bears the Art, / To kindle strong desire' although he himself 'ne'er feels the fire' (72). All three poems express awareness of the deceptions and dangers of love, and in each poem the speaker feels vulnerable to desire. The three poems all have similar metrical patterns, sixteen lines of alternating iambic tetrameter and trimeter lines, but are arranged in different stanzaic forms, with ababcdcd rhyme schemes. The titles, and the structural patterns, suggest that they might have been written with musical settings in mind.

'Ye Virgin Pow'rs' seems to have been a lyric which circulated widely. It is printed, unsigned, in *The Theater of Music . . . The First Book* (1685) with a setting by Thomas Farmer (44). This collection appeared in the same year as Behn's *Miscellany*; it is not clear which volume was published first. 'Ye Virgin Pow'rs' is also included in *The New Treasury of Music* (1695), a collection of previously published songbooks that includes *The Theater of Music. . . The First Book*. Several substantive differences between the Behn and *Theater of Music* versions of the poem suggest that neither work was the source for the other. The most striking difference is in the last stanza. The Behn version reads:

A heart whose Flames are seen tho pure,

> Needs every Vertues aid,
> And those who think themselves secure,
> The soonest are betrayed. (70)

In the *Theater of Music* the first two lines of the stanza are different: 'Tis fit the price of heaven be pure, / And worthy of its Aid' (44). The vivid image in the Behn version of a heart in flames is characteristic of Mrs Taylor's diction in the other two poems.

Mrs Taylor's brief songs about love conform to contemporary fashions in vocal music, and are also found in several surviving late seventeenth-century manuscript miscellanies. In a poetry miscellany at the Thomas Fisher Library at the University of Toronto 'Ye Virgin Pow'rs' is unattributed, entitled simply 'Song' (MS 9263, No. 14), its text only slightly different from Behn's version. Peter Beal notes that Edinburgh University Library MS La. III. 98, a manuscript which assigns five poems to Behn (four incorrectly), also includes what he calls 'the apocryphal:"Song" (Ye Virgin Pow'rs, defend my heart) by Mrs Taylor' (3).[10]

In a Bodleian manuscript miscellany 'Ye Virgin Pow'rs' is called 'A Song by a Lady, Mistrustful of her own strength' (Bod. S Rawl. poet. 173, f. 72-72v). It is followed by 'Strephon has fashion' with the title 'Song by a Lady. The heart at rest at home' (f.72v).[11] This carefully-compiled miscellany is entitled:

> The Muses's Magazine or Poetical Miscellanies. In two Parts.
> The first consisting of Choice Translations and Paraphrases
> selected from ye Ancients Done by the best of our Modern
> Poets. The Second Part consists wholly of original Poems.
> Selected from many of the best of our own Poets . . . 1705.

Inscribed on the backpaper of the binding of the miscellany is 'John Dunton his Book for which Mr Corbett at ye Addisons Head accepted one Half Guynea in full payment for it.' Dunton, a prolific publisher of poetry, was apparently not aware that Behn had published these two poems twenty years earlier as 'Mrs Taylor's.' Dunton did, however, identify the poems as by a woman writer – perhaps because he was following his source, or perhaps because the speakers are female.[12]

An unattributed version of 'Mertill though my heart should break' is in another manuscript miscellany, a bound collection of various kinds and sizes of paper in different hands (Bodleian MS. Rawl. poet. 172, f. 110). There are a number of substantive differences between the version of 'Mertill' in Behn's collection and in this manuscript, particularly in the third stanza, suggesting that they are not derived from each other. In the same hand on the same page, 'Mertill' is followed by a poem entitled 'Of the Dutchesse made by Mrs Taylor,' which begins 'Come all ye Nymphs and every swain.' This poem, 16 lines of iambic tetrameter, with an aabb rhyme scheme, employs a different form from that of the three Mrs Taylor poems printed by Behn. Although Ezell claims this 'may or may not be' the same Mrs Taylor, the juxtaposition of the two poems in the same hand, with the second poem ascribed to Mrs Taylor, suggests that 'Of the Dutchesse' is by the same Mrs Taylor whom Behn identifies as the author of 'Mertill.'

'Ye Virgin Pow'rs' continued to be read and sung after its inclusion in *The New Treasury of Music* in 1695 and in Dunton's manuscript miscellany of 1705. The poem also appears in John Aikin's *Essays on Song-Writing* (1772) which aims to collect 'the most excellent productions in song-writing' (iv). Aikin includes 'Ye virgin powers' (without the elision 'pow'rs') under the category of 'Passionate and Descriptive Songs' (127-8) and 'Strephon has fashion' in the category 'Witty Songs' (255), assigning both to Mrs Taylor.[13] In *Vocal Poetry* (1810), Aikin's later, much-revised edition of the collection, the two poems are printed together as 'Amatory Songs' (177-78). Aikin is vague about his sources. He writes that 'the chief source of good songs, are the miscellany poems and plays from the time of Charles the second to the conclusion of Queen Ann's [sic] reign' (vi) but offers no more specific information about his copytexts, or whether he used both print and manuscript sources. Aikin's version of 'Ye Virgin Powers' is closer to Behn's than to the version in *Theater of Music*, but minor differences between the two versions suggest that Aikin did not derive his texts from Behn.[14] I have not located his source, which apparently assigned the poems to Mrs Taylor.

I know of no material evidence that would illuminate how, or if, Behn might have known Mrs Taylor. *The Theater of Music . . . the First Book* in which 'Ye Virgin pow'rs' was printed includes in its subtitle *A Choice Collection of the newest and best Songs Sung at the Court, and Public Theaters*. Since Behn had friends in the theater as well as at court, she might have known Mrs Taylor through her connections there.

Given that three versions of 'Ye Virgin Pow'rs,' and one example each of 'Mertill' and 'Strephon' are known to survive in manuscript, these poems by Mrs Taylor may have circulated more widely in manuscript. 'Ye Virgin Pow'rs' was printed at least three times between 1685 and 1695, and again in 1772 and 1810. Yet these poems, and their author, virtually disappeared for more than 170 years until the editors of *Kissing the Rod* included Mrs Taylor in their collection. Neither Mrs Taylor nor any of her poems are listed in the Chadwyck-Healey full-text poetry database, nor in the *New Cambridge Bibliography* on which it is based. In spite of Behn's publication of her poems, Mrs Taylor has had little subsequent recognition.

The situation is different for Anne Lee Wharton (1659-1685), the other woman Behn identifies, though obliquely. Wharton was the wife of Thomas Wharton, who would become a Whig leader in Parliament after her death. Anne Wharton was highly respected in the late seventeenth and early eighteenth centuries, particularly for her poetic translations of biblical passages from Jeremiah and the Psalms, and for her paraphrase of the Lord's Prayer (now lost). Although Wharton wrote several light lyrics and songs, most of her surviving work focuses on affliction. During her life some of Wharton's work was read in manuscript; in the first few years after her death her poetry appeared in a number of different print miscellanies, including Behn's *Lycidus*.[15] A considerable proportion of her oeuvre is printed in different volumes of J. Nichols's *Select Collection of Poems* (1780). Although some of Wharton's poems have occasionally been anthologized since that time, her scattered poetry was not easily accessible until the recent appearance of Germaine Greer's and Susan Hastings's edition of *The Surviving Works of Anne Wharton*.[16]

Wharton is addressed, and one of her poems printed, in *Lycidus* (1688), Behn's last miscellany, which includes loosely connected groups of poems that engage a number of issues. Parts of *Lycidus* recall the ways in which poetry was produced and presented in non-professional, 'private' manuscript networks. The volume includes personal poems on topics such as the sending of small gifts and the reading, writing, and sharing of poetry. Most of the poems addressing women employ pastoral pseudonyms such as 'Antonia,' 'Laurinda, 'Cloris,' and 'Gloriana.' Two pseudonyms apply to identifiable women whose poetry is included – 'Urania' and 'Astrea.'

'Urania,' the name of the Muse associated with astronomy, is Anne Wharton,[17] whose 'To Mr Wolseley on his Preface to Valentinian. By a Lady of Quality' (95-6), is followed by 'Mr Wolseley's Answer to the forgoing Copy' (96-101), addressed to 'fam'd Urania' (96). 'Mr Wolseley's Answer' is annotated by the only marginal gloss in the volume, '*The Earl of Rochester, her Uncle*,' which is in italic type in the margin next to the line 'In her lov'd Lays his better part survives' (101). The second poem in *Lycidus*, the unsigned 'To Urania in Mourning,' (2-3) may also be addressed to Wharton. The speaker praises Urania's beauty in grief and asks her to 'spare / To my Distress one balmy pitying Tear' (3), a possible allusion to Wharton's elegy for Rochester, which was being read in manuscript not long after Rochester's death in 1680.[18]

Lycidus draws attention to Behn's relations with Rochester, his friend Robert Wolseley,[19] and his niece Anne Wharton. Behn had earlier alluded to her connections with Rochester and Wharton. *Miscellany* (1685) included Behn's elegy for Rochester, which she had apparently sent to Wharton, and Behn had printed 'To Mrs W. On her Excellent Verses (Writ in Praise of some I had made on the Earl of Rochester) Written in a Fit of Sickness' in *Poems Upon Several Occasions* (57-60) in 1684. Wharton's 'To Mrs A Behn on what she writ of the Earl of Rochester,' dated December 1682 by Greer and Hastings (314), was not printed until 1693, by which time both Wharton and Behn were dead.[20] In three of her print collections of poetry of the 1680s, then, Behn drew attention to her manuscript exchanges of poetry with Wharton and to their shared admiration for Rochester. In doing so, Behn also made public Wharton's approbation of the elegy.

Wharton died in January of 1685, the year after Behn and Wolseley had been associated in a project to stage Rochester's play *Valentinian* (an adaptation of Fletcher's play of the same name). Rochester's *Valentinian* was printed in 1685 with a prologue by Behn, and a preface and song by Wolseley. Wharton's poem to Wolseley in *Lycidus* thanks him for defending Rochester's reputation; Wolseley's reply chooses to emphasize her praise of his own work. Greer and Hastings suggest that Wharton herself might also have aided the *Valentinian* project (87; 326 n23). If so, Behn could have obtained the poems between Wharton and Wolseley either from Wharton, with whom she had exchanged poetry previously, or from Wolseley, who contributed several other poems and songs to *Lycidus*.

By printing Wharton's poem in *Lycidus*, and by obliquely identifying the author in the margin, Behn drew attention to her poetic contacts with two respected poets of high rank. Behn's works had been identified as Rochester's in both manuscript and print compilations;[21] when she 'claimed' these poems by publishing them in her own *Poems Upon Several Occasions*, the association with Rochester would enhance her poetic reputation. Behn was among the first to print any of Wharton's work, but not, significantly, until after her death. Although Wharton made no known efforts to print her poetry it was widely circulated and copied in the 'private' manuscript system, hence fairly 'public.' The poetic exchange between Wharton and Wolseley is found in two seventeenth-century manuscript miscellanies (Bodleian MS Rawl. poet. 159, ff. 192-93 and Folger MS X d 383). Wharton sent a number of poems to Bishop Gilbert Burnet, who on 9 January 1683 wrote: 'I send them about to all my female friends who know not what to think on you' (*Letters between the Rev James Granger* 243). While he encouraged her writing, Burnet passed on Lady Ranelagh's disapproval of some of Wharton's lines 'quarrelling with your Maker' in 'The Despair' (*Letters* 242), and repeated criticisms from others who had read her poems (*Letters* 241). Burnet also disapproved of Wharton's poetic correspondence with Behn. On 19 December 1682 he wrote of Behn, 'I am heartily sorry she has writ anything in your commendation . . . the praises of such as she is are great reproaches' (*Letters* 235). Burnet implies that by praising Wharton's poetry in print, and drawing attention to Wharton's correspondence with her, Behn gave Wharton a 'public' reputation that Burnet defined as a reproach.[22]

When Behn published Wharton's poem in *Lycidus,*[23] three years after Wharton's death, she identified Wharton only indirectly. However, other contemporary editors of miscellanies were not as discreet – or perhaps as anxious. Nahum Tate printed the elegy for Rochester in 1685 as 'By Mrs Wh—,' and a number of poems identified as Wharton's appeared in *The Idea of Christian Love* (1688) which also printed Edmund Waller's poems praising Wharton's poetry and piety. Wharton's works were also published in a number of other miscellanies during the next thirty years.

Behn's editorial decisions to name Taylor but not to identify Wharton directly in *Lycidus* (although she had alluded to 'Mrs W' in *Poems Upon Several Occasions* before Wharton's death) might have been affected by several concerns. Behn's social position in relation to Wharton, as seen by Burnet, for example, might have played a part in her decision. Behn's oblique identification of Wharton might also have seemed wise for a Tory political poet printing a poem by a woman from a powerful Whig family, presumably without permission. The differences in Behn's presentation and contextualization of poems by Taylor and Wharton, and their subsequent critical histories, could also indicate differences in the social status of the two poets. However, Wharton's high reputation from the 1680s to the 1720s was also due to the seriousness of her poetic themes.

I can only speculate about how and why Behn assembled the poems for *Lycidus*. The dialogues, addresses, and informal pieces suggest that some of the poems might have been part of a personal collection including poems to her, and her responses to them.   'Astrea's Booke,' which Mary Ann O'Donnell argues is partly in Behn's hand ('Bodleian MS Firth c.16'), is not the only collection of manuscript poetry that has been attributed to Behn. In March 1707 *The Muses Mercury*, a monthly miscellany of poetry compiled by John Oldmixon (1673-1742), printed Behn's 'On the First Discovery of Falseness in Aminta' from *Lycidus* as 'The Disoblig'd Love,' with some substantive variations. The poem is introduced in *The Muses Mercury* with the disclaimer:

> If it were proper to make publick what we have learnt of the Story of the Author of the following Verses, 'twou'd be an unquestionable Proof of their being *genuine*. For they are all writ with her own Hand in a Person's Book who was very much her Friend; and from thence are now transcrib'd for the *Mercury*. There are Fifteen or Sixteen Copies of Verses more, which will in due time be printed in this Collection. There's no Man who knows any thing of Mrs Behn's way of Writing but will presently see, that this Poem was written by her Self; and the rest are of the same Character. (March 1707, 60).

Although the 'Introduction' to the first issue, which solicits contributions to the *Mercury*, says that 'we shall Print Nothing that has been printed before' (January 1707), Oldmixon does not know, or admit, that Behn had already published the poem under another title. Oldmixon proudly emphasizes that the poem is transcribed in Behn's 'own Hand' in her friend's book. Several months later he invited sceptics to view the 'original Copies, under her own Hand' at the bookseller's (May 1707, 110).

In the 1690s, Oldmixon had written several plays and pastorals which were performed; these associations with the theater and other poets might have given him access to a source for manuscript works by Behn. After 1710 he became known as a Whig historian, political writer, and publisher. Oldmixon's memoir, which does not deal with the period in which he edited the *Mercury*, includes no explanation of how he came by the Behn manuscript.

It does, however, suggest that he often acquired and printed works in manuscript. The dedication to the Duchess of Marlborough reminds her that in 1710 he had returned to her one of her manuscripts that had come into his hands: 'Had I indeed been mercenar I might have made more Advantage, by trafficking with that Manuscript, than by all the awards and Gratuities I could ever expect from those Defenders and Patrons' (Oldmixon A3).

Altogether, in nine months *The Muses Mercury* printed twelve poems identified as Behn's, only two of which had not been previously printed in volumes Behn wrote or edited – *Covent Garden Drolery, Poems Upon Several Occasions, The Dutch Lover*, and *Lycidus* (O'Donnell, *Bibliography* 273-8). Substantive variants in all of the previously printed poems indicate that the print sources were not copytexts for the versions in *The Muses Mercury*.[24] Because the manuscript compilation from which Oldmixon claims to have transcribed the poems is not known to have survived, we have no further information about when the manuscript versions were composed or transcribed, or how they were arranged and contextualized in the manuscript. However, when Behn printed her own works, she printed versions of these poems that are different from those in the manuscripts published by the *Muses Mercury*, trying to assert editorial control over her own poetry by choosing which texts to print in her collections. Given the care she took in bringing her poems into print, it is ironic that after her death manuscript sources were used as copytexts for her poems while her published works were unknown or ignored. Oldmixon's comments suggest that he valued the versions of the poems included in the *Mercury* because of the privilege and authority their manuscript status conferred on them, and particularly because of their association with Behn's 'Hand.'

These brief case studies point to some of the paradoxical interrelationships between women's poetry in print and in manuscript. Wharton's work had been distributed, and sometimes criticized, in the 'private' manuscript system during her lifetime. In contrast, after her death her works were printed with praise and admiration, often grouped with poems praising her. Mrs Taylor's case is quite different. Poems identified as Mrs Taylor's circulated in both print and manuscript, suggesting that they were well-liked and popular. Yet in the 1680s and 1690s, when the poems were first printed and copied, there is no known contemporary allusion to the person who wrote them. By printing Wharton's work, Behn made public her coterie poetic connections with the serious-minded Wharton. In contrast, by publishing Mrs Taylor's signed work, Behn may have been acting as patron/editor for an obscure songwriter.

As a writer for the market, Behn took editorial control over much of her scattered poetry in the collections she published in the 1680s, where she printed most of the poetry she had composed to that date. She also printed works, by both men and women, that had been circulating in manuscript, collapsing some of the distinctions between the 'public' literary world reserved primarily for men of letters and the 'private' circles of manuscript transmission in which many women were writers. In the process, Behn emphasized her own complex connections with both 'public' and 'private' worlds. It is telling that after her death works in Behn's hand were ascribed a higher value than the books she had published, and that her poems found in manuscript collections were not recognized as the works she had so assiduously seen into print.

Notes

Early versions of parts of this essay were presented in the session on Early Modern Women and Genre at the Shakespeare Association of America, Cleveland, March 1998, where Julie Campbell made helpful comments, and at the Social Sciences and Humanities Congress, Ottawa, June 1998. Viviana Comensoli read a later version of the essay and contributed many useful suggestions. I am grateful to Wilfrid Laurier University for its research support in the form of a Short-Term Research Grant. I am grateful to the Bodleian Library, University of Oxford, for permission to quote from manuscripts in their collection.

[1] Gallagher argues that Behn constructs herself as a 'new fangled whore' (14), a strategy allying her with women performers of her plays who were perceived as 'public women.' Germaine Greer reads these images more literally when she raises the possibility 'that Aphra Behn began her career in the Americas or in mainland Europe as a courtesan' (*Slip-shod Sibyls* 188). Both Gallagher and Greer examine the extensive contemporary references which associate Behn's writing with prostitution. See also Jonathan Goldberg's comments on Gallagher's argument (54-6).

[2] In 1684, Jacob Tonson had published *Poems Upon Several Occasions*, a

collection of Behn's poetry followed by her translation of the first part of Paul Tallement's *A Voyage to the Isle of Love*. *Lycidus* includes the second part of the Tallemant translation.

[3] O'Donnell argues that 'Astrea's Booke' was compiled in the mid 1680s, the period when Behn published her two print miscellanies. 'Astrea's Booke' includes poems consistent with Behn's interests, but with only two exceptions the satires and poems in the manuscript are not found in Behn's published work ('Bodleian MS. Firth c. 16' 204). Many poems in 'Astrea's Booke' satirize people Behn supported ('Private jottings' 287).

[4] For the case that Behn probably edited this volume see Mary Ann O'Donnell (*Aphra Behn: An Annotated Bibliography* 213-17) and G. Thorn-Drury ('Introduction' to *Covent Garden Drollery*). Paul Hammond is less convinced that 'A.B.' was Behn (159).

[5] Lucy Hutchinson, who translated part of Lucretius, is one of the few late seventeenth-century women educated in classical languages.

[6] Dryden included Behn's 'Oenone to Paris' in his collection of translations of Ovid's *Epistles* (1680). Dryden's introduction describes Behn's contribution as an 'Imitation,' noting, 'I was desir'd to say that the Authour, who is of the Fair Sex, understood not Latine. But if she does not, I am afraid she has given us occasion to be asham'd who do' ([a4]). See Elizabeth Spearing's discussion of Behn's translations.

[7] Todd does not suggest why Behn might have wanted to publish three fairly conventional poems pseudonymously in a collection that includes so much of her own acknowledged work.

[8] The editors of *Kissing the Rod* identify Mrs Taylor with the 'Olinda' whose ode beginning 'Ah poor Olinda never boast' is included in Delariviere Manley's *Secret Memoirs and Manners . . . From The New Atalantis* (1709), printing the Olinda ode from *The New Atalantis* and the three Mrs Taylor poems that Behn includes in *Miscellany*. They also attribute to Mrs Taylor a drinking song by 'Lady Withens' published in 1720 (294-5). Their complex argument identifying 'Olinda' starts with an indirect allusion in one of the several keys to Manley's *roman-à-clef*, which leads to the entry for Sir Francis Wythens in the *Dictionary of National Biography*. The editors conclude that 'Mrs Taylor' is 'likely' the Elizabeth Taylor (d. 1708) who married Sir Francis Wythens or Withens in 1685, and who for many years during her marriage lived near or with Sir Thomas Colepepper of Aylesworth, Kent, marrying him after Wythens's death (294).

[9] Jeslyn Medoff, one of the editors of *Kissing the Rod*, briefly repeats this identification of Mrs Taylor in 'Daughters of Behn' (33-4) and it has been accepted by the editors of *The Feminist Companion to Literature* (1056-7). Janet Todd treats Taylor as a separate person from Behn in her recent *The Secret Life of Aphra Behn*, but adds no new information.

[10] The only poem ascribed to Behn in this manuscript accepted by modern editors as hers is 'Ovid to Julia' ('Fair royal maid, permit a youth undone'). See Todd's edition of Behn's *Poetry* (1:182-4). I have not seen the version of 'Ye Virgin Pow'rs' in this manuscript.

[11] Two poems in this manuscript appear in *Lycidus*: 'On an ungrateful and undeserving mistress' (49) and 'Cato's Answer to Labienus' (106).

[12] The editors of *Kissing the Rod* collate the two Mrs Taylor poems in Dunton's manuscript with Behn's versions (296; 298).

[13] Aikin includes a number of pieces by his sister Anna Barbauld. I am grateful to Lisa Vargo for bringing Aikin's collection to my attention.

[14] Aikin's version includes the flaming heart of Behn's text.

[15] After being published in a number of different miscellanies between 1685 and 1720, some of her work was also included in *Whartoniana* (1727), a collection of papers and documents associated with several generations of the Wharton family.

[16] I quote Wharton's poems from early texts, but all poems by or to Wharton can be found in the Greer and Hastings edition.

[17] Although 'Urania' is a common sobriquet in seventeenth-century poetry, Wharton was also addressed as Urania in Edmund Waller's 'Of the Paraphrase of the Lord's Prayer, Written by Mrs Wharton' in *The Idea of Christian Love* (1688) and Robert Gould's 1685 broadside elegy for Wharton (*Surviving Works* 301-5).

[18] A brief version of Wharton's elegy was published in *Poems by Several Hands . . . Collected by N. Tate* (1685); a longer version appears in *Examen Miscellaneum* (1702).

[19] Wolseley is discussed by Mary Ann O'Donnell in 'Private jottings' (288-90) and by Greer and Hastings (87-91).

[20] Wharton's poem to Behn appeared in *A Collection of Poems by Several Hands* (1685 [242-4]) and in a reprint of the volume with a new title *The Temple of Death* (1695 [242-4]), both published by Francis Saunders, the publisher of *Lycidus*.

[21] See David Vieth's discussion of this issue.

[22] In the political realm, however, Burnet did not think that Behn's praises would dishonour the recipients. In 1688 or early 1689, Burnet apparently asked Behn, who had long been a supporter of James II, to write a poem in praise of William of Orange on his attainment of the throne. Behn refused in 'A Pindaric Poem to the Reverend Doctor Burnet on the Honour he did me of enquiring after me and my Muse' (Todd 1:307-310; see Compton 140-49). Behn did, however, publish a poem praising James's daughter Mary, 'A Congratulatory Poem to her Sacred Majesty Queen Mary, Upon her Arrival in England' (Todd 1:304-307).

[23] Behn was ready to print the poem earlier, however, since *Lycidus* was licensed May 13, 1687 but not published until 1688.

[24] See Paul Saltzman's discussion of the variants between the two versions of 'Damon being asked a reason for loving' in *Covent Garden Drolery* and *Muses Mercury* (114-15).

Works Cited

Manuscripts
Bodleian MS Firth c.16, Oxford U
Bodleian MS Rawl. poet. 159
Bodleian MS Rawl. poet. 172
Bodleian MS Rawl. poet. 173
Folger Library MS X d 383
Thomas Fisher Library MS 9263, U of Toronto
Edinburgh U Library MS La. III. 798

Aikin, John. *Essays on Songwriting*. London: Joseph Johnson, [1772].
_____. *Vocal Poetry*. London: J. Johnson, 1810.
Barash, Carol. *English Women's Poetry, 1641-1714: Politics, Community, and Linguistic Authority*. Oxford: Clarendon P, 1996.
Behn, Aphra. *Lycidus: or the Lover in Fashion . . . Together with a Miscellany of New Poems by Several Hands*. London: Joseph Knight and Francis Saunders, 1688.
_____. *Miscellany, Being A Collection of Poems by Several Hands. Together with Reflections on Morality, or Seneca Unmasqued*. London: Hindmarsh, 1685.
_____. *Poems Upon Several Occasions*. London: Tonson, 1684.
_____. *The Works of Aphra Behn. Vol. 1. Poetry*. ed. Janet Todd. Columbus: Ohio State UP, 1992.
Beal, Peter. *Index of English Literary Manuscripts. Volume 2 1625-1700. Part 1*. London: Mansell, 1987.
Benedict, Barbara. *Making the Modern Reader: Cultural Mediation in Early Modern Literary Anthologies*. Princeton: Princeton UP, 1996.
Burke, Victoria. 'Women and Seventeenth-Century Manuscript Culture: Miscellanies, Commonplace Books, and Songbooks.' Diss. U of Oxford, 1996.
A Collection of Poems by Several Hands. 2nd edn. London: Francis Saunders, 1693.
Compton, Virginia. '"For when the act is done and finish't clean, / what should the poet doe, but shift the scene?": Propaganda, Professionalism, and Aphra Behn.' *Aphra Behn Studies*, ed. Todd. 130-53.
Examen Miscellaneum. London, 1702.
Ezell, Margaret J. M. *The Patriarch's Wife: Literary Evidence and the History of the Family*. Chapel Hill and London: U of North Carolina P, 1987.
_____. 'Revisioning the Restoration: Or, How to Stop Obscuring Early Women Writers.' *New Historical Literary Study: Essays on Reproducing Texts, Representing History*. eds. Jeffrey N. Cox and Larry J. Reynolds. Princeton: Princeton UP, 1993. 136-50.
The Feminist Companion to Literature in English: Women Writers from the Middle Ages to the Present. eds. Virginia Blain, Patricia Clements, Isobel Grundy. New Haven: Yale UP, 1990. 1056-57.
Gallagher, Catherine. *Nobody's Story. The Vanishing Acts of Women Writers in the*

Marketplace 1670-1820. Berkeley: U of California P, 1994.

Geduld, Harry M. *Prince of Publishers: A Study of the Work and Career of Jacob Tonson.* Bloomington: Indiana UP, 1969.

Goldberg, Jonathon. *Desiring Women Writing: English Renaissance Examples.* Stanford: Stanford UP, 1997.

Greer, Germaine. *Slip-shod Sibyls: A Recognition, Rejection and the Woman Poet.* London: Viking, 1995.

Hackett, Helen. 'Courtly Writing by Women.' *Women and Literature in Britain 1500-1700.* ed. Helen Wilcox. Cambridge: Cambridge UP, 1996. 169-89.

Hammond, Paul. 'The Prologue and Epilogue to Dryden's *Marriage-A-la-Mode* and the Problem of *Covent Garden Drolery.*' *Papers of the Bibliographical Society of America* 81 (1987): 155-72.

Hobbs, Mary. *Early Seventeenth-Century Verse Miscellany Manuscripts.* Aldershot: Scolar P, 1992.

The Idea of Christian Love. London, 1688.

Kissing the Rod: An Anthology of 17th Century Women's Poetry. eds. Germaine Greer, Jeslyn Medoff, Melinda Sansone, and Susan Hastings. London: Virago, 1988.

Letters between the Rev James Granger . . . and Many of the Most Eminent Literary Men of his Time. ed. J. P. Malcolm. [London, 1805].

Love, Harold. *Scribal Publication in Seventeenth-Century England.* Oxford: Clarendon P, 1993.

Manley, Delariviere. *Secret Memoirs and Manners . . . from the New Atalantis.* London, 1709.

Marotti, Arthur F. *Manuscript, Print, and the English Renaissance Lyric.* Ithaca: Cornell UP, 1995.

Medoff, Jeslyn. 'The Daughters of Behn and the Problem of Reputation.' *Women, Writing, History 1640-1740.* eds. Isobel Grundy and Susan Wiseman. Athens: U of Georgia P, 1992. 33-54.

Miscellany Poems. . . by the Most Eminent Hands. London: Tonson, 1684.

The Muses Mercury: or the Monthly Miscellany. London: Andrew Bell, January 1707-January 1707/8.

The New Treasury of Music. London: Andrew Bell, 1695.

O'Donnell, Mary Ann. *Aphra Behn: An Annotated Bibliography of Primary and Secondary Sources.* New York: Garland, 1986.

_____. 'Bodleian MS Firth c.16: A verse miscellany of Aphra Behn.' *English Manuscript Studies: 1100-1700.* eds. Peter Beal and Jeremy Griffiths. Oxford: 1990. 2:189-222.

_____. 'Private jottings, public utterances: Aphra Behn's published writings and her commonplace book.' *Aphra Behn Studies,* ed. Todd. 285-309.

Oldmixon, John. *Memoirs of the Press, Historical and Political, For Thirty Years Past, from 1710 to 1740.* London, 1742.

Ovid's Epistles, Translated by Several Hands. London, 1680.

Poems by Several Hands and on Several Occasions Collected by N. Tate. London, 1685.

Raylor, Timothy. *Cavaliers, Clubs, and Literary Culture: Sir John Mennes, James Smith, and the Order of the Fancy.* Newark: U of Delaware P, 1994.

Salzman, Paul. 'Aphra Behn: Poetry and Masquerade.' *Aphra Behn Studies*, ed. Todd. 109-29.

A Select Collection of Poems with Notes Biographical and Historical. 8 vols. London: J. Nichols, 1780.

Spearing, Elizabeth. 'Aphra Behn: The Politics of Translation.' *Aphra Behn Studies*, ed. Todd. 154-77.

The Temple of Death. London, 1695.

The Theater of Music: or a Choice Collection of the Newest and Best Songs Sung at the Court, and Public Theaters. The First Book. London: Playford, 1685.

Thorn-Drury, G. 'Introduction' to *Covent Garden Drollery: A Miscellany of 1672.* London: P. J. & R. Dobell, 1928.

Todd, Janet. *The Secret Life of Aphra Behn.* London: André Deutsch, 1996.

_____, ed. *Aphra Behn Studies.* Cambridge: Cambridge UP, 1996.

_____, ed. *British Women Writers: A Critical Reference Guide.* New York: Continuum, 1989.

_____, ed. *A Dictionary of British and American Women Writers 1660-1800.* London: Methuen, 1987.

Valentinian, a Tragedy, As 'tis Altered by the Late Earl of Rochester and Acted at the Theatre Royal Together with a preface concerning the Author and his Writings By one of his Friends. London, 1685.

Vieth, David. *Attribution in Restoration Poetry: A Study of Rochester's 'Poems' of 1680.* New Haven: Yale UP, 1963.

Wall, Wendy. *The Imprint of Gender. Authorship and Publication in the English Renaissance.* Ithaca: Cornell UP, 1993.

Wharton, Anne. *The Surviving Works of Anne Wharton.* eds. Germaine Greer and Susan. Hastings. Stump Cross, Essex: Stump Cross, 1997.

Whartoniana. London, 1727.

3

'Household Affaires are the Opium of the Soul': Damaris Masham and the Necessity of Women's Poetry

Margaret J.M. Ezell

Long have we here condemned been
to Folly & impertinence
but then it surely will be seene
There's in our Souls no difference
when we no longer Fetterd are
but like to them o[ur]^e selves appeare.

Damaris Masham, 'When deaths cold hand'[1]

The poetic career of Damaris Masham is an interesting case study of the cultural constraints faced by early modern women writers, not only constraints imposed by their contemporaries, but also those imposed by subsequent generations of readers and critics attempting to fit her within their cultural models of authorship. She is not an example of a woman silenced by her critics, but instead of a woman whose existence seems inextricably bound to powerful men in her life, acting as their mirror and defender, but not granted a voice of her own. Her male biographer George Ballard chose her as an exemplar of the female intellectual because of what he perceived as her ability to reproduce the ideas of her male mentors. As such, Masham seems in Luce Irigaray's terms to be 'mimicking' femininity, that is, acting out a feminine role to suit the expectations of her male-dominated circle and her culture – but, is her poetry simply a female voice articulating another's script? Or, as Irigaray suggests, is her performance of the female philosopher part of a process of her interrogation of her roles?[2] In concentrating on the men who surrounded her and her interactions with them, have we continued her own generation's erasure of her original audience – women?

The first challenge to recovering Damaris Masham as a poet is finding any trace of her poetic activity. We have no records at this point of women reading and responding to her verse. As a writer, Lady Masham was during her life and today best known publically as a polemical essayist and the earliest biographer of John Locke. Her verse has never been collected and only rarely commented upon; the majority of it was not printed during her lifetime and exists in print today only as a single entry in an anthology and as part of John Locke's correspondence.[3] She was, however, the object of comment and praise during her life time for her prose works, *Letters Concerning the Love of God* (1696) and *Occasional Thoughts in Reference to a Vertuous or Christian Life* (1705), which earned her a lengthy entry in George Ballard's *Memoirs of Several Ladies of Great Britain who have been Celebrated for Their Writings or Skill in the Learned Languages, Arts and Sciences* (1752), and which, as Ruth Perry has uncovered, was some twenty pages longer in Ballard's original draft (332-338 and 421-425). Although she seems to epitomize what Ballard fashions as an exemplary learned lady, Ballard makes no mention that Masham wrote poetry; likewise, some two hundred years later, her entry in Todd's 1987 *Dictionary of British and American Women Writers 1660-1800* describes her only as a 'theological writer' (214-215). It is interesting to speculate why we know so very much about one part of her literary life and so little about another.

> All Harsh opinions here shall cease
> products of ignorance & Pride
> where charity good will & peace
> no differences can ere divide.
> all freely seeke each others good
> where pride, nor Envy's understood.
> ('When deaths cold hand' 321)

On the one hand, the sentiments Masham expresses in this stanza are conventional enough: only after death, Masham seems to feel, will true happiness be found. What is less expected in these sentiments is her view that it is the ignorance and envy of others which are at the root of unhappiness in this life, rather than simply one's own personal weaknesses or actions. Masham seems to be suggesting that in this life, we are constantly watching and evaluating others. 'Harsh opinions' and lack of charity are the results not of the behavior of the one judged, but of the personal insecurities of the observer, which turn all others into rivals; the observer's incapacities create misinterpretations of the other's actions or abilities and further reinforce a competitive relationship between the one who sees and envies and the one who endeavors to find happiness.

The stanzas preceding this one describe the condition of life after death, 'ye Joyes of yt blessd state / Freindship refind, & purest love / . . . / Converse yts innocent & free / Bles'd Unione sweetest Harmonie' (320). Masham juxtaposes this state of mutual tolerance, understanding, and harmony with the astonishment of the 'honest bigot' who 'without mercy has damn'd all / Hee of his party cannot call'; when he finds 'Socrates & Pythagores / wth ye great Antonine' happily in residence, he is astonished and dismayed. Like those stern commentators on others' actions who generate 'Harsh opinions' as they constantly compare themselves to others, the 'honest bigot' cannot see the merit or worth of any individual not exactly his mirror. Masham, in contrast, can imagine a society which not only transcends differences of historical period, religion, and philosophy, but also appears to derive its joys from the interplay of differences rather than the enforcing of similitude. She imagines a life in which one is no longer required to perform specific roles in order to protect one's self from 'Harsh opinions' and envy of those who observe and judge.

What lies behind her poet's vision of a life of 'converse' which celebrates the harmonious expression of difference? How does her perception of gender feature in her interpretation of heaven's joys and of herself as a poet? Her own life situations as a daughter, wife, and mother, I believe, are intertwined with her poetic interests. The ways in which Masham's life has been presented to subsequent generations also provide interesting insights into the processes through which difference as defined through gender is controlled. Worldly society re-interprets or re-creates the awkward individual according to acceptable patterns of behavior and accomplishment, some of which in her verse she enacts, knowing perhaps that (in Irigaray's terms) she is 'staging' herself to meet the expected performance of femininity. The content of Masham's verse, in contrast, suggests how the woman on earth is continuously shaped by others' perceptions of her, imposing the self-conscious performance of a variety of feminine roles, some of which in her verse she enacts, knowing they are artificial.

Critics and commentators' urges to categorize may in part explain

Masham's seeming invisibility as poet. Ada Wallas's title for the chapter devoted to Masham in her early study *Before the Bluestockings* is a starting point: 'Locke's Friend, Lady Masham.' Throughout the accounts of her life and writings, Masham's biographers and commentators inevitably frame any commentary on her in reference to two powerful men: her father, Dr Ralph Cudworth, the Master of Christ's College, Cambridge and an important member of the Cambridge Platonists, and the philosopher John Locke, with whom she contracted a friendship in 1681 and who lived in her home for the last years of his life.

Ballard sets the pattern in his biography of Masham for how we talk about her, defining Masham's intellectual development and literary output as the expression of either her father's or Locke's ideas. 'Her father soon perceiving the bent of her genius, took such particular care in her tuition that in the early part of her life, she was distinguished for her uncommon learning and piety,' Ballard begins, although it is interesting to note that Cudworth's assumed care of her education did not include classical languages.[4] In tracing the passage of Masham from her father's supposed tutelage to marriage, the role of intellectual guide is not depicted as then being filled by her husband, Sir Francis Masham (he is, instead, routinely represented as 'rather stupid' by some commentators) but instead by John Locke. 'As she applied herself with great diligence to the study of divinity and philosophy, so she had great advantages therein from the directions of the famous Mr Locke,' but not apparently her husband (Ballard 332).

Concerning the contents of her books, Ballard again represents Masham's writings as being simply the expression of Locke's ideas, her ideas the fruit of his intellectual cultivation. 'Lady Masham (probably under the inspection of Mr Locke) wrote and published, without her name, a treatise,' Ballard observes in one reference. In another instance, he generalizes about the nature of Masham's and Locke's relationship that 'As she . . . owned much to the care of Mr Locke for her acquired endowments and skill in arithmetic, geography, chronology, history, philosophy and divinity, so she returned the obligation with singular benevolence and gratitude when he was a domestic in her family' (333, 337). Thus, the framework for interpretation seems clear: Cudworth and Locke provided the ideas, Masham the expression; Locke provided the source of accomplished attainments in intellectual studies, she provided the domestic comforts and nursing skills.

This urge to view Masham only in conjunction with either Cudworth or Locke is continued in twentieth-century references to her. We see, in the glosses on her letters to Locke and her poems, the editors' attempts to attribute her philosophical positions either to her father or her father's intellectual circle. The editors of *Kissing the Rod* continue this practice, for example, explaining Masham's condemnation of religious zealotry in 'When death's cold hand' as 'typical of the latitudinarian Christianity of the Cambridge Platonists among whom she spent the greater part of her life' (Greer 323). The editors of Locke's letters are quick to discover expressions of the thoughts of other (male) Cambridge Platonists in her views: the lengthy gloss on her reference to 'the Vehicles of the Platonists,' which in her letter immediately follows a quotation from Katherine Philips on the nature of friendship, contains no analysis of Philips, but instead a discussion of the use of the term 'Vehicle' in the writings of Henry More, Ralph Cudworth, and John Smith (2:735n2).

The most extended study of Masham, 'My Idea in Your Mind: John Locke and Damaris Cudworth Masham' by Sheryl O'Donnell, envisions Masham's married life as one long philosophical conversation with her male companions (other than her husband), but here, too, the representation of Masham as a woman writer is curiously charged. O'Donnell sees Masham's married life as,

> unfettered by the enervating details of housework and child care; bound only by the leisured disciplines of thought and writing . . . [not having] heavy domestic responsibilities in a household of ten servants. And the wife of an English baronet who stood for Parliament, regardless of her diminished financial status in the eyes of the law, had world enough and time for several rooms of her own. (28-29)

This last sentence is an interesting fusion of the image of the coy sexual female from Andrew Marvell's carpe diem masterpiece with that of the frustrated writer from Virginia Woolf's influential story of the doomed woman poet. Whether consciously or not, such a set of allusions points to a more general underlying pattern in the way intellectual women have culturally been examined: we know they are smart, but as important, what is their sex life like? In general, the biographical speculation about Masham and Locke has always revolved around whether she was indeed his physical mistress in addition to being his domestic 'governess,' the title by which she referred to herself in connection with Locke; the link between manipulative sexuality and getting the time and space for intellectual endeavors subtly colors our perception of both the woman and her literary efforts.

Is there any other way we can approach Masham as a poet and a writer? Actually, when one thinks about her as an individual over the course of her whole life – not just as a young girl in a university town, but also as a mature woman functioning in a domestic, material world – rather than her life as representing a series of philosophical positions, new possibilities for interpreting her work emerge. She did indeed spend her childhood and young adulthood, the first twenty-six years of her life, among the Cambridge Platonists; the ways in which she is discussed, however, make it sound as though the philosophical movement and the place itself completely engrossed her and determined her mode of expression. This view of her overlooks the references in her letters to her female relatives and friends with whom she passed her time away from Cambridge before her marriage and their importance in her young life. And, perhaps even more important, such a view overlooks the fact that she passed the remainder of her adult life, her twenty-three years as a wife, mother, and step-mother, living in a provincial country estate. As with O'Donnell's representation of Masham, commentators see the domestic arrangement at Otes as the perfect philosophical pastoral with no 'domestic' cares.

Forgotten in such assessments – constructed as they are on a series of interlocking references to Masham's male connections – is that while she was living in the Master's Lodge in Cambridge, she was not truly a part of that male company. Instead, Masham was raised in a small group of women, surrounded by a sea of intellectual men, most of whom were, it can be inferred from Masham's later references, apparently either indifferent or even hostile to the idea of intellectual, educated women. Cambridge does not seem to feature largely in her account of where she most wishes to live: in 1682 she writes to Locke to pity her because 'within these twoo [sic] Days I shall be Downeright sick with the Croud of Impertinent Company that this Place is always full of at a Sturbridge Faire, it is a Persecution of the kind that I am Confident exceeds all Imagination.' She continues that while winter will quiet down the town, 'Yet I shall not fancie to stay long in the Countrey, unless Necessities drive me to it,' and the necessity she fears might keep her in Cambridge is the simple domestic one that 'since my Sisters Familie is so increas'd that I cannot be there and doubt [not] that it will be the same at my

Lady Kings' (2:545). Masham was dependent on a female network of family and friends to provide her access to London and to provide an alternative mode of living to that in Cambridge.

We see her ambivalence about Cambridge and its intellectual environment, for example, in an early letter dated 1682 where she observes that she is out of sorts, having previously decided philosophically that 'I was a whole World to my self,' requiring nothing but books. Now, however, she finds that she is missing her friends and sister, and,

> I now experience so much the Contrary that Methinks I am Divided into as many Parts as there are Persons that I love, and that it is intollerable to live in a Place where it is not possible to spend one Houre in an agreable Conversation without being beholden to the Dead or the Absent Liveing for it, and that too in one of the most Famous Universities in the World. (2:518)

This same theme is found in other letters, most notably in one written in January, 1685, concerning her skeptical views on matrimony. She writes to Locke that she holds her negative views not because she has fallen out with a suitor, but because 'you know I have Liv'd Lately a great while in a Place where it has been a Complaint (as you may remember) that there was no Occasion for a Heart' (2:679).

Growing up in such a setting, where there is 'no Occasion for a Heart,' surrounded by male intellectuals although never permitted to be part of the institution of philosophy, the person with whom she had the most continuous contact throughout her life was not her father, but her mother. She has been largely overlooked in discussions of influences on Masham though simple arithmetic suggests that she is the continuing presence in her daughter's life, more so than her father or even Locke. In addition to raising her daughters in Cambridge, Damaris Craddock Andrews Cudworth (d. 1695) came to live with Masham at Otes in 1688, three years before Locke did. As an early commentator Peter Laslett notes in his article about Otes, 'little has been written about the lives of these wives and daughters incongruously scattered in the midst of institutions so emphatically masculine and so imperatively celibate' (536). Little is known, for example, of Masham's half sister with whom she hoped to go and stay in 1682: we know that she, too, was named 'Damaris' and that she was the child of Mrs Cudworth by her first husband, Thomas Andrews, that she married Sir Edward Abney, who had been a fellow in Christ's College 1655-61 (2:545n3, 546n3). The erasure of the presence of a female community inside this male one leaves us with the impression, reinforced by her biographer's accounts of her writings, that like some orphaned child, Damaris Cudworth was nursed not by humans, but by philosophy.[5]

Masham herself, however, writing in 1705 on the education of children cites mothers, not fathers, as the crucial influence on the child's education. She notes that 'the actual assistance of Mothers, will . . . be found necessary to the right forming of the Minds of their Children of both Sexes; and the Impressions receiv'd in that tender Age, which is unavoidably much of it passed among Women, are of exceeding consequence to Men through the whole remainder of their Lives' (*Occasional Thoughts* 8). And lest this again be simply dismissed as Masham mimicking Locke, let us remember that Locke formed his views on the education of children while living at Otes and observing Masham's nine stepchildren and her son, Francis.

While at Otes, she did indeed have the company of John Locke at intervals and later access to his extensive library. She also engaged in constant correspondence with a host of other intellectual figures while carrying out her domestic role. This should not distract us from the fact that the majority of her conversations were conducted with women and children; she was stepmother to Frances Masham's eight sons and one daughter, young Ester, who were living in the house while Locke was in residence, too. As Ruth Perry notes in her account of *Occasional Thoughts*, Masham 'sympathizes with those who have none but infants to talk to all day long' (97). Masham states that *Occasional Thoughts in Reference to a Vertuous or Christian Life* had been written and set aside for two years before she decided to publish it; the contents represent her conversations with her friends and her conclusions about the topics. 'There is no so constant and satisfactory a Pleasure, to those who are capable of it, as Rational Conversation gives,' she observes; she elaborates in a later place that 'these Persons who afford that agreeable Conversation I have mention'd, were in the greater part of them Ladies' (1, 8). And, when the ladies gathered to hold conversation at Otes, it was not on the platonic nature of the soul, but instead, 'it was not strange if they express'd much displeasure at the too general neglect of the Instruction of their Sex' (8).

In our accounts of her interests and her writings, these ladies, like Masham's mother, sister, and step-daughter, are lost. Our accounts instead reflect our inability to discuss her except in terms of either the Platonists or Locke. According to O'Donnell, 'Philoclea's favorite pose is one of Platonic distance from the material world, a sphere that came to include housewifery, husband, and children' (36). 'Pose' is an interesting choice here, as is the reference to Masham by her *nom de plume*. But does Masham in her letters, prose and verse truly represent herself as desiring to escape from all domestic ties and dwell in a land of masculine Platonic philosophy? In *A Discourse Concerning the Love of God* (1696), published according to Masham to show the 'unserviceableness of an Hypothesis lately recommended' by John Norris, her prime area of disagreement with Norris is his position that 'the Perfection of a Christian State [consists] in Contemplation; and that Duties of Social Life (for which 'tis plain Mankind was intended) to be low Matters, fit only to exercise the young Christian, not yet advanced into the spiritual state' (*Discourse* A3v, 4). Instead of a rejection of those 'social' domestic duties of wife and mother for the pleasures of philosophy, Masham instead seems to ground them as an essential part of living a full, Christian life. Her dismay over Norris's position arises from what she perceives as his urging of young people to abandon social and domestic ties as a distraction from a pure love of God; ironically her disagreement with Norris is over the position of social detachment which her subsequent modern critics have imagined that she herself coveted and possessed.

It is also important to note here that in addition to overlooking Masham's commitment to the material domestic world of human relationships and family, we have likewise overlooked her constant interest in and references to poetry as part of the necessities of her life, both by others and her own. That Masham from her early twenties had been interested in poetry and women poets is manifest throughout her correspondence and her prose texts. Locke's editors suggest that she took her *nom de plume*, Philoclea, from Sidney's *Arcadia* (2:473n1). In addition to poetry, she also refers to her familiarity with de Scudery's romances. She quotes Dryden in *Occasional Thoughts* to rebut the notion that sanctimonious chastity is a woman's chief virtue, 'Such Vertue is the Plague of Humane Life, / A vertuous Woman, but a Cursed Wife' (26); she quotes Cowley and Katherine Philips often in her correspondence with Locke to illustrate her points on the nature of platonic friendship.

In the first letter we have after her marriage, Masham writes to Locke, 'do not then think that the Spirrit of Care, and Familie Affairs shall Interely

Possess me How deepe soever I may seeme to Have ingag'd my self in them'
(2:727). This is not an escape from domestic ties and duties, nor a rejection of
them, as O'Donnell sees it – instead it is a recognition of the necessity of a
dual existence. Both wife and writer, she asserts, will continue to exist
simultaneously: 'the Love of my Friends therefore and the Best Kinds of
Usefull Knowledges so far as I am Capable of it, will still Possess my Heart as
much as ever They did.' She still continues to read and to write poetry, too,
after her marriage, curiously intertwining poetry with her domestic role.

This is not to say that she found it easy to play both her roles. In
September of 1685 she writes again of the self-conscious roles she fashions,
housewife, philosophical writer. 'You see that I cannot yet forget my Poetry
upon occasion,' she writes after quoting Katherine Philips, and, while

> the Vehicles of the Platonists . . . were Always much more my
> Favourites then the Muses; And it is not for Guilded Coaches,
> and Embroider'd Beds, Not yet the more important
> Considerations of a Familie, and Children, How Bountefully
> soever stor'd with Them, that will with me make them give Place
> to those Others, There being no Inconsistencie I hope between
> being still the same Philoclea, and indeavoring to Acquitt my
> self as my Lady . . . (2:735).

At the end of this letter, she writes ironically of her dual performances that
now that she is married and living in the country, 'I shall have a Great deal of
Real Business, and Where if I had none I must However seeme Busie to
Acquire the Necessarie Reputation of a Good Countrey Houswife,' and
having done so, she will have neighbors draw up an affidavit of her domestic
accomplishments and send it to Locke 'to Publish for the Honour of the
Muses; Who I dare say will think it no Disparagement to them' (2:737).

A month later, the newlywed writes in less sanguine tones about
balancing domestic and intellectual roles. In November 1685, Masham writes
'Tis in Vain that you bid me Preserve my Poetry; Household Affaires are the
Opium of the Soul' (2:757). She continues jokingly that her two personae are
competing for space in her closet: 'I can but Think how you would smile to
see Cowley and my Surfeit Waters Jumbled together; with Dr More and my
Gally Potts of Mithridate and Dioscordium; My receits and Accounts Books
with Antoninus's his Mediations, and Des Cartes Principles; with my Globes,
and my Spinning Wheel' (2:759). She asserts 'I can neither make any Verses

at this Time, nor remember any to the Purpose,' but in this same letter, she is once again quoting Davenant ('certainly nothing but the Aire of Essex would have brought this Poet to my mind'). In her next letter in early December, she writes that she has been seeking her entertainment 'in Books Altogether; and that Principally in Poetry, to which the Present Fancie most inclines me'; indeed, she has become so engrossed in poetry that she jokes that 'it is out of pure Crosness that I send You none, since I hardly write of Late to Any Body but your self in Prose' (2:762).

In this letter, she also raises the issue of women publishing poetry. Given that she is sending out quantities of verse to her friends, she wonders if she, like Katherine Philips, perhaps may find herself in print. 'Perhaps you may see me in Print in a little While,' she writes Locke – then he need not wait for her letters to bring him her verses. The only problem, Masham continues, is, 'I confess it has not much of my Approbation because (Principally) the Mode is for one to Dye first,' a reference the editors take to mean Anne Killigrew's *Poems*, published posthumously in 1686 (2:762n1). In this letter, reading and writing poetry have become the way to undo the 'opium' of household duties and to maintain her intellectual and literary community through correspondence; it also appears as a possible mode of public, printed expression.

In March of 1688, she is again sending verses to Locke and again raises the issue of women's printed verse. She tells Locke she will not apologize for not composing her whole letter in verse, 'I have Almost forsworne ever Leting it come on Againe, Since what was intended onely for my Owne Diversion I find has Unawares (to Use Mrs Philip's words) expos'd me to the Severities of the Wise and the Railerie of the Witt' (2:793). This arose from her 'Indiscretion in the first Place in Trusting to the Favorable Censure of my Friends, and theirs in the next in exposeing me to that of Those who were not so.' Obviously, the recipients of Masham's manuscript verses had enjoyed them sufficiently to circulate them and Masham was not always pleased with the response. 'Nevertheless I have sent you the Paper you Desire,' she continues, a poem on love and marriage written, she assures Locke, before she met Sir Francis, and now revised.

Her revisions include taking out the complimentary opening, since 'the Person it is Addres'd to Haveing as little share in it as Usually Friends in the Country Have, serveing in Reallities but for Pretence' (2:794). Having stripped it of its conventional epistolary framework, she asks Locke, 'If the

Author were Unknowne to you what Judgment you should from thence make
of Her; I have a Reason to Ask, and therefore desire you would tell me
sincerely.' The untitled poem concerns an unmarried woman's arguments
with her friend over whether a woman can both love and be wise. She warns
Locke that the subject owes nothing to 'any Philosopher of the Platonic Sect,'
and that 'you will see I am got now quite out of the Element of Housewifrie'
(2:794), and the playful, ironic speaker performs neither the role of the busy
housewife nor the Cambridge platonic mimic.

> Our Sins of Ignorance sure are Small,
> If any such can be at All;
> Else Mightie Love! what Hope Have I
> Ere to Appease thy Deitie,
> That Have a Thousand times, and more,
> Laugh'd at, and Defy'd Thy Power? (2:795)

As penance for having defied the god of Love, the speaker offers to 'convert'
her equally resistant female friend and argue why 'Love, Equally unto us is /
A Duty, and a Happiness.' First, the speaker states, 'Know Unbelief's a
Deadly Sin' in love. 'Nor ever Ask your Reason Why? / Though They should
give Thesemlves the Lye:'

> You'l Think Perhaps tis very Hard
> To be from Reason quite Debar'd,
> And strait will Cry, But Pray Why so?
> Why? Prethee Fool, How should I Know?
> Churchmen, and Lovers, Both Agree
> There's no Salvation else Can be,
> 's'not That enough for Thee, and Mee?

The culmination of this line of argument has the speaker warning the
unmarried woman that 'For 't has beene said without Controul / That not to
Love is want of Soul; / And if't Be so, without Dispute, / then who Love
Least, Is Most a Brute' (2:796). Reason, however, can be used to argue that
'Love, Equally unto us is/ A Duty, and a Happiness'. It is a duty, because
'The Text you'l find is very Plaine / Eve, was made onely for the Man, / Then
How can you your self Deceive / And think you're not some Adams Eve?'
(2:797).

Or on the Man Look with a Frowne
Who onley comes to Claime His owne?
And Begs but that You would Restore
The Ribb You Rob'd him of before;
And though for th' Hall of Westmister,
The Man no Justice can have There,
Yet surely Sister it is Plaine
He ought to have his Ribb againe. (2:797)

Thus is 'duty' comprised. That love is 'happiness' for women, however, seems to Masham to be a more challenging point to prove in this poem.

This playful self-conscious analysis of women's relationships with men and the construction of socially defined categories of what constitutes a woman's 'duty' and her 'happiness' points to another area where Masham's verses may not fit our expectations. In addition to a tendency to see Masham as a type of single-role performer of the masculine ideal of the learned lady, divorced from material circumstances of her sex and thus privileged over other women, we also tend to stress the philosophical basis for her interest in poetry and in her selection of topics. For example, the editors of *Kissing the Rod* have interpreted the manuscript poem 'When death's cold hand' as Masham's attempt, using the Neoplatonic model provided by Cudworth and his friends, to 'conciliate conflicting opinions about the relationship between the mind and body rather than resolve the issue, closing with resignation amid lingering tension' (322). However, in addition to the philosophical framework, it is a strongly argued position about the treatment of women as projections of masculine desires which lies far, far afield from the concerns of the Cambridge Platonists.

After death, Masham observes,

. . . our weake sex I hope will then
Disdain yt stupid ignorance
wch was at first impos'd by men
   their owne high merits to inhance
And now pleade custome for pretense
   to banish knowledg witt and sense. (321)

Only after death, argues Masham, when the souls are free from gendered flesh, will it be seen that there are no differences in the sex of souls. Only then will women stop appearing in the 'dress' designed for them by men, 'when we no longer Fetter'd are / but like to them our selves appeare.'

The specific reference here is to leaving aside the fleshly body, the female form with its gendered codes for reading it, and appearing as one truly 'is' rather than as one is perceived to be. The reader is prepared for this turn to gender by the preceding analogy of men's worldly business and children's contests. After death, 'Strip'd then of Earth,' Masham writes, 'Ye greatest actions men have praisd / or mightiest Heroes practisd ere / ye huge designe ye Vast desires / Ambition in ye soul inspires' (lines 63-66) can be viewed from a larger perspective and it can be seen that 'The business then of life will show / as childrens play to men appears / on wch some minuts they'l bestow / in smiling at their hopes & feares' (lines l67-70). In Masham's poem, men's activities and business, so important in the masquerade of the material world, are converted into children's games viewed with domestic toleration by the enlightened soul. Women's intellects, so often belittled and dismissed by men as childish, are likewise 'strip'd' of their false garb to reveal their true forms, and to assume their true function and potential. It is a position she likewise expressed in her later prose works, but it is clearly an early and ongoing theme of her verse, and one at odds with her as a mimic of the Cambridge philosophical institutions.

Having grown up in the material world of Cambridge University rather than dwelling purely in the realms of philosophy, it was certainly clear to Masham that while philosophers may generate sublime theories, they also generate heat without light. In her poetic accusations of masculine colonization of the feminine spirit, their treatment of their wives, sisters, daughters, and female acquaintances, the philosophical male is also clearly under attack. In one letter, Masham refers to Cambridge conversation as characterized by 'Learned Dulness' and 'the Impertinent Wrangl'lings of the Schools,' which she admits are marginally better than country conversations devoted to 'repeated Entertainments of the Price of Corn, and the Best Management of a Dairie' (2:736). She makes joking reference in another poem in which she addresses her 'sister' on the topic of reason and love, 'Our Sins of Ignorance sure are small,' to the way in which her analysis of the nature of women's love has processed 'in a True Pedantick Cant / Like a Right Cambr: disputant,' for she has both proved and disproved the true nature of Love (2:799).

These are not topics which engaged the pens of the Cambridge Platonists. You will search in vain through Ralph Cudworth or Henry More's writings for references to women's education or the difficulties faced by a 'learned lady,' although, obviously, each knew highly intelligent and articulate women. You find such concerns, as Ruth Perry notes in her account of the impact and influence of Astell, in the contemporary writings of Mary Astell, Mary Chudleigh, Judith Drake, and Anne Finch (106).[6] What we have tended to overlook in our focus on Masham's philosophical origins is her participation in a women-centered discourse in both prose and verse concerning women's roles. What we find in her verse is her understanding of her own position relative to the institution of philosophy as embodied in the Universities and her own perception of her place among her female relatives and friends. Finally, what her verse offers us that her prose does not is a clear sense of her attempts to balance both the domestic roles of wife, daughter, and mother with those of philosopher and independent thinker, a balancing act which seemed to find in poetry a stable ground from which to consider her various roles and to attempt to speak in her own voice.

Notes

[1] All references to this poem of Masham's will refer to the entry in *Kissing the Rod* 318-23.

[2] The concept of 'mimicking' or the 'staging' by women of the masculine definition of femininity and its potential for subversion appears as a part of Luce Irigaray's exploration of the construction of femininity in western patriarchal culture through her deconstruction of psychoanalytic theory. See in particular the essays which make up *Ce Sexe qui n'en est pas un* (1977), translated by Catherine Porter as *This Sex Which Is Not One*.

[3] In addition to the poem cited above printed in *Kissing the Rod*, the surviving manuscript poems by Masham are part of John Locke's papers held in the Bodleian Library, MS. Locke.c.32, ff.17-19 and Locke c.17, ff. 130-3. These have been published as part of Locke's correspondence in *The Correspondence of John Locke* 2:571-73, 795-800.

[4] Masham lightly concludes one of her early letters to Locke in 1682 by describing how she will attempt to be composed at one of her brother's departures for the East Indies, 'like the Daughter of a Philosopher' (2:546), thus identifying herself by her father's intellectual position; however, she also reminds Locke in 1684 when he is sending her books on the philosophy of

Labadie that she does not read Latin (2:640n3), which casts an interesting light on the extent she was 'educated' by her father.

[5] Jeslyn Medoff has drawn attention to a parallel, possible community of educated women, also linked to Masham. The step-mother of the early feminist poet Sarah Fyge was Mary Beacham, Damaris Masham's niece. As Medoff notes, 'There is the possibility that Mary herself was well-educated, reared in a family that supported the idea of eloquent daughters. If so, she may have been a more important educational influence on Sarah than the father' (36).

[6] Perry, however, rather overstates the case when she concludes that Judith Drake, Masham, Elizabeth Thomas, Chudleigh, and Elizabeth Elstob were waiting on Astell to publish to enable them to change their lives, that Astell 'showed them how to take themselves seriously as thinkers and writers' (106) – by 1700 when Astell published, Masham had obviously been taking herself seriously as a writer and thinker for decades. Perry's list, however, does underline the fact that Masham was part of a chorus of women's voices discussing women's roles, in addition to being trained as a Cambridge Platonist.

Works Cited

Ballard, George. 'Lady Masham' *Memoirs of Several Ladies of Great Britain.* ed. Ruth Perry. Detroit: Wayne State UP, 1985. 332-338.

Greer, Germaine, Jeslyn Medoff, Melinda Sansone, and Susan Hastings, eds. *Kissing the Rod: An Anthology of 17th Century Women's Verse.* London: Virago P, 1988.

Irigaray, Luce. Trans. Catherine Porter. *This Sex Which Is Not One.* Ithaca: Cornell UP, 1985.

de Beer, E. S., ed. *The Correspondence of John Locke.* 8 vols. Oxford: Clarendon P, 1978.

Laslett, Peter. 'Masham of Otes: the Rise and Fall of an English Family.' *History Today* 3 (1953): 535-543.

Masham, Damaris. *A Discourse Concerning the Love of God.* London, 1696

———. *Occasional Thoughts in Reference to a Vertuous or Christian Life.* London, 1705.

Medoff, Jeslyn. '"My darling pen": The autobiographical poetry of Sarah Fyge (Field, Egerton).' Diss. Rutgers U, 1994.

O'Donnell, Sheryl. 'My Idea in Your Mind: John Locke and Damaris Cudworth Masham.' Perry, Ruth and Martine Watson Brownley, eds. *Mothering the Mind: Twelve Studies of Writers and Their Silent Partners.* New York: Holmes & Meier, 1984. 26-46.

Perry, Ruth. *The Celebrated Mary Astell: An Early English Feminist.* Chicago: U of Chicago P, 1986.

———, ed. *Memoirs of Several Ladies of Great Britain* . Detroit: Wayne State UP, 1985.

Todd, Janet, ed. *A Dictionary of British and American Women Writers 1660-1800.* London: Methuen, 1987.

Wallas, Ada. *Before the Bluestockings.* London: G. Allen & Unwin Ltd., 1929.

PART II

Poetic Conventions and Traditions

4

Mary Wroth's Guilty 'secrett art': The Poetics of Jealousy in *Pamphilia to Amphilanthus*

Clare R. Kinney

In Mary Wroth's *Pamphilia to Amphilanthus*, the first woman known to have authored a sonnet sequence in English must perforce reshape the conventions of Petrarchism to accommodate the anomalous situation in which a female poet/lover records her painful emotional enthralment to a male beloved.[1] Her renegotiation of the Petrarchan paradigm results in both suggestive supplementations and telling subtractions. *Pamphilia to Amphilanthus*'s material framing, for example, is unprecedented: it is printed as a kind of appendix within the 1621 published portion of Wroth's *Urania* and, as Wendy Wall has noted, the presentation of the lyric sequence as the work of the romance narrative's heroine, with its concomitant insistence upon the fictionality of Pamphilia the female poet/lover, distances the author from her potentially scandalous, intermittently autobiographical, and perhaps all too authoritative representation of female desire (336-37).[2] At the same time, Wroth produces a sonnet sequence in which the object of the speaker's love is almost invisible: Amphilanthus is never addressed by name, never represented in the fetishizing terms of a blazon, and the reader is almost half-way through the sequence before she even encounters a masculine pronoun gendering the person the poems celebrate.[3]

But if the hybrid romance-lyric text created by the splicing of *Pamphilia to Amphilanthus* on to the *Urania* finesses the issue of Wroth's 'culpability' as a woman author who refuses to confine herself to devotional or moral matter, and if the sonnets eschew certain fashionings of the beloved that might be construed as transgressive (given that the male body is not, officially, culturally imaginable as an object of female desire), her lyrics nevertheless articulate an anxiety about a rather particular kind of misrepresentation or 'wrong conseite' (P11.13). The customary Petrarchan provocation to writing is the chaste resistance, disdain or indifference of an idealized woman; poetic productivity is born out of erotic frustration. In a cultural context where chastity is a gendered virtue, however, the situations of the male and female Petrarchist can not be symmetrical: when Wroth/Pamphilia identifies herself with a shepherdess bewailing her lover's inconstancy who records on the bark of a willow 'this tale of haples mee' (P7. 35), that tale may be quite different from the one imagined by her uncle Philip Sidney's Astrophil when he implores Stella to 'pity the tale of me' (*Astrophil and Stella* 45). A reading of *Pamphilia to Amphilanthus* is not only likely to be informed by foreknowledge of the *Urania*'s very thorough chronicling of Amphilanthus's errancies and infidelities, but also inflected by an extra-textual awareness of the vicissitudes of Wroth's own situation as lover of the philandering William Herbert. And the sequence's lyric speaker is in the end less concerned with the culpability of her desire (or the culpability of her choice to frame that desire in poetry) than with the challenge to her 'constant art's idealizing representations offered by a powerful counter discourse: the 'secrett art' of Jealousy.

Jealousy, it should be emphasized, is not an emotion which usually aggravates the sufferings of the male lover in the Petrarchan tradition. The nearest we get to an invocation of it in the *Rime Sparse* is the *invidia* the poet experiences when he sees a visiting dignitary salute Laura with a kiss (*Rime Sparse* 238). Sidney's Astrophil represents himself as being (comically) jealous of the intimacies permitted Stella's lapdog and her pet sparrow (*A&S* 59, 83), but the only sonnet in his sequence which takes jealousy as its subject displaces it on to Stella's husband, and concludes by asking wickedly, 'It is not ill that such a devil wants horns?' (*A&S* 78). In *Pamphilia to Amphilanthus*, by contrast, there is a suggestive tension, almost a dialectic, between the sequence's official poetics of constancy – a poetics whose logical conclusion turns out to be the silencing of the speaker – and an officially deplored but poetically highly productive poetics of jealousy.[4] It is this tension which I hope to explore in this essay, and since I believe it is to be enacted at the level of style and syntax in the significant indeterminacies of Wroth's deceptively decorous lyrics, my approach here will be a quite consciously formalist one as I investigate the way in which her sequence repeatedly complicates and destabilizes the utterances of the officially constant subject.

Pamphilia to Amphilanthus, it should be emphasized, configures the relations between constancy and jealousy in a manner that distinguishes its

protocols rather significantly from those of Wroth's *Urania*. Mary Ellen Lamb
has offered an incisive account of the way Wroth's romance locates the 'heroics
of constancy' championed by the long-suffering Pamphilia in opposition to the
behavior of less exemplary female characters – characters who frankly articulate
their anger and jealousy, characters who become 'disposal site[s] into which rage
over inconstant lovers . . . can be placed to prevent contamination from spreading
further into the romance' (168).[5] The sonnet sequence does not have the same
formal resources for deflecting away from its female speaker any suspicion of
culturally transgressive behavior. What it offers instead are double-voiced lyrics
whose internal contradictions disclose telling divisions and contradictions within
the lyric subject and become focal points for the articulation of a very particular
kind of metapoetic anxiety.

  Three poems into her sequence, Pamphilia asks Cupid to take possession
of her beloved:

> Shine in those eyes which conquer'd have my hart;
> And see if mine bee slack to answere thee:
>
> Lodg in that brest, and pitty moving see
> For flames which in mine burne in truest smart
> Exiling thoughts that touch inconstancie,
> Or those which waste nott in the constant art. (P3.3-8).

The speaker's representation of her constant heart and constant art is subtly
inflected at the very moment of its articulation by a syntactic indeterminacy to be
found in many of Wroth's lyrics. Line 5 is somewhat confusing – it seems to
have Cupid both moving pity in the beloved's breast and seeing pity moving
there – but what follows is even more ambiguous. Given the lack of any
possessive pronoun qualifying 'inconstancie,' are we to understand that the
flames of the speaker's incandescent love purge (a) all thoughts which might
'touch' (relate to or ignite) her own inconstancy, or (b) all thoughts that entertain
the notion – touch upon the possibility – that her lover might be inconstant? Or
is it that the putatively less than constant thoughts are the beloved's, and that
Love is being asked to exile from his breast all fancies that might promote or
ignite his inconstancy? Other poems in the sequence make it quite clear, to be
sure, that the 'constant art' is not exercised in response to the erotic frustration
recorded by the male Petrarchists – the impasse created by the lady's chaste
distance, where the putative inconstancy of the love object is not even an issue.

'I, that ame of all most crost / Having, and that had, have lost' declares
Pamphilia: her desire – unlike that of Astrophil – is not crying out for the food it
never had (A&S 71) but speaks to a hunger once satisfied and now unassuaged: 'I,
that must nott taste the best / Fed must sterve, and restles rest' (P59.1-2, 15-16).[6]
The scandal – the guilty secret – of Pamphilia's poems lies in their disclosure that
even when the female Petrarchist assumes a relatively culturally acceptable
position of stoic endurance, her poetic productivity may not be engendered, like
the male's, by what are constructed as the virtues of the other (the female chastity
and silence which provide the enabling conditions for the poet to articulate
himself as a speaking subject) but by the provocation to the imagination supplied
by the beloved's infidelity.[7]

        We are not especially accustomed to finding representations of female
jealousy in the literary texts of this period;[8] asked to flesh out an early modern
'poetics of jealousy,' a reader would most likely invoke the Elizabethan and
Jacobean playwrights' pervasive interest in masculine fear of cuckoldry – most
notably in those dramas where a male character's wrongful suspicions, 'born of
themselves, begot upon themselves,' have such disastrous and far-reaching
consequences.[9] There are, of course, good historical reasons for this almost
exclusive emphasis on male anxiety about sexual betrayal. In a culture absolutely
invested in hierarchical notions of sexual difference – and in a society where
every man's honor is perceived as being closely linked to his success in
controlling the chastity of his woman – such scenarios address pervasive fears
concerning the material challenge to a system of patrilineal inheritance posed by
the 'incontinent' female body as well as the threat to masculine identity inherent
in the possibility that a woman may never be fully possessed or her desires fully
circumscribed.[10] Mark Breitenberg has argued, indeed, that male sexual jealousy
'is both constitutive and symptomatic of the normative operations of early
modern patriarchy rather than an aberration' (175), going on to suggest that plays
like Othello and The Winter's Tale 'stage cases of unjustified jealous rage in
order to foreground male jealousy as a discursive energy that does not require a
referent' (182). It is all the more interesting, then, to find the kind of dangerous
copia or imaginative excess associated in the drama with the morbid suspicions
of an Othello or a Leontes reconfigured in Wroth's lyric practice as the (in this
case rather less fantastic) imaginings which at once oppress the poet and produce
their own kind of 'discursive energy.' Such imaginings lead not to acts of
murderous violence but rather to the elaborate equivocations of the 'constant art'
– an art which, for all its intermittent insistence that the lover's miseries spring

from her own unworthy suspicions,[11] constantly threatens to reinvent itself as a poetics of jealousy.

Readers of *Pamphilia to Amphilanthus* have noted the difficulty verging upon hermeticism of Wroth's poems, their tendency to speak an 'almost inscrutable private language,' their 'aporetic ambiguity of reference' (Masten 67, Walker 189).[12] I would suggest that their most subversive and significant syntactic ambiguity (a kind of radical duplicity if you will) is to be found at the very moments when the lyric speaker vigorously attempts to purge the insinuations of jealousy from her poetry. This phenomenon is particularly conspicuous in the sonnet in which Pamphilia most explicitly repudiates the 'secrett art':

> An end fond jealousie alas I know
>   Thy hidenest, and thy most secrett art
>   Thou canst noe new invention frame butt part
>   I have allreddy seene, and felt with woe,
> All thy dissemblings which by fained show
>   Wunn my beeleefe, while truth did rule my hart
>   I, with glad mind imbrace'd, and deemd my smart
>   The spring of joy, whose streames with bliss showld flow;
> I thought excuses had bin reasons true,
>   And that noe faulcehood could of thee ensue;
>   Soe soone beeleefe in honest minds is wroght;
> Butt now I find thy flattery, and skill,
>   Which idly made mee to observe thy will;
>   Thus is my learning by my bondage bought.   (P69)

Jealousy, with its inventions and framings, its dissemblings, fainings and flattering skill, sounds like the consummate false artist (or treacherous lover). (Indeed, in a sonnet sequence in which the wayward male beloved is barely visible, it is almost as if Jealousy substitutes for Amphilanthus as an object of representation.) But the very indictment of its practices engenders ambiguity. The inverted syntax of lines 7-8 appears to suggest that under jealousy's control, the speaker came to deem her 'smart' what should properly have been perceived as the 'spring of joy' (presumably the slandered beloved). But the lines hint at an alternative reading in which the speaker comes to equate the smart of jealousy with 'the spring of joy' – as if jealousy becomes the wellspring of feeling itself. This referential drift is emphasized by the oddly floating clause 'while truth did rule my heart' (one would expect, surely, to read 'while error ruled my heart'). Is this 'truth' the fundamental faith in her beloved that has finally allowed her to renounce jealousy? Or is this a moment at which the very act of denouncing jealousy parenthetically reinscribes the truth claims of jealousy? If so, the poem obliquely concedes that the secret art of jealousy isn't something invasive, inimical, external to the poet, but rather her authentic voice, the heart of her matter. That voice indeed threatens to resurface in the sestet of the sonnet – at first sight, a further repudiation of jealousy, but in substance remarkably like an address to a faithless lover:

> I thought excuses had bin reasons true,
>   And that noe faulcehood could of thee ensue;
>   Soe soone beeleefe in honest minds is wroght;
> Butt now I find thy flattery, and skill,
>   Which idly made mee to observe thy will;
>   Thus is my learning by my bondage bought.

Jealousy, after all, does not deal in excusing.

The poem is all the more interesting because Wroth's own voice seems to speak particularly clearly through her Pamphilia persona in its penultimate line. Thanks to the work of May Paulissen, who first suggested that Wroth's sequence seemed to offer repeated instances of punning references to a lover named Will (46, 196), and Josephine Roberts's later mustering of evidence that Mary Wroth's own Amphilanthus was her cousin William Herbert (24-26), readers of Wroth tend to be hypersensitive to potential wordplay on 'will' in her poetry. When the lyric speaker declares that jealousy's flattery and skill 'made mee to observe thy will,' she may also be suggesting that her attention has been fixed upon jealousy's version of the beloved: thy Will. Presumably the poet, no longer bound to jealousy's will/Will, should now employ her own 'constant art' to represent her version of Will. But as we have seen, from the earliest sonnets of *Pamphilia to Amphilanthus*, Wroth/Pamphilia has had great difficulty in figuring forth an unequivocally 'true' love.

Wroth's poems, as I have already mentioned, do not offer any sustained representation of an idealized beloved (whether he be Amphilanthus or William Herbert); their emphasis is rather upon their speaker's privation, her 'molesting' memories of lost delight, her besetting doubts and fears. They also intermittently bear witness to the fact that 'griefe is nott cur'd by art' (P9) in a manner that anticipates the creative paradoxes hinted at in P69's attempt to banish jealousy once and for all:

Iff I were giv'n to mirthe 't'wowld bee more cross
  Thus to be robbed of my chiefest joy;
  But silently I beare my greatest loss
  Who's us'd to sorrow, grief will nott destroy;
Nor can I as those pleasant witts injoy
  My own fram'd words, which I account the dross
  Of purer thoughts, or recken them as moss
  While they (witt sick) them selves to breath imploy,
Alas, think I, your plenty shewes your want,
  For wher most feeling is, words are more scant,
  Yett pardon mee, Live, and your pleasure take,
Grudg nott, if I neglected, envy show
  'T'is nott to you that I dislike doe owe
  Butt crost my self, wish some like mee to make.   (P45)

The sonnet begins by noting an all too familiar loss; its speaker then claims that her words cannot console her or do justice to her 'purer thoughts,' even as she criticizes the copious writings of other poets. Informing these 'witt-sick' writers that 'Your plenty shows your want,' she interestingly appropriates the words of Ovid's Narcissus, who, staring at his own reflection, laments: 'inopem me copia fecit' (*Metamorphoses* 3.466). Wroth/Pamphilia seems to be castigating the solipsism and emptiness of other Petrarchists' 'narcissistic' lamentations. This is not in itself a particularly original move – one is reminded of Sidney/Astrophil's declaration that 'Dumb swans, not chattering pies, do lovers prove; / They love indeed, who quake to say they love' (*A&S* 54). But Wroth's syntax, once again, is suggestively ambiguous, and allows for the possibility that it is rather her 'own fram'd words' that are 'witt sick,' and that the accusation 'your plenty shewes your want' has been turned back upon her own writings – that the very plenitude of her repeated testimonies to loss underlines her own 'want.'[13] The reading cannot be sustained for the whole poem, which finishes (most unusually) with the lover apologizing to the other poets for her bad temper. It offers, however, yet another of those suggestive counter-narratives that so often disrupt the middles of Wroth's sonnets. In the context of this counter-narrative, the 'want' revealed by undesired superfluity would not only refer to the present absence of the beloved but might also point towards the lack of and desire for a faithful lover who might be faithfully and economically made present in the poet's 'constant art.'

    The complicated and slippery dialogue between that constant art and the all too cunning (and potentially much more copious) 'secret art' of jealousy in *Pamphilia to Amphilanthus* painfully emphasizes the poet's own consciousness of the problems involved in both signifying the beloved and in signifying the beloved's truth. In P24, one of the rare lyrics in which Wroth/Pamphilia addresses her lover directly (and one which, as Heather Dubrow has pointed out, is tellingly reminiscent of some of Shakespeare's sonnets to his own unreliable young man [145]), the speaker describes his 'Image' visiting her in sleep, and concludes:

> Then since my faith is such, soe kind my sleepe
> That gladly thee presents into my thought:
> And still true lover like thy face doth keepe
> Soe as some pleasure shadowe-like is wrought.
> Pitty my loving, nay of consience give
> Reward to mee in whom thy self doth live.   (P24.9-14)

A familiar enough theme – the poet as the custodian of the best version of the beloved – is here complicated by the ambiguous phrasing of line 11. Is it the speaker's sleep which is always 'true-lover-like' in reproducing his face even in her dreams, or are we to understand that (only?) in her dreams can she keep him 'still true-lover like,' continue to represent him as a true, faithful, lover. If the latter is the case, her plea for pity and reward may also become a plea that he make the 'shadowe-like' pleasures offered by the imagination signify in waking life: that he lend substance to those shadows. We are left wondering whether the sonnet is simply reasserting Wroth/Pamphilia's constancy in loving, or whether it is the 'secrett art' of suspicion that solicits the addressee's constancy to the version of him that the 'constant art' has produced.

Wroth's most sustained attempt to disentangle the constant art from the art of Jealousy is to be found in her 'Crowne of Sonetts dedicated to Love.' These lyrics constitute the most formally ambitious sub-sequence of *Pamphilia to Amphilanthus*; in sustaining the intricate design wherein the concluding line of one poem becomes the beginning of the next across fourteen sonnets, Wroth both emulates her uncle Philip Sidney's linked dizains in *The Countess of Pembroke's Arcadia* (188) and improves upon her own father's abortive *corona* (Robert Sidney's attempt to master this form grinds to a halt in the middle of its fifth sonnet [Croft 174-181]). More importantly, the 'Crowne' becomes a testing ground for an attempt to define and embrace a vision of a higher Eros which will purge the 'phant'sies' of the jealous imagination even as it engenders an alternative and less duplicitous aesthetic.[14] The first sonnet of the Crowne begins:

In this strang labourinth how shall I turne?
  Wayes are on all sids while the way I miss:
  If to the right hand, ther, in love I burne;
  Let me goe forward, therin danger is;
  If to the left, suspition hinders bliss,
  Lett mee turne back, shame cries I ought returne.   (P77.1-6)

A little earlier in the sequence, Pamphilia had imagined herself as the prisoner of a 'strang cage' engendered by 'Cruell suspition' and 'bace jealousie' (P66); the 'strang labourinth' recasts this image of psychic imprisonment, and if the intention here is to undo jealousy's artful constructions, it seems particularly fitting that Pamphilia begins by asking 'how shall I turne?' – how shall I trope? How shall I figure an alternative erotic and an alternative aesthetic for myself? Her concluding decision to 'leave all and take the thread of love' (P77.14) tellingly revises a line from an earlier sonnet in which a father is overheard warning his son not to be 'Led by the hatefull thread of Jelousy' into emotional captivity (P27.10). The thread of love, by contrast, leads the speaker, in the second sonnet of the Crowne. 'straite . . . unto the soules content / Wher choyse delights with pleasures wings doe move, / And idle phant'sie never roome had lent' (P78.1-3). The court of Heavenly Cupid has no place for 'idle phant'sie,' suspicious imaginings: its constant art will not, it seems, be entangled with a poetics of jealousy.

    The poet-lover's intermittently neoplatonic imagery of Higher Love repeatedly insists upon (or strives to fix) a new stability of reference: love has become 'the roote of peace, / The lasting lampe fed with the oyle of right; / Image of fayth' (P78.10-12). Indeed as Wroth/Pamphilia expands her account of the secure pleasures of love's realm, inviting her reader as well as herself 'to bee in his brave court a glorious light,' the *corona*'s third sonnet offers a striking formal alternative to the labyrinthine syntax, and destabilizing enjambments encountered in many of the poems of *Pamphilia to Amphilanthus*. Thirteen of its fourteen lines are end-stopped, and its almost liturgical repetition of Love's virtues is emphasized by a particularly homologous rhyme scheme: the rhyme words might/white/light/requite repeat themselves through three quatrains; the final couplet rhymes might/light (P79).

    The 'chaste art' (P81.8) of Higher Love which the poems explicitly celebrate is complemented, then, by a conscious chastening or refining of the poet-lover's art, although, as Barbara Lewalski points out, Wroth's rather idiosyncratic neoplatonism posits no final rejection of either the earthly beloved

or the poems which celebrate him.[15]   The poet's idealizing reconception of
heterosexual relations and her sense of the new 'turns' that her art might take are
very much interdependent. The sixth sonnet of the Crowne celebrates Love's
capacity

> To joine two harts as in one frame to move;
>   Two bodies, butt one soule to rule the minde;
> Eyes which must care to one deere object bind,
>   Eares to each others speech as if above
>   All els they sweet, and learned were; this kind
>   Content of lovers wittniseth true love,
> Itt doth inrich the witts, and make you see
>   That in your self, which you knew nott before,
>   Forcing you to admire such guifts showld bee
>   Hid from your knowledg, yett in you the store.   (P82.3-12)

This Love explicitly fosters the equality of affection so painfully missing from
the experience recorded in the earlier sonnets – there is something very poignant
in the speaker's insistence on the Heavenly Cupid's power to bind 'eyes which
must care to one deere object.' The sonnet moves almost seamlessly, moreover,
from Love's power to create a perfect mutuality to its potential to 'inrich the
witts' of the individual lover, to promote a new esteem of one's own capacities.
This claim is reasserted even more emphatically in the seventh sonnet, which
moves from a tribute to the 'just desire' kindled by Heavenly Cupid to the
insistence that

> Love will a painter make you, such, as you
>   Shall able bee to drawe your only deere
> More lively, parfett, lasting, and more true
> Then rarest woorkman, and to you more neere.   (P83.9-12)

Most immediately, these lines speak to the lover-poet's heightened powers of
mimesis, her ability to render the beloved more faithfully in her art. But that
loaded phrase 'more true' (whose heavily stressed monosyllables tempt the reader
to resist the enjambment which immediately follows) suggests that the refinement
of the constant art can also fix the beloved's identity in accordance with
Pamphilia/Wroth's desires, rendering him more faithful and 'moore neere,' not
only depicting him more closely but drawing him closer to her.[16] The earlier
fantasy of the poet's power to summon in sleep a 'true lover like' image of

Amphilanthus is here revisited under the authorizing aegis of Heavenly Cupid.
What we are witnessing, of course, is a re-construction of the power of the
desiring imagination, the redeeming of 'phant'sie' purged of jealousy. Indeed in
the eighth sonnet of the *corona*, after declaring that 'briers / Of jelousie shall
heere miss wellcomnes' (P84.7-8), the speaker feels sufficiently confident to
reintroduce (as if now purged of problematic connotations) the very notion of
'phant'sie,' instructing true lovers: 'Never to other ends your phant'sies place /
Butt where they may returne with honors grace' (P84.13-14). And yet, for all the
Crowne of Sonetts' fervent testimony to the power of a constant art, the 'thread
of love' eventually unravels. The last line of the last sonnet in the *corona*
reiterates the question 'In this strang labourinth how shall I turne?': in retrospect,
the dream of making present in one's heart and art a constant lover may itself be
just another 'idle phant'sie' or 'wrong conseit' haunting the interior maze.
As the *corona* concludes, Pamphilia's old adversary returns even as she
repledges her allegiance to Heavenly Cupid:

> The tribute which my hart [art?] doth truly pay
>   Is faith untouch'd, pure thoughts discharge the score
>   Of debts for mee, where constancy bears sway,
>   And rules as Lord, unharm'd by envyes sore,
> Yett other mischiefs faile nott to attend,
>   As enimies to you, my foes must bee;
>   Curst jealousie doth all her forces bend
>   To my undoing; thus my harmes I see.
> Soe though in Love I fervently doe burne,
> In this strange labourinth how shall I turne?   (P90.5-14)

In line 11, the poet figures jealousy as a force independent of circumstances, but
I'm tempted to suggest that it is the remembered particularity of experience that
subverts the ideal vision (and alternative aesthetic) promoted by the Crowne of
Sonetts. This is emphasized by the very grammar of the *corona*'s undoing. The
final pledge of the constant art/heart to Love begins a little earlier, in the
penultimate sonnet of the Crowne, which recapitulates the virtues of Higher Love
before shifting its focus to the speaker's own oath of fealty to King Cupid:

> Free from all fogs butt shining faire, and cleere
>   Wise in all good, and innosent in ill
>   Wher holly friendship is esteemed deere
>   With truth in love, and justice in our will,

> In love thes titles only have theyr fill
>   Of hapy lyfe maintainer, and the meere
>   Defence of right, the punnisher of skill,
>   And fraude; from whence directions doth apeere,
> To thee then lord commander of all harts,
>   Ruller of owr affections kinde, and just
>   Great King of Love, my soule from fained smarts
>   Or thought of change I offer to your trust
> This crowne, my self, and all that I have more
> Except my hart which you beestow'd beefore.   (P89)

The first person pronoun of line 12 is the first instance of an 'I' since Pamphilia lamented 'I must thes doubts indure with out allay' (P77.11) in the Crowne's opening sonnet; as soon as the speaker took up the thread of love to search for the 'soules content,' experience had become idealized and generalized. The *corona*'s preferred pronouns are the 'we' which allies the speaker with the true lovers of Heavenly Cupid's court and the 'you' which invites the reader or readers to follow her 'thread of love.' As Kim Walker has suggested, the *corona*'s undoing seems to be closely associated with the reemergence of the first person, the desiring 'I' (188). What exactly is happening here?

Even before the first person pronoun is used in line 12, it is perhaps anticipated in the fourth line of the sonnet. Heavenly Cupid's realm holds the promise of 'truth in love, and justice in our will.' The last phrase reinvokes in a general sense the experience of 'just desire' promised to the servants of Love in the seventh sonnet of the *corona*. But if Wroth's familiar pun on will/Will is also operative here – tellingly associating an ideal 'truth in love' with a Will who deals justly with the speaker – then the possessive 'our' is already sliding out of the first person plural and towards the first person singular as 'our will' becomes 'my Will.' The hint of a discontinuity between the claims the lover is making for Love's powers and her personal experience of desire's inequities – the trace memory of a Will who has not always done her justice – seems to trigger a disruption of the *corona*'s own enactment of a more constant art. Eight lines later, the return of the previously repressed 'I' is followed by an assertion of agency (the speaker freely offers herself and her allegiance to the King of Love) which, however, quickly collapses into a narrative of disempowerment. Pamphilia cannot give Cupid her heart because Cupid has already bestowed it elsewhere; the self-division announced here seems to anticipate the reemergence of the jealousy which oppresses the lover in P90. To be a singular female speaking subject in *Pamphilia to Amphilanthus* is to be of two minds, to be undone by the jealousy that reclaims the constant heart and constant art.

One might compare this collapse of the idealizing trajectory of the *corona* to a similar testimony to self-division in Sidney's *Astrophil and Stella.* In sonnet 71, Astrophil spends thirteen lines celebrating Stella's capacity not only to embody virtuous beauty but also to engender virtuous behavior in the lover, only to reverse the neoplatonizing movement of the lyric in its last line: 'But ah, desire still cries: "Give me some food."' The male speaker is unable, in the end, to transcend the urgency of his own desire, and indeed it is his very inability to resist it that permits the sequence to continue: his desiring 'I' will carry on soliciting Stella's sexual surrender in the succeeding lyrics. Pamphilia/Wroth's announcement of her renewed subjection to the assaults of jealousy offers us a new spin on Astrophil's retreat from the fantasy of self transcendence; if her 'constant art' cannot in the end circumscribe a constant object, cannot fully assure the speaker of 'truth in love and justice in our will,' then the 'I' which continues to tread the 'strange labourinth' in P90 must perforce re-'turn' to a language inflected by the contingencies (and most particularly the gendered asymmetries and inequalities of the Petrarchan scenario) which inform the woman poet's attempt to participate in the idealizing discourses privileged by her historical moment.

Yet to be jealous is also to have an art. After the unravelling of the *corona*, *Pamphilia to Amphilanthus* can only imagine a final victory over the proliferating conceits of the jealous imagination which comes at the expense of all poetic production. The last lyric of the sequence begins: 'My muse now hapy, lay thy self to rest / Sleepe in the quiett of a faithfull love, / Write you noe more, butt lett thes phant'sies move / Some other harts, wake nott to new unrest' (P103.1-4); it concludes: 'And thus leave off, what's past showes you can love, / Now lett your constancy your honor prove' (13-14). Pamphilia's 'constant art' will now be manifest in her conduct, not her verse. The poetic affirmation of an end to the vicissitudes of the desiring self also requires an end to all representations of the desiring self. A certain familiar doubleness still lingers: is the speaker's Muse to sleep in the quiet certainty that her beloved is faithful, or to sleep in the knowledge that whatever he is up to, she has confidence in her own ability to love constantly? But without the 'phant'sies' of jealousy, the rest is silence.

Notes

[1] For discussions of Wroth's dialogue with Petrarchism, see, for example, Lewalski (251-263); Jones (141-54); Dubrow (134-161); Waller (194-219); Miller (29-30; 155-159); Walker (171-190).

[2] Wall notes that although Sidney's *Astrophil and Stella* was eventually added to early modern editions of his *Arcadia*, there is no link between the lyric speaker of *Astrophil and Stella* and any of the characters who compose poetry in the *Arcadia* (336).

[3] The lyric in question is P47 in Josephine Roberts's numbering of *Pamphilia to Amphilanthus*. (I employ Roberts's 'P' numbering in all citations).

[4] I here disagree with Elizabeth Hanson's assertion that Wroth's lyrics are characterized by a 'rigorous repression . . . of contradictions' (183); I would suggest that it is in the complicated relationship between the 'constant art' and the art of jealousy that we find the 'dialectical relationship between gender and genre' she finds missing in *Pamphilia to Amphilanthus* (186).

[5] In fact, the proliferation of narrators and narratives in the *Urania* allows Lamb to suggest that no speaker attains 'any hegemony of position' therein: the capacious romance even permits the heroics of constancy so passionately voiced and enacted by Pamphilia to be quite roundly criticized by the work's secondary heroine, Urania (143).

[6] See also the emphasis on the 'molesting' memory of a good once enjoyed and then lost in P4.

[7] See also Lamb (167). The gendered reinflection of the Petrarchan scenario may be seen in the work of an earlier poet, Gaspara Stampa (1523-54), whose lyrics speak very specifically to the pains of jealousy suffered by a woman whose lover is frequently absent and less than reliable in his affections (see, for example, Stampa #56, #125, #126). In contrast to Pamphilia, however, Stampa does not describe jealousy as a defect in her own love. For a suggestive discussion of Stampa's Petrarchism, see Braden (122-128); commenting on her intermittently forceful denunciations of her fickle Collaltino, he observes: 'The empowering role that frustration plays in male Petrarchism is here supplied by abandonment and loss' (125).

[8] One striking exception, however, is Philip Sidney's sympathetic treatment of Gynecia in the *Arcadia*.

[9] For an excellent discussion of representations of male jealousy in early modern drama which pays particular attention to the generic implications of the

performance of jealousy, see Maus.

[10]   Both Danson (passim) and Breitenberg (175-201) discuss the relationship suggested in Shakespearian drama between jealous speculation and the threat to the male sense of self represented by female interiority, i.e. the very possibility of the 'self possession' of the officially 'feme covert.' Breitenberg touches upon Wroth's treatment of jealousy, glancing at P66 ('Cruell suspition, O! Be now at rest'), but in a reading which completely ignores its context within the rest of the sequence, declares it to be an indictment of the jealousy of the male beloved (199); there is no space in his argument for the jealous female subject position. By contrast, Robert Burton's extended discussion of jealousy in *The Anatomy of Melancholy* insists that it is no use arguing about which sex is the more jealous: 'Comparisons are odious . . . men and women are both bad, and too subject to this pernitious infirmity' (282).

[11]   See, for example, P11, P27, P66.

[12]   See also Dubrow (134, 151).

[13]   The possibility of this reading was initially suggested to me by Amy Siddons.

[14]   Mary Moore's detailed and suggestive reading of the 'Crowne of Sonetts' explores the relationship of the labyrinth/*corona* to Wroth's gendered aesthetic, but her emphases differ substantially from my own, and she does not discuss the concluding sonnets of the *corona* ('The Labyrinth as Style').

[15]   Lewalski observes that 'chastity is sometimes linked to constancy in the *corona*, but in the sense of fidelity to one, not the renunciation of desire' (260).

[16]   See also Miller (157).

Works Cited

Braden, Gordon. *Petrarchan Love and the Continental Renaissance.* New Haven: Yale UP, 1999.

Breitenberg, Mark. *Anxious Masculinity in Early Modern England.* Cambridge: Cambridge UP, 1996.

Burton, Robert. *The Anatomy of Melancholy.* eds. Thomas C. Faulkner, et al. Vol 3. Oxford: Clarendon, 1994.

Croft, P. J., ed. *The Poems of Sir Robert Sidney.* Oxford: Clarendon P, 1984.

Danson, Lawrence. '"The Catastrophe is a Nuptial": The Space of Masculine Desire in *Othello, Cymbeline,* and *The Winter's Tale.' Shakespeare Survey* 46 (1993): 69-80.

Dubrow, Heather. *Echoes of Desire: English Petrarchism and its Counter Discourses.* Ithaca: Cornell UP, 1995.

Hanson, Elizabeth. 'Boredom and Whoredom: Reading Renaissance Women's Sonnet Sequences.' *Yale Journal of Criticism* 10 (1997): 165-91.

Jones, Ann Rosalind. *The Currency of Eros: Women's Love Lyric in Europe 1540-1620.* Bloomington: Indiana UP, 1990.

Lamb, Mary Ellen. *Gender and Authorship in the Sidney Circle.* Madison: U of Wisconsin P, 1990.

Lewalski, Barbara K. *Writing Women in Jacobean England.* Cambridge: Harvard UP, 1993.

Masten, Jeff. '"Shall I turne blabbe?": Circulation, Gender and Subjectivity in Mary Wroth's Sonnets.' *Reading Mary Wroth: Representing Alternatives in Early Modern England.* eds. Gary Waller and Naomi J. Miller. Knoxville: U of Tennessee P, 1991. 67-87.

Maus, Katharine Eisaman. 'Horns of Dilemma: Jealousy, Gender and Spectatorship in English Renaissance Drama.' *ELH* 54 (1987): 561-83.

Miller, Naomi J. *Changing the Subject: Mary Wroth and Figurations of Gender in Early Modern England.* Lexington: UP of Kentucky, 1996.

Moore, Mary. 'The Labyrinth as Style in *Pamphilia to Amphilanthus.' SEL* 38 (1998): 109-25.

Ovid. *Metamorphoses.* Trans. Frank Justus Miller. 3rd edn. Vol. 1. Cambridge: Harvard UP, 1977.

Paulissen, May N. *The Love Sonnets of Lady Mary Wroth: A Critical Introduction.* Salzburg: Institut für Anglistik und Amerikanistik, Universität Salzburg, 1982.

Petrarch. *Petrarch's Lyric Poems.* ed. and trans. Robert M. Durling. Cambridge: Harvard UP, 1976.

Roberts, Josephine, ed. *The Poems of Lady Mary Wroth.* Baton Rouge: Louisiana State UP, 1983.

Sidney, Sir Philip. *Astrophil and Stella. Sir Philip Sidney.* ed . Katherine Duncan-Jones. Oxford: Oxford UP, 1989.

____. *The Countess of Pembroke's Arcadia.* ed. Maurice Evans. Harmondsworth: Penguin, 1987.

Stampa, Gaspara. *Selected Poems.* eds. and trans. Laura Anna Stortoni and Mary Prentice Lillie. New York: Italica P, 1994.

Walker, Kim. *Women Writers of the English Renaissance.* New York: Twayne, 1996.

Wall, Wendy. *The Imprint of Gender: Authorship and Publication in the English Renaissance.* Ithaca: Cornell UP, 1993.

Waller, Gary. *The Sidney Family Romance: Mary Wroth, William Herbert, and the Early Modern Construction of Gender.* Detroit: Wayne State UP, 1993.

5

'An Emblem of Themselves, in Plum or Pear': Poetry, the Female Body and the Country House

Jacqueline Pearson

In about 1611, a period marked by anxieties about disorder and the beginning of the argument between king and parliament over the limits of royal authority which culminated in the 1640s in civil war, a new poetic genre emerged – the country house poem. While there were women practitioners, they were few: Alastair Fowler's substantial *The Country House Poem: a Cabinet of Seventeenth-Century Estate Poems and Related Items* finds only Aemilia Lanyer, Margaret Cavendish and Anne Finch. Country house poems display revealing contradictions. The country house serves as a metonym for the state or civilization itself, though the poems reveal deep anxieties about the collapse of authority and order by the very vigor and repetitiveness by which the presence of these virtues is asserted. They may also stage a utopian vision of universal participation in country house culture, thereby representing society as an organic unity where all have shared interests and acquire equal benefits, thereby mystifying and naturalizing social inequality. A central passage in Jonson's 'To Penshurst' (lines 61-75, a substantial part of a poem of 102 lines) describes the poet enjoying the lavish resources of country house culture. Such passages, however, paradoxically suggest anxieties of exclusion which become explicitly central in some poems, like Lanyer's 'The Description of Cooke-ham.'

Moreover, at a time when women's status as citizens was most problematic, these poems figure both an idealized authority and the greatest threats to it through the female body. In addition, the country house poem is not only explicitly political, it often draws self-conscious attention to its own poetic nature, which may itself constitute a political project. The choice of form – rhyming couplets, or, more rarely, complex stanzaic forms – has direct relevance to the political vision, asserting mimetically the order which the poems praise. Even the nature of the rhymes may, I shall demonstrate, serve political as well as poetic functions. Moreover, the female body often figures the poetic authority and processes of representation through which the poem functions. Recently we have been reminded that 'it is virtually impossible to separate out gender as a category unrelated to class position' (Coiro 358), and the female body becomes central to a discourse of class as well as gender in these poems, and also plays a key role in the politics of poetic representation. Investigating the ways these images are manipulated will cast light on early modern women poets, and the specific ways they experienced anxieties of authority, exclusion, and poetic influence.

In seventeenth-century poetry, nature and architecture are never politically neutral spaces. In Geoffrey Whitney's 'Patriaque Cuique Cara: To Richard Cotton, Esquire' (1586) the estate's beehives embody an ideal order – 'A Commonwealth, by this, is right expressed: / Both him, that rules, and these, that do obey' (19-20) – which mirrors that of Cotton's estate at Combermere. That the country house is presented as 'a political or moral microcosm' (Fowler 21) is implicit from the origins of the genre. Gender is, moreover, a significant issue. Whitney accepts his age's science, itself shaped by social attitudes: the worker bees are female (17), their ruler male. This 'master bee' (7), who 'hath no sting' (11) but is protected by loving subjects, suggests not only the pacific Cotton but also Queen Elizabeth, who possessed 'a male body politic in concept while a female body natural in practice' (Levin 121). Nonetheless, the only natural structure of authority for Whitney is that of the male over the female, although the monarch was a woman and Cotton had inherited his Combermere estate from a female relative (Fowler 33).

Elsewhere the female body becomes explicitly central to the *paysage moralisée*. In Thomas Carew's 'To my Friend G. N. from Wrest' (1640), the landscape is surreally fecund: 'the pregnant Earth / Sends from her teeming womb a flowery birth' (9-10). The description of the brewing of March beer describes Bacchus impregnating Ceres, 'Begetting so himself on her' (103) that he is simultaneously both the father and the begotten child. This makes explicit the usually mystified role of the female in transmitting to the next generation patrilineal property and culture in which she herself has no real share.

There are obvious reasons for the association of women with the country, garden and estate. Nature was traditionally gendered as feminine, a symbolic system which confirmed the exclusion of women from culture and citizenship, but could be used by more radical women against itself (Pearson, 'Gender and Narrative' 179-90). Gardens figure Eden, which in the seventeenth century had political as well as religious resonances. The Eden metaphor, however, clearly provided problems for depicting the female subject. Sir Thomas Salusbury's 'Kensington Grove' (1637) compares the Earl of Carbury's house to 'Eden's sacred bowers' (4), the 'best remembrance . . . what Eden was' (33), with the newly-married couple as an unfallen Adam and Eve. But praising Frances Altham Vaughan as a second Eve proves ambiguous since the poem implies that the virtues appropriate to a prelapsarian woman – lack of 'coyness' (11), for instance – may not be suitable for a seventeenth-century matron. The relationship between nature and culture becomes problematic precisely at the site of the female body.

There was another reason why Jacobean women were identified with the country estate. Repeatedly between 1614 and 1627 Kings James and Charles issued proclamations ordering gentry to return to their estates, poeticized in James's 'An Elegy Written by the King Concerning his Counsel for Ladies and Gentlemen to Depart the City of London According to his Majesty's Proclamation' (c. 1622). James's injunction focuses on an allegedly natural congruence between women and the country, the 'orb and proper sphere' (29) of the elite class woman: those who resist their natural place are compared to transgressive women like Eve and Lot's wife (50, 24). Both men and women are, presumably, at fault for neglecting the true duties of rural landowners, but James firmly blames women primarily, with 'Eve's offense' corrupting 'honest Adam' (50).

Images of ideal order and authority, then, are founded on the female body, which also paradoxically symbolizes the most potent threats to that order. Finally, poetic representation itself may be seen as contingent upon the female body. To some extent this simply reproduces the gendered metaphors of creativity – of Muses, Athene, Daphne – which early modern writers borrowed from the classics (Pearson, 'Women Reading' 84), or the commonplace that the beloved woman inspires the production of poetry: in Waller's 'At Penshurst' (1) (c. 1635), Saccharissa invests both Penshurst and the poem with order, for she has a 'power like that of harmony in sound,' shaping a 'confused heap' into 'fair figures' (Fowler 181). These claims are too conventional to constitute empowerment of the female subject, but again they could be renegotiated by women writers to legitimate their own access to culture.

The claim that the female body is crucially enabling to poetic culture can, however, have a dark side. The nightingale, personified as Philomela, both a natural creature and a metaphor for poetry and the poet, opens up a transitional space between nature and culture, which could be useful for women writers like Lanyer and Finch in reflecting their own condition as both culturally silenced and yet possessed of a voice. But in the originating Ovidian narrative, Philomela, raped and with her tongue cut out, provides a disturbingly contradictory image of a feminized art. In 'Upon Occasion of His Majesty's Proclamation' (1630), for instance, Sir Richard Fanshawe describes the nightingale paradoxically as a 'harmless Siren' who 'prettily . . . tells a tale / Of rape and blood' (Fowler 125). For male poets, the mutilated Philomela may suggest ambivalence about the feminizing metaphors of poetic creativity.

The country house poem, then, includes political and metapoetic discourses in both of which the female body takes a central place. The female body may be characterized by absence or presence, or by a weird combination of the two, as in the poems of Andrew Marvell, whose garden poems veer between positioning the female body at the center of its discourse and making it conspicuous by its absence. In 'The Picture of Little T. C. in a Prospect of Flowers,' the 'Nimph' (2) is a female Adam dominating not only the poem but language itself as she names the creatures, while conversely, in 'The Garden,' the absence and silence of the female is precisely what permits its paradisal world of solitary contemplation, and in 'The Mower against Gardens' the female body is present only through its absence, as gardening is figured as unnatural sexuality, 'Forbidden mixtures' (22), adultery, rape, harems and eunuchs, even procreation 'without a Sex' (30). 'Upon Appleton House' creates a semiotic landscape which functions as a coded 'language' of 'Signs' which the observer must learn to 'read' (571, 582). In this landscape everything represents something else: a garden represents England torn by civil war, a flower-bed provides 'the just Figure of a Fort' (286), a forest punningly embodies a family tree. At the center of this semiotic landscape is the body. 'No Creature loves an empty space; / Their Bodies measure out their place' (15-16): the *holy Mathematicks* (47) of the 'Lines' (42) which punningly refer both to the architecture and the poem, 'In ev'ry Figure equal Man' (48). However, while the (male) body of Vitruvian man figures the stability of building and poem, the female body both represents and offers the most potent threat to national and family stability. The body of Maria Fairfax, 'pure, and spotless as the Eye' (726), assures stability and order, as does the body of her grandmother, 'the blooming Virgin *Thwates*' (90). But as virginity assures it also threatens social stability. Premarital female virginity upholds a patrilineal system by guaranteeing the true succession of property, but virginity can also figure a disturbing self-sufficiency, a sexuality potentially both lesbian and autoerotic, as the 'Virgin' (186) bodies of the 'Suttle Nuns' (94) threaten the ordered heterosexual economy of the Fairfax family.

In Jonson's 'To Penshurst' and poems by Aemilia Lanyer and Anne Finch, the female body takes a central role in an economy which is not only political but also self-consciously metapoetic. Penshurst was the family estate in Kent of the Sidney family, in 1612 the home of Sir Robert Sidney, brother of the poet, and thus an embodiment of literary as well as political order. Jonson depicts it as a utopian community marked by generosity, communality and mutual respect, where Sidney is defined by his presence: 'thy lord dwells' (102) are the climactic final words of the poem, showing Sidney's awareness of all the duties of a landowner, including 'hospitality' (60). Ann Baynes Coiro identifies Jonson's 'edgy support of the aristocratic status quo,' and calls *The Forrest* (1616), the collection in which 'To Penshurst' was first published, 'a book structured by a weird ambivalence about public life and private life,' with one purpose of the poem being 'a fantasy redress of Jonson's own social unease' (Coiro 369-71). Such ambivalence can be seen in the poem particularly around its treatment of gender and the female body.

Jonson's poem constitutes a conservative, though not unconflicted, celebration of old values and hierarchies. As a poem stressing 'the importance of lineage' (Riggs 180) it appropriately operates through two intersecting straight lines, one horizontal and one vertical, both showing the importance attached by the poet to linear hierarchies. First, the poem moves systematically upwards – literally so, from the 'lower land, that to the river bends' (22) to the 'middle grounds' (24) and then 'the tops' (25), but also symbolically, as it ascends the Great Chain of being from inanimate objects through plants and animals to the human hierarchy – peasants, aristocrats, the king – and finally to God himself (93). Penshurst constitutes a stable hierarchy modelled on the Great Chain of Being, and is thus legitimated not only politically but also theologically. At the same time, the poem enacts a second linear trajectory, moving inward from the outskirts of the estate – the woods, trees, mount – into the house itself, first into its public and then gradually into its most private rooms. The ultimate private space is the womb of Barbara Gamage Sidney, which ensures the survival of the family and the cultural and political values it represents. Lady Sidney, wife of Sir Robert, becomes a key figure in the poem, a 'good lady' (84), 'noble, fruitful, chaste' (90).

However, while Jonson affirms hierarchy, the act of penetration which allows him to enter the aristocratic house's most private spaces undercuts this affirmation, perhaps demonstrating the poet's 'ambivalence' and 'unease.' These anxieties are reemphasized by the fact that at each site where the poem's linear trajectories are interrupted, a female body is to be found. As the poem ascends the Great Chain of Being, its coherent upward movement momentarily falters at the first appearance of Lady Sidney. Her name has been given to an oak and a copse on the estate (18-19), and at this point the systematic hierarchy from plants to animals to humans is disrupted. On the poem's horizontal axis, too, Barbara Sidney constitutes the problematic center of the house and the poem, both impregnably 'chaste' (90) and with her 'noble parts' penetrated by the poet and laid open as a text to be 'Read' (97) by the common reader. Moreover, while at the beginning of the poem Jonson, in 'seeking to enhance the renown of Penshurst . . . must disparage the renown of rival estates' (Evans 122), he performs an identical manoeuvre at the end, denigrating all other women through praising the chastity of Lady Sidney, 'A fortune in this age but rarely known' (92). Such strategies define the poem's ambiguity about the female body which both ensures and challenges the hierarchies Jonson celebrates.

In Jonson's poem, the female body is imprinted on the landscape, which is haunted by dryads (10) and Muses (14), and has an oak and copse named for Lady Sidney (18-19). This identification of landscape and female body becomes most intense and problematic in the depiction of the 'ripe daughters' of farmers who carry to the owners of the great house 'An emblem of themselves, in plum, or pear' (54, 56). The female body and the products of the landscape become indistinguishable, naturalizing Jonson's conservative construction of gender difference. Moreover, the female body becomes a metaphor for exchange, social, sexual, and, since line 56 draws conscious attention to the working of metaphor, poetic. Jonson describes previously the planting of a tree to celebrate Sir Philip Sidney, 'his great birth, where all the Muses met' (14). Male creativity is mediated through the power of the female muses, as male birthright and authority are mediated through female bodies, like those of the ripe daughters sent to gain husbands by advertizing their own fruitfulness, and that of Lady Sidney, whose chastity guarantees true succession. Male authority, familial, political and poetic – the authority of fathers, Sidney, King James and the poet – depends on controlling the potential power and unruliness of women.

'To Penshurst,' then, enacts contemporary contradictions about the female body, social stability, and poetry. Stability depends on the compliance of the female, the great lady as well as the ripe daughters of the peasantry, but the female body threatens as well as sustains that order. The poem's metapoetical discourse echoes this ambiguity: its linear structures and performance of the act of penetration identify the poet as by definition male, while the female serves as a metaphor for text, landscape, poem. When women wrote country house poems, they needed at least a different means of gendering poetic creativity, and possibly a more fundamentally revisionist form. It is in this context that we should see Lanyer's 'The Description of Cooke-ham' and Finch's country house poems.

Aemilia Lanyer has become the best-known of early modern women poets, with at present three full editions (Rowse, 1978; Woods, 1993; Purkiss, 1994), a wealth of critical comment, and at least two complete books with substantial bibliographies (Grossman 1998, Woods 1999), which allow her relations to existing discursive practices to be better understood. Lanyer's 'The Description of Cooke-ham' was certainly published, and probably written, before Jonson's 'To Penshurst,' and it is hard to believe that the later poem was unaware of the earlier, since they share rhymes, metaphors, and other details too specific to be simply the result of shared conventions (Barroll 36-40). While internal evidence suggests that Jonson's poem, although not published until 1616, was composed in 1612 (Fowler 57), Lanyer's forms a coda to her remarkable protofeminist religious poem, *Salve Deus Rex Judaeorum*, published in 1611. 'The Description of Cooke-ham' should, indeed, be read in the context of *Salve Deus*, its images of Eden rooted in that poem's defense of Eve, and its audacious strategies with gender congruent with those of *Salve Deus*, which presents a feminized Christ and immasculated female dignitaries who become avatars of Solomon, St Peter, Aaron, and even God Himself (Pearson, 'Women Writers' 46).

In Lanyer's poem women both inspire and write poetry, and the act of composition is made more explicitly visible than in Jonson's. The poem is a 'work of grace' generated by the 'desires' (12) of the female patron and the 'power' of the female poet. Lanyer is all too aware of how 'great a difference is there in degree' (106) between herself and her 'great friends' (105), but she also claims that 'When I am dead, thy name in this may live' (206), a conventional claim which nonetheless is one in a series of acts of class subversion. While in Jonson's poem religion is a conservative force underpinning traditional class and gender politics, for Lanyer religion undoes traditional hierarchies. Christ, 'a seeming tradesman's son' (*SDRJ* 1715), is actually God; God subverts hierarchies, for 'Unto the mean he makes the mighty bow' (*SDRJ* 123), 'Making the powerful judged of the weak' (*SDRJ* 1536); and the lower-class female poet benefits from this, for 'the weaker thou dost seem to be / In sex or sense, the more his glory shines' (*SDRJ* 289-90). All are equal before God – 'Although we are but born of earth, / We may behold the heavens, despising death' (113-4); but the imperfect rhyme adds a discordant and uncertain note which interrogates the poem's frustrated dream of female power and solidarity.

While Jonson's poem optimistically demonstrates the participation of all in country house culture, Lanyer pessimistically shows the exile from the country house not only of the poet but also of the women of the noble family. While Penshurst is an idealized patriarchy, in which the female body assures and represents lineage and poetic achievement, Cookham is a fragile, temporary matriarchy where the female body is ineluctably tragic, defined by absence, instability and exile, unlike the presence of the patriarchal family in 'To Penshurst.' While the lord of Jonson's estate by definition 'dwells,' noble women left estates to marry or when widowed, and in lamenting this Lanyer's poem constitutes a 'dissent from the Jonsonian celebration of patrilineal dynastics' (Grossman 140). While Penshurst was the ancestral estate of the Sidney family, Cookham was not the family home of the Clifford women, but was leased from the king: the great estates of the Earl of Cumberland had been bequeathed away from his daughter, so on his death both his wife and daughter were deprived of the family home (Coiro 363-4). Lanyer's plangent poem laments the disinherited status of women in Jacobean society, which the female poet shares with the greatest of noblewomen. Cookham constitutes 'a lost female paradise' (Lewalski 204), where relations between women correct the fallen heterosexuality of Adam and Eve, but which is now as unattainable as the prelapsarian world. In this lost Eden, the female body is absent, deferred – the poet, unable to kiss Anne Clifford, kisses instead a tree she has kissed (165-72); or it is constantly metamorphosed into substitutes, as the mutilated Philomela is transformed into a nightingale (32), a nymph into an echo (199), and the virtuous female Cliffords into male worthies, Moses, David and Joseph (85-91).

While Jonson's poem is structured on two linear axes, Lanyer's, in keeping with its association of the female body with themes of disinheritance, deferral, absence and exile, adopts a significantly looser, spiral structure, its prototype not the straight line but the circle. I have written elsewhere (Pearson, 'Women Writers' 47) of the significance of the circle in *Salve Deus Rex Judaeorum*, whose narrative is structured in concentric circles with, at the center, the vindication of the originary woman, Eve. For seventeenth-century writers the circle was a female symbol, even a euphemism for the vagina: Donne, for instance, structures 'A Valediction: Of Weeping' on a series of expanding circles – tears, coins, pregnancy, fruits, zero, globe, earth, moon, spheres – which force our attention to the sexual drama of parting (Donne 89). For Lanyer, the circle was similarly useful in imprinting the feminine on the poem and dissolving the linear and hierarchical trajectories embodied in works like 'To Penshurst.'

The circle of 'The Description of Cooke-ham' is described by the farewell to the estate with which it begins (1, 6) and ends (205). Within this are other circles, reminiscent of the wombs-within-wombs structure of *Salve Deus Rex Judaeorum*. These circles may be constituted by repeated images, like Philomela (31, 189), phrases, like 'pleasures past' (13, 118), homophones, like 'wither' / 'whither' (135, 182), and even rhymes, like 'away' / 'stay' (141-2, 147-8, 197-8), 'tree' / 'thee' (33-4, 45-6, 59-60, 191-2), 'came' / 'frame' (17-18, 131-2), 'grace it' / 'deface it' (19-20, 201-2). Repetition is, moreover, not only the medium of the poem but also part of its subject: 'memory' (117, 155), the imaginative repetition of the past, is central to the poem, which issues injunctions to 'Remember' (119) and praises the Cliffords for not 'Forgetting' their subordinates (151). The poet even remembers Anne Clifford when she 'did repeat the pleasures which had past' (163). Lanyer's repetitions create the drama of memory and regret which is central to the poem, and her use of the spiral translates the female body into a mimetic verse form, undercutting her age's linear hierarchies of class and gender.

The poem comprises two main movements, with a break at line 126: the first presents an idealized vision of the matriarchal utopia of Cookham, the second laments its destruction with the departure of Margaret and Anne Clifford. A buffer between these two movements is provided by the attack on fortune and the inequity of class hierarchy in lines 103-26, positioned centrally to the poem as the defense of Eve constitutes the center of *Salve Deus Rex Judaeorum*. The rhyme of the first couplet of the final section ('leave' / 'conceive,' 127-8) echoes that of the last couplet of the previous section ('grieve' / 'relieve', 125-6). This continuation of rhyme stresses the continuity behind the apparent break: in the unequal society Lanyer inhabits, the tragic future is implicit even in the utopian past. Some of the poem's repetition dramatizes intense regret. The rhyme 'away' / 'stay' echoes through the last section, bringing the two opposites, absence and presence, into equilibrium. Elsewhere repetition connects the final phase with earlier sections, casting the last section as a painfully ironic inversion of a happy past. Early in the poem, for instance, the rhyme 'tree' / 'thee' demonstrates the utopian harmony of nature and its female rulers (33-4, 45-6, 59-60), while later the same rhyme expresses absence rather than presence: 'each stately tree / Looks bare and desolate now for want of thee' (191-2). Similarly the rhyme 'grace it' / 'deface it' expresses a positive in the early part of the poem ('all ornaments to grace it, / . . . no foulness to deface it,' 19-20), while later it is recast in the negative to emphasize the loss of the feminized utopia – 'The house cast off each garment that might grace it, / Putting on dust and cobwebs to deface it' (201-02).

Two images can be related to these spiral structures and repetitions, the mirror and the echo. As I have argued elsewhere (Pearson, 'Women Writers' 50-1), *Salve Deus Rex Judaeorum* plays on the double association of the mirror as an attribute of Venus and hence a female symbol, and an Elizabethan metaphor for an instructive text, and this ambiguity is useful to Lanyer as a means of legitimizing her own entry as a woman into print culture. The mirror, of course, also reflects: in the dedication 'To all virtuous ladies in general,' Virtue 'deigns herself to see' in the mirror which is the poem (7). The mirror, while not explicitly mentioned in 'The Description of Cooke-ham,' may be invoked in its strategies of reflection and repetition, again inscribing the feminine on the poem.

More demonstrably, 'Delightful Echo' (199) connects the poem's representations of gender and its strategies of repetition. The echo poem became a favourite virtuoso piece in the late sixteenth and early seventeenth centuries. Gascoigne's entertainment for the queen at Kenilworth in 1575 featured a dialogue between a wild man and Echo: echoing his 'did lay', she celebrates the sponsor of the lavish entertainment, 'Dudley,' the Earl of Leicester (Hollander 29). Like many royal entertainments, Gascoigne's may have dramatized not uncritical worship but 'struggle' between queen and people (Wall 133), in this case challenging women's ability to speak independently, and hinting at the benefits to the people of the queen's marriage to Leicester. For Gascoigne Echo represented the incompleteness of the female. For Jonson, who makes much use of Echo in plays and masques, she 'figure[s] the practice of Renaissance imitation' (Loewenstein 6) and is used to claim a place for the (male) poet within literary traditions (Loewenstein 95).

Unlike Jonson, Lanyer does not use Echo primarily to identify herself with hegemonic literary or political structures. Like Philomela, Echo draws attention to and problematizes women's language, offering a series of ambiguous images of female speech. As a punishment for gossiping, Echo was deprived of independent speech: later she pined away for love of Narcissus and lost bodily form altogether. She might, as for Gascoigne, represent the incompleteness of the female. But Echo might also through apparently compliant repetition offer disturbing insights beyond the original speaker or a subversion of his speech, as in Webster's almost contemporary *The Duchess of Malfi* (c. 1612), where after her death the Duchess speaks as an echo, identifying herself to Antonio (*'I, wifes-voyce'*), warning him against his proposed meeting with the Cardinal (*'Be mindfull of thy safety ... O flye your fate'*), and predicting the tragedy to come (*'Thou art a dead Thing'*) (V.3.33-44). Like Lanyer, Webster uses Echo to chart the tragic shift from a female-dominated utopia to a world where femininity figures only as loss, exile and silence.

Like Philomela, Echo represents the silencing (and in the case of Echo the making invisible) of the female. In 'The Description of Cooke-ham' Echo is silenced in the very process of being named – 'did now for sorrow die' (201). Yet she can also be used, like Philomela, by the female poet to achieve an ambiguous authority and 'presence' through 'Absence, denial, negation, loss' (Goldberg 37). Lanyer's interest in Echo depends on her status as the 'very patron of liminality' (Loewenstein 5), who marks the transition between past and future, speech and silence, presence and absence, deconstructing binary opposites, a strategy always fruitful for the woman writer (Moi 104-7). She also presides over 'moment[s] of generic instability' (Loewenstein 61) – is 'The Description of Cooke-ham' an independent poem or part of *Salve Deus Rex Judaeorum*, a celebration or a critique of aristocratic country house culture? Above all, Echo offers space for the exploration of ambiguities around gender, language and literary tradition. While the myth attacks women's speech as both excessive and unoriginal, Lanyer reclaims Echo to challenge assumptions about female speech and silence, both using her as a metaphor for the restrictions on female access to language and killing her off to claim artistic autonomy rather than only the ability to parrot (male) language and literary traditions.

In 'The Description of Cooke-ham,' even more literally than in 'To Penshurst,' poetic creation is dependent on the female, the poet herself and the Cliffords, by whose will the poem is created and in whose presence the landscape becomes ordered like the poem: 'all things else did hold like similes' (22). This is reflected even in the poem's rhyming patterns. As Maureen Quilligan has pointed out, 'noticing where Elizabethan poets consciously choose to use feminine rhymes may tell us something about the complex interrelations between the politics of poetry and sexuality in the English Renaissance' (Quilligan 312). In the seventeenth century, 'poetic form ... was a politicized practice' (Wolfson

20). Elizabethan literary critics like Sir Philip Sidney, Sir John Harrington and Samuel Daniel borrowed from the French the distinction between masculine rhymes, where the rhyme falls on the stressed syllable, and feminine rhymes, where the rhyme falls on the unstressed syllable (Shepherd 41; Smith, 2:221, 383). Generally they regarded the rhymes much as they regarded the genders in society, with feminine rhymes viewed as weak and fit only for minor poetic forms. 'To Penshurst' has no feminine rhymes at all: Jonson's utopian community is solidly patriarchal with the female contained within the house and within the masculine rhymes . 'The Description of Cooke-ham' has eleven pairs of feminine rhymes. This partly reflects the more plangent tone of Lanyer's poem, the poetic equivalent of a minor key: but it is also an instrument of the poem's radical sexual politics.

This reflects the practice in *Salve Deus Rex Judaeorum*, which 'abound[s] in feminine endings' (Mueller 107). Here, in a poem of some 2660 lines, I count at least 82 pairs (or triplets) of feminine rhymes. As Mueller argues, one specific purpose may be to critique Daniel's poetics, as Lanyer critiques his representation of women elsewhere in the poem (Mueller 107). Feminine rhymes tend to cluster at points where gender becomes a pressing issue, in the poems to multiple female dedicatees (especially Susan Bertie and Mary Sidney Herbert) and the digressions addressed to Margaret Clifford, in the dream of Pilate's wife, and the description of Christ's passion with its focus on his relations with women. It is as if Lanyer were struggling to devise a specifically female language in contrast to the male-dominated forms she had inherited.

In the dedications and early stages of the poem, feminine rhymes express strongly positive qualities, often attributing them to real contemporary women – 'dignities' / 'excellencies' (Purkiss 241, lines 13-15), 'majesty' / 'piety', 'beauty' / 'duty' (Purkiss 244, lines 91-4). As the poem continues, though, the passion of Christ becomes full of negative feminine rhymes, 'unrespected' / 'rejected' (735-6), 'no sov'reignty' / 'cruelty' / 'tyranny' (826-30), 'iniquity' / 'impiety,' 'claiming'/ 'blaspheming' (926-9). This does not, I think, mark a retreat from the protofeminism of the rest of the poem: Christ as Man of Sorrows is feminized, and the traditionally negative associations of these feminine rhymes are placed on the men, Judas (735-6), men who defraud women of 'equal[ity]' (826-30), and the men present at the crucifixion whose corrupt uses of language contrast with Christ's (feminized) silence and the tears of the daughters of Jerusalem (962-6). In the triumphant conclusion, Christ's resurrection and the theological authority of women like Margaret Clifford return feminine rhymes to a predominantly positive register, though the awareness that the final judgement is still to come can create a tense balance of positive and negative – 'sweetness' / 'discreetness' (1753-5), 'eternal' / 'infernal' (1778-80). In *Salve Deus Rex Judaeorum*, then, the feminine and the ideal of female language are imprinted on the poem at every level, thematic and formal.

In her survey of rhyming practices in Sidney and Spenser, Maureen Quilligan finds a consistent use of feminine rhymes to articulate 'patriarchal chaos' and 'political upset' (313, 315). For Lanyer in 'The Description of Cooke-ham,' feminine rhymes are more likely to reflect positive qualities and presence, and to constitute a meditation on the possibility of a gynocentric utopia – 'pleasures' / 'treasures' (15-16), 'beauty' / 'duty' (101-2), 'memory' / 'continually' (155-6). As the two noblewomen and the poet leave the estate, masculine rhymes displace feminine: 'give' / 'live,' 'hest' / 'breast,' 'remains'/ 'chains' (205-10), or feminine rhymes take on a newly negative resonance: 'their very leaves did wither / Changing their colours as they grew together' (135-6), 'The winds and waters seemed to chide together, / Because you went away, they knew not whither' (181-2). Like the echo rhymes, feminine rhymes are deployed in imaginatively repetitive or chiastic patterns to mark the poignant movement from the affirmative beginning to the pessimistic conclusion. The imminent absence of the Clifford women transposes the feminine rhymes from positive to negative register.

The country house poem survived the cultural shifts of the late seventeenth century and continued to interest poets in the different climate of the early eighteenth: and its women practitioners continued to be preoccupied by images of the female body and the idea of a female language. I conclude with a brief examination of some poems of Anne Finch, Countess of Winchilsea, who emerges as the most imaginative and inventive reviser of the Jonsonian country house poem, and a successor to Lanyer in her adaptation of the form for protofeminist purposes. As women poets, despite the hundred years that separate them, Finch and Lanyer share some images, like the paradoxical figure of Philomela, and poetic strategies: it is important to both, for instance, to 'imagin[e] a community of heroic women' (Barash 265; see Lewalski).

Many of Finch's poems center on the country house and the role of the woman within it. Finch and her husband were Stuart sympathizers who withdrew from the public world of politics at the Williamite settlement (McGovern), and many poems praise the order of the country estate in contrast with chaotic national politics, especially through Finch's favorite metaphor of 'shade/s'

(*Selected Poems* 18, 21, 28, 34, 53, etc.). Nonetheless, the key to Finch's attitude to the country estate is its ambiguity. Although the country house offered the safe domestic space she craved, it also removed her from the public role of the Augustan poet (Rogers), which she both fears and desires. In 'The Introduction', for instance, she offers a vigorous defense of the woman poet, but ultimately retreats to the 'retired' (59) space of the private house, unconvincingly claiming to be 'content' (64) there. The female body and female poetry must accept their 'wants' and their 'contracted' nature (61). As Carol Barash argues, this poem and others centered on the country house enact a 'tension' between Finch's proposal of a feminized 'model of literary authority' and the poet's 'refusal' to speak with that authority (Barash 272). However, some poems succeed in resisting such closure, usually by dealing with women's entry to language and literature indirectly rather than confrontationally. The most powerful of these poems is 'A Nocturnal Reverie', a poem as political as Jonson's and Lanyer's country house poems. By opening up an alternative to both a female domestic and a male public space the poem 'shifts the relationship between public and private political spheres' (Barash 261). I shall conclude with an examination of this, after a brief discussion of two less well-known poems.

Fowler's anthology includes two country house poems by Finch, 'To the Honourable the Lady Worsely at Long-leate' (c. 1690) and 'Upon my Lord Winchilsea's Converting the Mount in his Garden to a Terrace, and other Alterations and Improvements in his House, Park and Gardens' (c. 1702), neither of which was published in her lifetime. The first sees the great estate of Longleat as itself a female body (53-5). Finch's insistence that the 'splendours' of the estate are 'above metaphor' (46-7) undercuts the poetic authority of 'Denham or . . . Cowley' (44), but not that of the female poet, since her art is closely identified with the feminized landscape: 'my pen (smooth as their turf)' (59). The place cannot be described in 'syllables' (76) or 'words' (81), but can only be enjoyed 'silent' (82): but this silent language, like that of Echo in Lanyer, is one in which the female poet by virtue of her sex is expert, as the (female) 'free soul' (43) in 'A Nocturnal Reverie' has special insight through 'silent musings' (41) into 'Something too high for syllables to speak' (42). 'To Lady Worsley' praises Thomas Thynne, first Viscount Weymouth, and his daughter Frances Thynne Worsley, and 'his presence and her charms' (97) create the idyllic world of Longleat. As in 'The Description of Cooke-ham,' the parent-child dyad recapitulates a prelapsarian world as an unfallen Adam and Eve in 'paradise' (110), in whom for Finch even gender difference is abolished, for 'paternal wit' can be seen in the face of the daughter (96).

'Upon my Lord Winchilsea's Converting the Mount' adopts many of the established conventions of the country house poem – it compares the place with classical *loci amoeni* and ends with praise of the owner (Fowler 398) – but it shows a subversive engagement with these conventions, since it implies a marked ambivalence about the improvements it ostensibly praises, and the long central section (23-49) undoes the praise at beginning and end. This ambivalence is emphasised by the gendering of improvements, for the house and the estate are consistently feminine (41-2, 72-8), the improvers masculine (1, 6), so that improvement becomes an enactment of the 'power . . . absolute' (32) of men over women and the feminized estate. (Finch deleted lines about the 'too prevailing art' of a previous lady of the manor who was herself responsible for improvements [Fowler 398], perhaps so as not to compromise the poem's gender-dynamics.) The fourth Earl of Winchilsea is compared with Caesar ('came, and saw, and overcame' 14), and with Alexander the Great destroying Persepolis (44), violent and ambiguous embodiments of male power. Male power defeats the 'robbed palace' (42), and the only recourse to this act of despoliation is 'secret whispers' (34), presumably including this unpublished poem.

Carol Barash writes of Finch 'generating a web of metaphors – solitude, inwardness, darkness, what Julia Kristeva called "abjection" – that would become, over the course of the eighteenth century, figures both of women's emotions and the power of poetic language' (Barash 261). This can be clearly seen in 'A Nocturnal Reverie,' where Finch's landscape journey rewrites, even satirizes, that of Jonson's 'To Penshurst' or Marvell's 'Upon Appleton House.' Whereas Jonson gradually enters the house, and Marvell begins within the house and at the end of the poem prepares to re-enter it, in 'A Nocturnal Reverie' the country house, although glimpsed, is never arrived at or entered. Despite the rise of domestic ideology (Davidoff and Hall 149-92), for Finch woman has no real place within the country house, or within the state which it figures, and the poem ends, not like 'To Penshurst' with the presence of the lord, but with a vision of country-house life as one of endless and pointless deferral – 'pleasures, seldom reached, again pursued' (50). The 'free [female] soul' (43) prefers a transcendant spiritual realm beyond androcentric language and institutions, or its earthly reflection in nocturnal nature, to the rule of 'tyrant man' (38). Culture is moved to the margins, while a feminized landscape locates the origins of poetry in a feminine nature, embodied for Finch, as for Lanyer, in the evocative figure of Philomel (4). Finch's landscape is feminized in the sense that it is full of shapes recapitulating the curves and concavities of the female body – the 'distant cavern' (2), the hollow shape of the foxgloves (15), the 'hills' and 'swelling haycocks' (27-8), even the pun on the verb 'hollowing' (6). Its inhabitants are female animals, nightingale, owl (5-6), glow-worms (17), partridge (34), with only the male horse (29) creating momentary 'fear' in the female speaker (31). Both the public sphere of tyrant man and the private sphere of routine feminine tasks are adjudged inferior to this third space, a feminized sphere of the free soul, nature, and poetic composition, all identified as by definition feminine.

Unlike Lanyer, Finch does not imprint the feminine on the landscape through feminine rhymes, either in 'A Nocturnal Reverie' or in her other country estate poems. Augustan poetics tended to relegate feminine rhymes to comic and satiric contexts, and Finch conforms to this, as in 'A Tale of the Miser and the Poet' (Lonsdale 12-14), which satirizes the materialism of modern society, and functions through a high proportion of feminine rhymes: by my count, 72 of its 100 lines use feminine rhymes. Finch's use of anaphora, though, performs a similar task to Lanyer's echo rhymes. Of fifty lines, ten begin with 'When,' nine with 'And', three with 'Or,' and three with 'Whilst' or 'While': the opening phrase 'In such a night,' perhaps borrowed from *The Merchant of Venice* (McGovern 80) and meant to evoke the edgy romanticism of Jessica and Lorenzo, is also repeated three times. This repetition, as in Lanyer, creates a spiral effect, drawing implied (female) circles which play against the Jonsonian (male) linear order of the heroic couplet. It could be argued, moreover, that 'A Nocturnal Reverie' evokes the Kristevan semiotic, the pre-Oedipal phase linked to the mother, perceived as 'contradictions, meaninglessness, disruption, silences and absences in the symbolic language' (Moi 162). The 'free soul,' by returning to the maternal body of nature, achieves poetic language and frees the power of the feminized semiotic from 'tyrant man', and the poem evokes this through spirals, anaphora, ambiguities, absences (like that of the country house that the conventions lead us to expect the poem to celebrate). This remarkable poem, 50 lines which constitute a single sentence, offers a critical inversion and rereading of Jonson's hierarchical and gendered vision, and extends Aemilia Lanyer's project of devising spiral, non-hierarchical forms representing both political order and poetic language through the female body and the free female soul.

Works Cited

Unless otherwise stated, all poems are quoted from Fowler; Aemilia Lanyer from Purkiss; Marvell from Margoliouth; and Anne Finch's 'A Nocturnal Reverie' and 'A Tale of the Miser and the Poet' from Lonsdale.

Barash, Carol. *English Women's Poetry, 1649-1714: Politics, Community,and Linguistic Authority*. Oxford: Clarendon P, 1996.

Barroll, Leeds. 'Looking for Patrons.' *Aemilia Lanyer*. ed. Grosssman. 29-48.

Coiro, Ann Baynes. 'Writing in Service: Sexual Politics and Class Position in the Poetry of Aemilia Lanyer and Ben Jonson.' *Criticism* 35 (1993): 357-376.

Davidoff, Leonore and Catherine Hall. *Family Fortunes: Men and Women of the English Middle Class 1780-1850*. London: Hutchinson, 1987.

Donne, John. *The Complete English Poems*. ed. A. J. Smith. Harmondsworth: Penguin, 1971.

Evans, R. C. *Ben Jonson and the Poetics of Patronage*. Lewisburg: Bucknell UP, 1989.

Finch, Anne, Countess of Winchelsea. *Selected Poems*. ed. Denys Thompson. Manchester: Carcanet, 1987.

Fowler, Alastair, ed. *The Country House Poem: A Cabinet of Seventeenth-Century Estate Poems and Related Items*. Edinburgh: Edinburgh UP, 1994.

Goldberg, Jonathan. *Voice Terminal Echo: Postmodernism and English Renaissance Texts*. New York: Methuen, 1986.

Grossman, Marshall, ed. *Aemilia Lanyer: Gender, Genre and the Canon*. Lexington: U of Kentucky P, 1998.

_____. 'The Gendering of Genre: Literary History and the Canon.' *Aemilia Lanyer*. ed. Grossman. 128-42.

Hollander, John. *The Figure of Echo: A Mode of Allusion in Milton and After*. Berkeley: U of California P, 1981.

Lanyer, Aemilia. *The Poems of Aemilia Lanyer: Salve Deus Rex Judaeorum*. ed. Susanne Woods. Oxford: Oxford UP, 1993.

Levin, Carol. *The Heart and Stomach of a King: Elizabeth I and the Politics of Sex and Power*. Philadelphia: U of Pennsylvania P, 1994.

Lewalski, Barbara K. 'Of God and Good Women: The Poems of Aemilia Lanyer.' *Silent but for the Word: Tudor Women as Patrons, Translators and Writers of Religious Works*. ed. Margaret P. Hannay. Kent: Kent State UP, 1985. 203-224.

Lonsdale, Roger, ed. *Verse by Eighteenth Century Women: An Oxford Anthology*. Oxford: Oxford UP, 1989.

Loewenstein, Joseph. *Responsive Readings: Versions of Echo in Pastoral, Epic, and the Jonsonian Masque*. New Haven: Yale UP, 1984.

Marvell, Andrew. *The Poems and Letters of Andrew Marvell*. ed. H. M. Margoliouth. 3rd. rev. edn. 2 vols. Oxford: Clarendon P, 1971.

McGovern, Barbara. *Anne Finch and her Poetry: A Critical Biography*. Athens: U of Georgia P, 1992.

Moi, Toril. *Sexual/Textual Politics: Feminist Literary Theory*. London: Routledge, 1985.

Mueller, Janel. 'The Feminist Poetics of "Salve Deus Rex Judaeorum."' *Aemilia Lanyer*. ed. Grossman. 99-127.

Pearson, Jacqueline. 'Gender and Narrative in the Fiction of Aphra Behn.' *Review of English Studies* 42 (1991): 40-56, 179-190.

_____. 'Women Reading, Reading Women.' *Women and Literature in Britain 1500-1700*. ed. Helen Wilcox. Cambridge: Cambridge UP, 1996. 80-99.

_____. 'Women Writers and Women Readers: The Case of Aemilia Lanyer.' eds. Kate Chedgzoy, Melanie Hansen and Suzanne Trill. *Voicing Women: Gender and Sexuality in Early Modern Writing*. Keele: Keele UP, 1996. 45-54.

Purkiss, Diane, ed. *Renaissance Women: The Plays of Elizabeth Cary; the Poems of Aemilia Lanyer*. London: Pickering & Chatto, 1994.

Quilligan, Maureen. 'Feminine Endings: The Sexual Politics of Sidney's and Spenser's Rhyming.' *The Renaissance Englishwoman in Print: Counterbalancing the Canon*. eds. Anne M. Haselkorn and Betty S. Travitsky. Amherst: U of Massachusetts P, 1990. 311-326.

Riggs, David. *Ben Jonson: A Life*. Cambridge: Harvard UP, 1989.

Rogers, Katharine M. 'Anne Finch, Countess of Winchilsea: An Augustan Woman Poet.' *Shakespeare's Sisters*. eds. Sandra Gilbert and Susan Gubar. Bloomington: Indiana UP, 1979. 32-46.

Rowse, A. L. *The Poems of Shakespeare's Dark Lady: Salve Deux Rex Judaeorum by Emilia Lanier*. London: Jonathan Cape, 1978.

Sidney, Sir Philip. *An Apology for Poetry: or, the Defence of Poesy*. ed. Geoffrey Shepherd. Manchester: Manchester UP, 1973.

Smith, G. Gregory, ed. *Elizabethan Critical Essays*. 2 vols. Oxford: Oxford UP, 1904.

Wall, Wendy. *The Imprint of Gender: Authorship and Publication in the English Renaissance*. Ithaca: Cornell UP, 1993

Webster, John. *The Duchess of Malfi*. ed. F. L. Lucas. New York: Macmillan, 1959

Wolfson, Susan J. *Formal Charges: The Shaping of Poetry in British Romanticism*. Stanford: Stanford UP, 1997.

Woods, Susanne. *Lanyer: A Renaissance Woman Poet*. NewYork: Oxford UP, 1999.

6

'So May I With the *Psalmist* Truly Say':
Early Modern Englishwomen's Psalm Discourse

Margaret P. Hannay

Why did Anne Vaughan Lock respond to the Petrarchan tradition in a sonnet sequence, probably the first in English, meditating on Psalm 51? Why did the Countess of Pembroke compose 126 different verse forms – including quantitative verse, two sonnet forms, *ottava rima*, *rime royal*, and some highly original verse patterns – to paraphrase the Psalms? What sustained these women as they began writing poetic forms never before attempted by an English woman?

The answers, I believe, may be found not so much in the words of Lock and Pembroke as in their literary context.[1] Psalm paraphrase was a genre that rivaled the Petrarchan lyric in sixteenth-century Europe. As Roland Greene observes, the Book of Psalms 'belongs with Petrarch's *Rime sparse* as a master text through which the writers of the age tested their capacities . . . not only as worshippers and theologians but as poets and critics' ('Sir Philip Sidney's Psalms'19; see also Lewalski 32-53). The choice of Hebrew, Latin, or vernacular versions of the Psalms could be a religious marker, and congregational singing of vernacular Psalms became a distinctively Protestant form of worship, but the Psalms themselves were embraced by all Jews, Catholics and Protestants as a divinely inspired expression of human experience.[2] Among Christians the cultural importance of Psalms transcended class, gender, and Catholic or Protestant affiliation even in the religious wars. Paraphrasing Psalms became a standard activity for prisoners on both sides of the religious conflicts, such as penitential Psalms by Sir Thomas More, Henry

Howard, Earl of Surrey, Anne Askew, and Queen Mary Stuart; the Countess of Pembroke's uncles John Dudley, Earl of Warwick, and Robert Dudley, later Earl of Leicester, varied the formula by poetic versions of prayers for vengeance against their enemies in their metrical renditions of Psalms 55 and 94 (*Arundel Harington Manuscript* 1:338-41). Psalms might serve as 'battle hymns of the Lord' in the religious wars, as Stanford Reid has demonstrated (36-54), or give courage to martyrs, including both the Protestant Lady Jane Grey and the Catholic cardinal John Fisher. Psalm paraphrase and meditation could be safely used in times of political crisis, even to express anger and a desire for vengeance, because Psalms were a sanctioned form of discourse for both men and women, for both Catholics and Protestants. The choice of a particular Psalm might make a strong political or personal statement, but the Psalms remained the words of David and the words of God. Using Psalm discourse was thus, in a sense, the ultimate strategy of indirection, whether the censorship to be countered was externalized state censorship or internalized gender restrictions.

'All this is *trita et obvia*,' as Deborah Shuger observes of the pervasive importance of religion in all areas of early modern thought; nevertheless, such discourse has, until recently, often been 'curiously invisible in modern Renaissance scholarship, which, for complex political, ideological, and institutional reasons, brackets off religious materials from cultural analysis and vice versa' (2; see also Trill 30-55; Graham 213-17). Likewise Janel Mueller has recently argued for 'theoretically constituting religion on a par with the triad of race, class, and gender as a material determinant of human experience and expression' (41). Recognizing the importance of such religious discourse is essential in our readings of the works of early modern women, who so automatically used words of scripture, and particularly the Psalms, to articulate their deepest thoughts.[3]

Aside from the political use of the Psalms, which I have discussed elsewhere (*Philip's Phoenix* 84-105; see also Reid 36-54; Prescott, 'Evil tongues' 163-86), there were four primary uses of the Psalms in early modern England, as Rivkah Zim notes: for personal expression, for religious instruction, for singing, and for devotional poetry (41). Such 'practices of piety are central' to constructions of 'Renaissance selfhood,' Shuger argues (190). In each of these Psalm discourses women participated fully, both in private and in public, as readers, as singers, as writers. Children in a devout Protestant household would participate in daily group recitation and singing of the Psalms in a vernacular version, usually the prose version of Miles Coverdale included in the *Book of Common Prayer* and the metrical versions of Sternhold and Hopkins. Children in a devout Catholic household might hear the Psalms in the mass, or even hear their mother singing the metrical Psalms of Richard Rowlands. The words of the Psalms so permeated early modern consciousness that quoting Psalms often became the deepest personal expression of the inner life for both men and women, but because of cultural restrictions on a woman's speech and writing, the Psalms became a foundational discourse for women writers.

Psalm meditation and paraphrase were encouraged for Christian women because the Psalms were read as a dual allegory, of Christ and of the Christian life. 'David's infolded voices express Christ and ourselves as well as his own circumstance,' as Anne Prescott reminds us ('King David' 134; see also Lewalski 301-2; Zim 6, 43-74). Psalms could thus become life-writing, as their words were used to express a woman's own interiority. Women prayed in the words of the Psalmist in the midst of political and religious conflict, or in the throes of childbirth, or when they felt betrayed by family and friends, or when they mourned the death of a family member, or when they approached their own death. Because Christians usually recited, sang, and meditated on the Psalms in their own vernacular language or in Latin, the very fact of translation from the Hebrew created a gap between the original words of the Psalmist and the words as they were transmitted, a space that permitted women as well as men to intertwine their own voices with that of 'David.'

Although some devout Jews and Christians today do maintain a living tradition of daily meditation on the Psalms, the use of Psalms to express one's deepest thoughts is a habit now largely absent from popular culture. Material culture can remind us of the centrality of that form of discourse in the early modern period. English women carried tiny Psalters in their pockets and stitched needlework covers for Psalters as gifts for daughters or friends (Klein 459-93; Donawerth). Copies of Sternhold and Hopkins' Psalms, often scored with music, were frequently decorated with various symbolic covers. The embroidery might signal David's authorship, as in a binding of embroidered white satin with David holding a slingshot on the lower cover and holding Goliath's head on the upper cover. Or it might symbolize the godly woman, as in a cover of tapestry stitch on canvas depicting a woman holding an open book inscribed with the word 'Faith.' Or it might show a tulip reaching toward the sun, one of the most common motifs, to symbolize the soul reaching toward God. Often the Psalter was bound *dos-o-dos* (or back to front, so that the books opened in opposite directions) with the other essential book for the godly woman, the New Testament.[4]   Esther Inglis, in her calligraphy Psalter for Elizabeth, was extending the tradition of women exchanging Psalters, as was Pembroke's dedication of the Sidneian *Psalmes* to Elizabeth in that same year of 1599 (Ziegler, 'Jewels' and 'More').

Psalms were used constantly for religious instruction. Such Psalm meditation was familiar from medieval practice, included in traditional books of hours, and encoded in the *Book of Common Prayer*. This daily meditation, often practiced as group recitation by the entire household, meant that the words of the Psalms were known from earliest childhood. Women had been taught to recite Psalms daily to confess their sins to God and to rejoice in God's blessings; they heard sermons on the Psalms, meditated on them, and studied scholarly commentaries.   Mothers used Psalms to instruct their children in reading as well as in doctrine. Psalm quotations were also included as part of the standard catechisms and were sometimes rendered as verse or song to make memorization easier.

Psalm singing, which had become an essential part of church and household worship, also moved out into the popular culture. Those who had wished to replace secular lyric with sacred song included Savonarola, Erasmus, Luther, and Tyndale. Luther's Psalms were first introduced in congregational singing, but in England and France Psalm singing spread from the court to the countryside. Marot's Psalms were first sung at the French court, and the Psalms of Sternhold and Hopkins at Edward's English court (Diefendorf 41-64; Leaver).   Coverdale had also wanted carters and ploughmen to whistle 'psalms, hymns, and such godly songs as David is occupied withal' and women to sing them as they spin, instead of '*hey nony nony, hey troly loly* , and such like phantasies' (*Remains* 537). Evidently, his wish was granted, for by 1579 Anthony Gilby complained that Psalms were being sung more 'for fashion sake, then for good devotion and with understanding' ('Epistle to the Reader', in Calvin, sig. *6; see also Hannay, 'House-confined maids' 44-71). That is, Gilby was concerned that the Psalms were indeed used instead of '*hey nony nony* '; there is considerable evidence that women did sing them whether they were spinning or not, but usually 'for good devotion and with understanding.'

Psalms became an essential part of women's musical repertoire. They sang Psalms daily in public and private worship, and as they went about their household duties. Like the Geneva Protestants, many women believed that 'there are no songes more meete, than the *Psalmes* of the Prophete David' (*Forme of prayers* sig. B2). Most sang the ubiquitous versions of Sternhold and Hopkins, but more educated English women might also have sung the *Psaumes* of Clément Marot and Théodore de Bèze, and by the end of the sixteenth century there were many English versions in print to choose from, most notably *The whole Psalter* by Matthew Parker with settings by Thomas Tallis, and *Psalmes, Sonets, and songs of sadnes and pietie made into Musicke of five parts* by the composer William Byrd. Grace Sherrington Mildmay may have been alluding to Byrd's version, particularly of the penitential Psalms, when she recorded that she daily 'spent some tyme in playing on my lute, and setting songs of five parts thereunto, and practised my voice in singing of psalmes, in making my prayers to God, and confessing any sinnes' (Mildmay 220; see also Weigall 125; Warnicke, 'Lady Mildmay's Journal' 55-68; Pollock 94-109; Martin 33-82). Some women may have written their own settings for private use. Two of the penitential Psalms paraphrased by the Countess of Pembroke, Psalm 51 and 130, were set for soprano voice and lute in what Linda Austern suggests is part of a collection compiled by an individual woman for her own performance. Pembroke's quantitative versions of Psalms 120-27 were also revised, probably by a later hand, to reduce their metrical and poetic complexity; they appear to have been revised for singing to the Sternhold and Hopkins tunes (*Collected Works* 2:308-36). Her version of Psalm 97 seems to have been adapted for singing in *All the French Psalm Tunes with English Words* (Doelman 162-3).

No wonder then that Anne Lock in 1560 and the Countess of Pembroke in the 1590s undertook their audacious literary compositions using the content that was so familiar to them – and the most culturally sanctioned.[5] Anne Lock lived in Geneva during the composition of the 1557 Geneva Psalter, revised in 1559 and then included in the 1560 Geneva Bible. (A friend and patron of John Knox, she had left Marian England to worship with the exiled Protestant community in Calvin's Geneva.) During this same period, the English Protestants in exile were preparing the Sternhold and Hopkins Psalter for congregational singing, so that rendering the Psalms into verse was a community activity. Setting aside the sonnet form for a moment, we see that Lock's presentation of the Psalms was in a format that had already become standard by 1560, giving a verse and then commenting on it. The first such English Psalter, printed separately from other scriptural passages, was

George Joye's translation of Martin Bucer, or 'Feline,' printed with 'every Psalme havynge his argument before / declarynge brefly thentent and substance of the whole Psalme' (1530). This sets the early pattern for English translation of European commentaries: George Joye also translated Ulrich Zwingli's Psalms and commentary, Coverdale translated Luther's exposition on Psalm 23, and so on. More original Psalm versions and meditations and prayers were published in English by Coverdale and Thomas Becon. Numerous metrical Psalm translations in European vernaculars had also been printed by the time Anne Lock wrote, including the German Psalms of Luther and Johann Agricola, Marot's *Trente Psaumes*, Coverdale's *Goostly psalmes and spirituall songes*, Robert Crowley's *Psalter of David*, various versions of Sternhold and Hopkins (beginning in 1549), and selected Psalms by Thomas Wyatt, Henry Howard, Earl of Surrey, John Hall, William Hunnis, and Frances Seager (Zim 211-59; Hobbs 222-5; Rohr-Sauer 119-24). Such works were not peripheral, as they may seem to our secularized era, but highly valued. Their sheer numbers indicate a lively market for such Psalters.

Women too had a tradition of Psalm translation and meditation. In the fifteenth century, for example, Dame Eleanor Hull translated a lengthy Old French commentary on the penitential Psalms into English, and Christine de Pisan composed allegorized French meditations on the penitential Psalms (Hull; Pisan; Willard). Two anonymous translations, of Savonarola's exposition of Psalm 51 and of John Fisher's Psalms, may have been the work of Katherine Parr (James 200-9). Anne Askew's metrical version of Psalm 54 was published by John Bale, and Lady Elizabeth Fane's meditations on twenty-one Psalms (no longer extant) were published by Robert Crowley. Thus when Lock set out her version of Psalm 51, the most familiar of the penitential Psalms, she entered this rich tradition, meditating on individual verses of a Psalm like so many writers before her. Her marginal prose translation of the Psalm does not seem to match any known English version; Susan Felch has recently concluded that it is Lock's own translation from the Gallican Latin Psalter (*Works of Anne Vaughan Lock* lvii). Composing extended meditations on penitential Psalms had been an approved devotional practice for many centuries, and the use of marginal glosses to the scriptures was a standard feature of Protestant texts. Lock's sonnets are titled 'Written in Maner of a *Paraphrase*,' a term that had 'achieved some generic stability by 1560', as Felch observes. 'In England, it had come to mean a species of commentary particularly suited to the Protestant church,' particularly since the

New Testament paraphrases of Erasmus had been translated into English and put into every parish church ('Anne Lock').

Psalm commentary and paraphrase were thus both well established genres among English Protestants. What is unprecedented is Lock's literary form, since she meditated in English sonnets. Writing on the Continent, she must also have had early access to the Petrarchan sonnet tradition, perhaps as represented in Joachim du Bellay's *L'Olive*, the first French sonnet sequence, as well as in Tottel's *Miscellany*. (On her use of the sonnet form see Spiller 92-93; Morin-Parsons 30-32.) Lock may have known (or known of) secular poems by women such as Pernette Du Guillet, Tullia d'Aragona, Louise Labé, les Dames des Roches, Veronica Gambara, Vittoria Colonna, and Gaspara Stampa (Wilson 99-259; Jones; Stortoni). She must also have known of at least one woman who could serve as a role model, Marguerite de Navarre; she may have read *Le Miroir de l'âme pécheresse* rather than Elizabeth's English translation published by Bale, and she may have known Marguerite's secular lyrics included in *Les Marguerites de la Marguerite des princesses*. She may also have known of Vittoria Colonna's use of the sonnet for sacred, as well as secular, topics. Perhaps Lock chose to redeem the sonnet form for godly poems in England, even as Marot used French dance tunes for the *Psaumes*, and Martin Luther used the tunes of drinking songs, such as his adaptation of Psalm 46 familiar in English hymnody as 'A Mighty Fortress is Our God.'

From an artistic standpoint the sonnet form may have appealed to Lock because of its traditional use to express subjectivity (Dubrow; Kennedy; Kuin). Psalms, like love lyrics, raise questions of interiority and the divided self. Philip Sidney may later show Astrophil torn between reason and desire, but he had been anticipated by St Paul, who said, 'what I wolde, that do I not: but what I hate, that do I . . . Now then, it is no more I, that do it, but the sinne that dwelleth in me' (Romans 7:15, 17; Geneva Bible). Quotations from the penitential Psalms were frequently used to express the conflicted self, bewailing the state of one's sins, begging for God's help, and vowing to sin no more. Calvinist doctrine emphasized this tendency to look inward as 'the believer attempted to monitor the rightness of an inner core of self' (Graham 214). The self is thus split between action and analysis, between doing something and watching oneself perform that action, as the believer constantly struggles to bring the inner and outer selves into harmony. Although original sin means that the person can never achieve full sanctity, the struggle itself is seen as beneficial, for sin cannot be expunged until it is recognized and confessed to God. The Psalms are particularly helpful in this process of constant renewal. Calvin says: 'Bycause they discover all the inner thoughtes, [Psalms] do call or drawe every one of us to the peculiar examinatien of himself, so as no whit of all the infirmities to which wee are subject . . . may abyde hidden.' Through such self-examination 'the hart is clensed from the most noysome infection of hypocrisie and laid open to the light' (sig. *6v). In this medical metaphor, the godly must discover hidden sins or 'infirmities' and bring them to the light so that they may be healed. Some modern readers may find the recurring sense of guilt distasteful, but the psychological impact for 'the godly' was ultimately joy. All that was required for wholeness was confession to God and then the 'sacrifice of praise,' thanking God for 'his Fatherly providence and care towards us' (Calvin, sig. *7). The Psalms are 'the Anatomy of all parts of the soul, in as much as a man shall not find any affection in himself, whereof the image appeareth not in this glass,' Calvin says (sig. *6v). Yet looking in the glass of the Psalms 'does not merely reflect subjectivity, it organizes it,' as Alan Sinfield notes (*Faultlines* 166). The Protestant reader of Calvin's commentary, for example, sees the self that is reflected in the words of the Psalmist as read through Calvin's eyes. Anne Lock's sonnets certainly were read in the context of Calvin's sermons, for they are appended to her translation of his series of four sermons on Isaiah 38. For her sonnet sequence on the divided self Lock appropriately chooses Psalm 51, a Psalm that presents the 'trobled sprite' as pleasing to God in its recognition of sin, asks for God's mercy in restoring the self to health and wholeness, and promises that the speaker will then give thanks and 'leape for joy, to shewe myne inward chere.'

Thus by 1560 Lock had a sonnet tradition; she had a tradition of Continental women poets; and she had a tradition of metrical Psalms and meditations, particularly on the penitential Psalms. She braided these three strands together to produce her sonnet sequence, 'A Meditation of a Penitent Sinner: Written in Maner of a *Paraphrase* upon the 51. Psalme of David,' apparently the first in English (Roche 155-57; Greene, *Post-Petrarchism* 129-35). More than thirty years later, the Countess of Pembroke undertook an even more extensive poetic project when she completed the metrical Psalms that her brother Philip Sidney had left unfinished when he died. She wrote to honor him, she said in her dedicatory poem 'To the Angell Spirit,' but that is not a complete explanation, for she chose to print the *Arcadia* as her brother had left it, deciding that it could not be completed without him. As her secretary Hugh Sanford explained, 'Sir Philip Sidneies writings' could not be 'perfected without Sir Philip Sidney' (*Arcadia* [1593], sig. A4). So why finish Sidney's Psalm paraphrases?

Pembroke's decision to write metrical Psalms may well have been influenced by Lock, whose poems she knew; given their mutual connections, it would not be surprising if she had met Lock herself, despite the difference in their social rank. (Pembroke does quote two of Lock's phrases [Hannay, 'Unlock my lipps' 19-36], and among other personal connections, Lock's second husband Edward Dering served at Salisbury Cathedral, just a few miles from Wilton, and Lock's second printed translation was dedicated to Anne Russell Dudley, Countess of Warwick, Pembroke's aunt.) But an equally important impetus was the genre itself, both in its international importance and in its perceived suitability for a woman's voice. Metrical Psalms in the vernacular had become, by the early 1590s, even more recognized as a genre, one that engaged nearly as many English poets as the Petrarchan tradition. Not only Philip Sidney, Wyatt, and Surrey had written English metrical Psalms, but also poets like Abraham Fraunce, George Gascoigne, and Edmund Spenser, and even those more known for their theological works like Thomas Becon and Matthew Parker. As English poets tried to emulate Petrarch's *Rime sparse*, so they tried to emulate the *Psaumes* of Marot and Bèze.

Unlike the Petrarchan sonnet, the metrical Psalm was, in one sense, ungendered. Poetic versions of the Psalms, particularly the penitential Psalms, had become so acceptable a sign of devotion that the confessions of sin in Anne Lock's sonnet sequence on Psalm 51 often do not sound significantly different in tone from those of her male contemporaries. The 'I' in each verse is ungendered, representing the individual human in dialogue with the divine. As Wilcox reminds us, the soul is traditionally portrayed as female, so that 'we might describe the soul's condition as a sacred parody of the relationship of human female to human male in the Renaissance, depicted in a vocabulary of silence and attentiveness similar to that of contemporary conduct books for women' (11). In a sense, the male poet thus stands in exactly the same subordinate relationship to God as the female poet.

Paradoxically, Psalms for 'godlie' women were also highly gendered, in that the words of the Psalmist provided a means for them to write, even to circulate their words publicly, without a challenge to their chastity. When a woman recites Psalm 51 in a standard English version, such as the Geneva Bible, she thereby promises God that if her sins are forgiven 'Then shal I

teache thy waies unto the wicked, and sinners shal be converted unto thee' (Ps.
51:13). That is, she has, even by quotation alone, found a way to circumvent
cultural restrictions against female speech by presenting her words as godly
service. When such words are presented in poetic paraphrase, they become
even more empowering, as when Lock prays

> Lord loose my lippes, I may expresse my mone,
> And findyng grace with open mouth I may
> Thy mercies praise, and holy name display. (Sonnet 17)

The Countess of Pembroke's version invokes a similar opening or freeing of
the 'lipps' as the natural and divinely sanctioned response to God's gracious
forgiveness: 'Unlock my lipps, shut up with sinnfull shame: / then shall my
mouth o lord thy honor sing' (51. 43-44).[6] Sin, not gender restriction, here
becomes the only reason for silence; if sin is forgiven, then the immediate
result is to 'display' God's praise with 'open mouth' or to 'sing' God's
'honor' (Hannay, 'Unlock').

The full explanation for the Psalms of Lock and Pembroke can thus be
found only in the wider religious and cultural context, for Psalms became a
foundational discourse for early modern women, one that invited them into a
variety of literary genres. If we look at function rather than form, we see that
because Psalms traditionally were used for personal devotion, women could
use those words to articulate their own sense of self in forms of life-writing.
Because Psalms traditionally were used for spiritual instruction, women could
use those words to undertake a teaching role not unlike that of published
sermons. Because metrical Psalms traditionally were used for private and
public song, women could use those words to compose poetry. Psalms thus
provided early modern English women with an entry into at least three major
types of literary discourse: life writing, spiritual instruction, and devotional
poetry. Of course these three modes of Psalm discourse were intertwined, so
that private life writing could be framed as religious instruction and presented
to a wider audience, particularly in hagiographic works printed by co-
religionists or relatives after the writer's death. Metrical Psalms might
originate either as a deliberate teaching device, like Luther's vernacular
versions of the Psalms, or as individual meditation, like Matthew Parker's
Psalms, but if they were printed or set for singing by the individual, the
household, or the congregation, they became religious instruction.

Each of these major Psalm discourses progressively allowed more freedom in handling the words of the Psalms. Life-writing tended to use the Psalms as a coded language, so that the meaning was expressed in the framing of direct quotations from familiar vernacular Psalters; occasionally a pronoun might be altered to fit the speaker's gender, but usually no other significant alterations were made in the words of the vernacular Psalms. Religious instruction tended to assemble and rearrange phrases from the Psalms, interweaving them with other scriptural quotations, and occasionally making explicit allegorical interpretations. Such works often included set form prayers, wherein the reader was to identify with the 'I' of the prayer. (On the seventeenth-century Royalist redefinition of the Puritan Psalms to justify Anglican set-form prayer, see Loscocco.) Once again, alterations in the actual quotations from vernacular Psalms were few. Paradoxically, metrical Psalms were the most faithful renditions contextually and the freest verbally. That is, the writer presented an entire Psalm in order, verse by verse, instead of adapting isolated quoted phrases to other contexts, as in life-writing or religious instruction. Yet the genre of metrical Psalms traditionally permitted significant expansion, as the author meditated on the Psalms, and it allowed considerable freedom of interpretation if the writer studied the Hebrew Psalms and/or consulted the voluminous and often conflicting scholarly commentaries. Because of the need to fit the meaning into rhyme and meter, metrical Psalms by definition became paraphrases, thereby providing the most scope for the individual voice. The innovative works of Lock and Pembroke wove together all these strands. Both incorporated personal experience into their words; both wrote Psalm versions used for religious instruction; both were scholars who incorporated ideas from various biblical versions and commentaries; both were poets who recast entire Psalm(s) into sophisticated Continental literary form.

Life-Writing

Considered appropriate for private meditation and public worship in Jewish and Christian tradition, the words of the Psalmist were seen as infinitely malleable, applying directly to the situation of the individual reader as the Greek church father Athanasius so famously explained in words translated in the opening of the Sternhold and Hopkins Psalter: 'It is easy . . . for every man to finde out in the Psalmes, the motion and state of his owne soule' (sig *7^v; see also Parker, sig. C1). These words could fit almost any emotional state, since the Psalms variously express thanksgiving, anger, fear, doubt, envy, pain, guilt, despair, and utter joy. Many Psalms chart a transition from one state, usually doubt and sadness, to another, usually faith and joy. Philip Sidney explains how the Psalms may be 'used with the fruit of comfort by some, when, in sorrowful pangs of their death-bringing sins, they find the consolation of the never-leaving goodness.' They also may 'be used by whosoever will follow St James's counsel in singing psalms when they are merry' ('Defence' 80). When people meditated on the Psalms they were thus able to express their own subjectivity in sacred words, as when Wyatt articulates such 'inwardness' by identifying Israel with his own inner condition, speaking of 'Inward Sion, the Sion of the ghost' and of the 'heart's Jerusalem' (Wyatt; Greenblatt 115). Women were full participants in this tradition.

Psalms can thus enact the same ritual dimension that Roland Greene finds in the lyric sequence, 'to superimpose the subjectivity of the scripted speaker on the reader' (*Post-Petrarchism* 5-6). Yet at the same time the reader superimposes her own subjectivity on the scripted speaker. As they had been taught, women made the words of the Psalms their own – and thereby reading became rewriting.

Most gendered are the prayers written by and for women in childbirth. As Charlotte Otten observes, the Christian woman was encouraged to adapt Psalm 22, traditionally described by the church as 'The Complaint of Christ on the Cross,' to her own suffering. Equating 'her assignment to bear children with Christ's assignment to die, she finds herself closer to God than in any other state.' She therefore 'does not hesitate to change the male-gendered nouns and pronouns' in the Psalm, and where women are not present, she adds them. To 'Our fathers trusted in thee' in Psalm 22:4, for example, she adds 'and mothers were wont to put their trust in thee'; 'sisters' as well as the biblical 'brethren' will praise God for deliverance ('Women's Prayers' 19-20; see also Wilcox 15). During Elizabeth's reign such gender substitutions were ubiquitous, further encouraging other women to insert themselves and their own situation into an appropriate Psalm. Thomas Bentley, for example, regenders his reprint (in Gilby's translation) of Bèze's Psalm 18:50. For 'king' Bentley substitutes 'queene', for 'David' he writes 'Elizabeth,' and for the masculine 'seed' he writes 'posteritie': 'For verelie thou hast marvellouslie preserved thy Queene, and not onlie ELIZABETH hir selfe, whom thou hast annointed Queene, but also thou hast shewed singular favour to her posteritie that shall remaine for ever, Amen' (*Monument of Matrones* 2:257).

Psalms were ideally suited to express what Debora Shuger aptly terms the 'decentered and complex subjectivity' of 'the Calvinist saint' who struggles with doubt and with the divergence between the desire to be godly and the reality of sin (105). The penitential Psalms were frequently transcribed, rephrased, and sung to articulate such self-awareness. Such meditations, probably typical of women's devotions, are included in a manuscript of prayers compiled by young Elizabeth Beaumont Ashburnham, later Richardson, who is primarily known as the author of *A Ladies Legacie to her Daughters* (Folger MS V.a.511; Burke and Hannay). She repeatedly uses the phrase a 'broken and a contrite heart' from Psalm 51, like the liturgy, for example, and in 'A confession of sinnes and a prayer for remission' she paraphrases Psalm 130:3, 19:12-13, and 25:7 in a single sentence: 'For gracious Lorde, if thou shouldest marke all y^t is done amisse who should be able to stand in thy sight, for who can vnderstand ye multitude of their owne faultes, therefor clense mee I humblie beseeche thee, from my secrete faults, and keepe thy seruant from presumptuous sinnes, Let y^m not raigne ouer mee, neither remember, o god, the fraylties of my youth' (fol. 72). Such interwoven quotations were usually produced from memory, not by hunting through an open Bible. When she thought about her sins, she thought in the words of the Psalms that she had repeated daily since early childhood; the originality of her expression consists in the way the quotations are ordered and embedded in her own discourse. Psalms thus became autobiographical meditation even when the words were direct quotations from familiar English translations.

The Psalms also allowed women to articulate other emotions, to speak their fears and even to express their anger. 'The voyce of Anne Askewe out of the 54. Psalme of David' is a clear example of the genre. The paraphrase of this Psalm, already familiar in Coverdale's version, follows the original closely except for added comments on her approaching execution. The Psalm allows her to articulate her anger against her judges, those 'faythlesse men,' as well as her plea that God will help her in 'thys dystresse' and 'revenge my wronge.' Susan James sees a similar use of the Psalms as an outlet for Katherine Parr's anger (203).

In the sixteenth century women employed Psalms as a mode of

thought, but this autobiographical use of the Psalms is most evident in seventeenth-century miscellanies, diaries, and poems. Alice Thornton, for example, quotes from Psalm 107:42 when she says that God saved her from a slanderous attack: 'God . . . took the matter in to his own hand to stop the mouths of my adversaries' (159). Likewise Anne Clifford intersperses Psalm quotations with her own words in her diary, particularly in the final year of her life (*Diaries* 229-68). Aged, ill, confined to her room, this matriarch repeats to herself the comforting words of the Psalms, particularly the phrase, 'Yea though I walk through the valley of the shadow of death, I will fear no evil' (Ps. 23:4). Such Psalm references are the best indication of her inner state, since most of the diary records events rather than feelings.

An Collins uses words of the Psalms to similar effect in her poetry, as an expression of the speaker's mental state. Her identification with the words of the Psalms is most complete in a stanza based on sections of Psalm 119:

> So may I with the *Psalmist* truly say,
> Tis good for me that I have been afflicted,
> Before I troubled was, I went astray,
> But now to godlinesse I am adicted;
> If in Gods Lawes I had not took delight,
> I in my troubles should have perisht quite. (73)

As she speaks 'with the Psalmist' the words truly become her own. Her use of Psalm 119, her reflections on affliction, and her expressed identification with the Psalmist are similar to those of Anne Lock, who says 'Then we with *David* shall confesse / that God from heaven above / (By humbling us) does well expresse / his mercie and his love' in her poem on 'The necessitie and benefite of affliction' (*Works* 189). These poems are not Psalm translations, but rather indicate that Collins and Lock, like Richardson, Thornton, Clifford and many other devout women, often articulate their own experience through the familiar words of the Psalmist.

Such personal application of the Psalms provided many women with an acceptable form for self-expression in a culture that exalted silence as a feminine virtue. This self-expression might be circulated in a variety of ways – kept within the family in diaries, commonplace books, or in mothers' advice books (sometimes published posthumously by family members); sung within the household; copied in manuscripts within a literary coterie; printed in collections meant for religious instruction, like Thomas Bentley's *Monument*

(1582). What women may have originally written as private expression of religious devotion could thus be more widely circulated through scribal or print publication, amplifying their voices so that other women were inspired to follow their example.

Religious Instruction

Women have always instructed children and younger women, but religious instruction became an increasingly important function for women during the Protestant Reformation. Bentley's *Monument* was particularly influential in validating, preserving, and circulating women's words of instruction, including their Psalm versions and meditations. This compilation gives women entry into a genre not significantly different in theological content from printed sermons or prayers by male authors. Bentley tells 'the Christian Reader' that he presents the works of these 'heroicall authors and woorthie women' to serve 'as perfect presidents of true pietie and godlinesse in woman kind to all posterie,' presenting them as instruction for 'the simpler sort of women' (sig. B1). That is, Bentley compiles godly works by learned aristocratic women for those of the humbler and less learned (but still literate) lower classes. Such spiritual instruction of those who were younger, of lower rank, or of less education was considered part of the standard duties of the Protestant English woman, though that instruction would more usually be oral rather than written, and kept within the home rather than made public. Mother's advice books were often framed with the written words of the dead mother taking the place of the normal oral instruction by a living mother (Wayne 56-79; Wall 283-96; Brown, *Mothers Legacies* and *Over her dead body*). Elizabeth Jocelin, for example, fearing that she would die in childbirth, left her husband a letter saying that she would write only because she could think of no other way 'to expresse my motherly zeale' to her unborn child (*Mother's Legacie* sig. B3).

As the mother instructs the child, so those of highest rank instruct those of the lower ranks. Bentley includes prayers and devotional meditations by Marguerite de Navarre as translated by Elizabeth, the works of Katherine Parr previously published under her own name, and then (roughly in order of rank) writings of Lady Jane Grey (Dudley), Lady Elizabeth Tyrwhit, Lady Frances Abergavennie, Anne Askew, 'maister Bradfords mother,' an anonymous 'godlie harted Gentlewoman,' and Dorcas Martin.

Bentley begins with the work of queens – Elizabeth's own translation of Marguerite de Navarre, Katherine Parr's *Prayers Stirryng the Mynd unto Heavenlye Medytacions*, which reworks selections from Book III of Thomas à Kempis's *Imitation of Christ,* and Parr's *Lamentacion of a Sinner* (see John King, 'Patronage' 47; Mueller 26). Parr's collections of *Prayers* uses the Psalms in the most direct way, by interspersing whole verses in the midst of her prayers, as her quotation from Psalm 91:1 to note her current danger. 'For it is not with me, as it was, when . . . I was defended under the shadowe of thy wynges from all perils and daungers' (95). Such embedded quotations express her own experience and also allow a ritualized individual voice, inviting the reader to identify with the 'I' of the Psalm. Lady Jane Grey's use of Psalm quotation is similar when she articulates her own despair in 'A certaine effectuall praier, made by the Ladie Jane Dudley, in the time of hir trouble, a little before hir death' (*Monument* 2:98-100). Imprisoned in the Tower, she prays that God will be 'a strong tower of defense' (Ps. 61:3). The personal is then framed as instruction when her subsequent assurance of God's care is presented by Foxe and then Bentley as an example for all Christians, as is her 'exhortation' to her younger sister Katherine, written in her Greek New Testament on the night before her execution. Here she commends God's word to Katherine as greater riches than all the lands their family had lost. 'Desire with David (good sister) to understand the lawe of the Lord your God' (101). Her brief allusion sums up the theme of Psalm 119, an extended meditation on the laws of God, which declares, 'I have had as great delight in the way of thy testimonies, as in all manner of riches' (v. 14). Her instructions to her sister then become, through print, her instructions to all Christians (Foxe 6:424).

Like Lady Jane's words to her sister Katherine, the words of Lady Frances Manners Abergavennie are contextualized as moral guidance presented to a specific young woman. Abergavennie committed these words 'at the houre of hir death' to her only daughter Mary Fane 'As a Jewell of health for the soule, and a perfect path to Paradise,' Bentley says, but adds that her words are 'verie profitable to be used of everie faithfull Christian man and woman' (*Monument* 2:139). That is, by printing her words, authorized as a deathbed legacy to her child, Bentley expands their significance, presenting them as suitable instruction for other women – and for men. He obviously anticipates their use in public as well as private worship, for one prayer is headed 'A godlie praier for the true worshipping of God, which may be used in the Church before common praier' (158). Abergavennie frequently quotes words from the Psalms, as in her echo of Psalm 1, 'keepe me from the counsels of the foolish and ungodlie' (161), but she makes no attempt to paraphrase a specific Psalm; rather, phrases from the Psalms have been internalized as part of her own self-articulation and her instruction of younger women, a method also employed by Lady Elizabeth Tyrwhit, Princess Elizabeth's governess, in her *Morning and Evening Praiers, with divers Psalms, Himnes and Meditations*. (Susan Felch has analyzed the differences between the original edition and Bentley's reprint in Tyrwhit, *Works*.) Tyrwhit's 'Psalms' are not translations, or even paraphrases, of the biblical Psalms, but meditations on Christian doctrine that incorporate, combine, enlarge on, or interpret biblical citations. Words from the Psalms are interspersed with references to Christ, the church, and the atonement to serve as spiritual instruction.

The instructional mode is most evident in the translation of a French catechism, *An Instruction for Christians,* by Dorcas Martin (1537-99), wife of the Mayor of London and, as Micheline White has recently established, an important Puritan activist in her own right – and a relative of Anne Lock (White, 'Biographical Sketch'). The catechism was an essential element in the spiritual reformation of England, as Bentley underscores when he admonishes his readers to imitate Martin by teaching 'their whole familie in the principall points of christian religion' (B4r). The Martins, like other more radical Protestants, believed that godly instruction must be given in the home in order to compensate for what they perceived as inadequate instruction by the ministry (White, 'Cunning' 92). *An Instruction for Christians* begins with two quatrains that paraphrase Psalm 119:37 and 133 in ballad measure as a prayer undoubtedly meant to be sung, perhaps to one of the tunes in the familiar Sternhold and Hopkins Psalter:

> From vaine desires and worldlie lusts,
> Turne backe mine eies and sight:
> Give me the spirit of life and power,
> To walk thy waies aright.
> Direct my footesteps by thy word,
> That I thy will may knowe:
> And never let iniquitie,
> Thy servant overthrowe. (221)

Martin's verse is not poetry in the sense of *belles lettres*, but rather lines set to music for spiritual edification. The aim is essentially the same in the verse as it is in the prose 'praier to saie afore one begin to studie his lesson. Out of the 119 Psalmes. verses, 9, 18, 34' (227-28), which interweaves quotations from the Psalm with words thought suitable for the child's voice, as the prayer 'that I may prepare my selfe now to serve thee once, in that estate and vocation, to the which it shall please thee to ordeine me when I shall come to age.' Mothers' advice books use quotations from the Psalms in a similar way, as Dorothy Leigh adapts Psalm 1:2 in her instruction to *'Meditate in the Law of the Lord day and night*, (as the Psalmist saith) and then thou shalt bee fit to bring forth fruit in due season: then shalt thou bee fit to serve God, thy King, and Countrey, both in thy life, and in thy death' (sig. B7). Such embedded quotations from the Psalms offer a place for the reader to receive spiritual instruction by identifying with the speaker, becoming the 'I' of the piece, even as the Psalms functioned in individual use of the *Book of Common Prayer* or the songs of Sternhold and Hopkins. The words of these devout Protestant women are not here individualized in the sense of life-writing, nor do they aspire to literary merit. From their perspective, they had much more important concerns than the merely personal or literary.

So did the devout Catholic Elizabeth Bernye Grymeston. Her *Miscelanea. Meditations. Memoratives* (1604) is set out for her child's instruction, prefaced with a letter to her son Bernye Grymeston. Spiritual guidance, not original composition, is her stated goal (sig. A3). Psalm versions, gathered along with other poetic and prose meditations for her son's instruction, demonstrate her 'ability to assimilate and even to alter quotations from many sources for her own purposes,' as Betty Travitsky observes (51). How the work is framed, selected, reproduced and/or adapted may be more significant than authorship of individual portions of the work. Grymeston herself declares that she would not 'set downe that haltingly in my broken stile, which I found better expressed by a graver author' (sig. A3^V).

As with all miscellanies and commonplace books, authorship is a vexed question in her *Miscelanea*. She may appear to be the author of significant verse paraphrases of the Psalms included in her *Miscelanea*, but this devout Catholic woman has transcribed the 'Odes in imitation of the seven poenitentiall Psalmes' of Richard Rowlands[Verstegan]. (Hughey and Hereford 61-91; Zim 129; Beilin 267-71; authorship is (falsely) attributed to her by the *DNB*.) Grymeston freely adapts the order of Rowlands' stanzas so that they tell her own story. These borrowed words, as she says, set forth 'the true portrature of [her] minde' (sig. A3ᵛ). For her these verses served as the words of the Psalmist, words that could be adapted to her own condition; the intermediary work of the poet became invisible. This transparency is a significant factor in the freedom that Anne Lock and Mary Sidney experienced in setting forth Psalms in verse.

Metrical Psalm Paraphrase

In an important sense those who composed metrical Psalms believed that they were not undertaking original composition. The very proliferation of Psalters had reinforced the idea that the content was unchanging; the goal of faithfully rendering that content was universally accepted, even though the words of individual Psalters varied. As Pembroke explained, they were simply attiring King David's divinely-inspired words in English. Her intent was 'That Israels King may daygne his owne transform'd / In substance no, but superficiall tire: / And English guis'd' (*Collected Works* 1:113). Perhaps this was partially a discursive strategy, a way to allow a woman's voice to enter the English poetic tradition by claiming that her words were not original. As such, it was highly effective. But Pembroke was also deeply concerned with the responsibilities of transmitting sacred text (Rienstra and Kinnamon). The responsibility was heavy because metrical paraphrase could be received as scripture. As Grymeston used the penitential Psalms of Rowlands for devotional meditation, so John Harington evidently used Pembroke's *Psalmes*. His two manuscripts of the Sidneian *Psalmes* are rubricated for Morning and Evening prayer, indicating that they too were read for devotional meditation and instruction just as one might turn to Coverdale's prose Psalms included in the *Book of Common Prayer*. Since the poet became invisible, the poet's gender evidently could become irrelevant.

Metrical paraphrase thus became a third important Psalm genre for English women, a genre that provided English women like Lock and Pembroke entry into the poetic tradition. Psalm paraphrase and meditation, even poems as sophisticated as those by Lock or Pembroke, were seen as appropriate for the female voice because the content of the Psalter was more important than its form. As we have seen, women, like men, were encouraged to read and restate the words of the Psalms as their own in various forms of life-writing. Devout women in positions of responsibility were encouraged to instruct those of lower rank, less education, or younger years than themselves; their teachings frequently included extensive quotations from the Psalms, some of which were in verse. Thus, even if the verses presented so publicly by Bale, Foxe, and Bentley had little artistic merit, they established a precedent. Godly women were praised for writing verse, particularly if they spoke through the words of the Psalms. When Lock meditated on Psalm 51 in a sonnet sequence or Pembroke rendered it in rime royal, they were immeasurably improving the literary quality of verse by English women, but they were still conforming to the content of works by women whom Bentley praised as examples of godliness.

The most important of these precedents was undoubtedly the metrical version of Psalm 13 attributed to Elizabeth in Bale's publication of her translation of Marguerite's *Miroir*. Bale himself is now usually believed to have written the Psalm, but his original readers would not necessarily know of that disputed authorship. The Countess of Pembroke, for example, seems to allude to that Psalm in her dedication to Elizabeth, when she says that Elizabeth will 'Sing what God doth,' an echo of Psalm 13:6 (*Collected Works* 1:104). This Psalm, too, is appropriate to the voice of the reputed speaker and, even if it is not by Elizabeth, putting it into her voice 'lent her royal authority to this kind of poetry', as John King observes (*English Reformation* 219).

When Pembroke dedicated her *Psalmes* manuscript to Elizabeth, she boldly entered what might be termed an international competition to produce complete poetic Psalters. English poets were embarrassed by the ubiquitous Sternhold and Hopkins version. John Donne, for example, said that prior to the Sidneys, the English Psalms had been 'More hoarse, more harsh than any other'; they were 'So well attyr'd abroad, so ill at home' ('Upon the Translation of the Psalmes,' *Divine Poems* 34-5; see also Todd; Swaim). Perhaps the primary reason for this inadequacy was that poetry had been sacrificed to the desire for accuracy in translation. Those who revised the Sternhold and Hopkins Psalter, for example, further weakened the poetry because 'we thought it better to frame the ryme to the Hebrewe sense, then to bynde that sense to the Englishe meter' (*Forme of prayers* sig. B4). Pembroke explained that the Sidneian *Psalmes* were an attempt to 'better grace' those Psalms than 'what the vulgar form'd', her harsh assessment of the pounding meters of the Sternhold and Hopkins Psalter (*Collected Works* 1:113). Donne believed that the Sidneys had succeeded: 'They shew us Ilanders our joy, our King, / They tell us *why*, and teach us *how* to sing' ('Upon the Translation' ll. 21-22). Pembroke created an extensive body of poetry in her paraphrases of Psalms 44-150, running almost 300 pages in our edition. She sought to render the Psalms into the best English poetry, using 126 different verse forms and many of the rhetorical figures recommended by George Puttenham and others (Woods 169-75, 290-302; Alexander 195-96; *Collected Works* 1:56-74). She elaborated metaphors, entering imaginatively into the text, yet she rarely sacrificed accuracy to poetry, consulting virtually every important translation and commentary available to her in English, Latin, and French, and frequently choosing the rendition closest to the Hebrew (Steinberg; *Collected Works* 2:9-32). In this she was following the lead of others who wrote vernacular metrical Psalms, including Martin Luther, who sought 'to turn a Psalm into a hymn' so that the meaning was 'cleare and as close as possible to the [Hebrew] Psalm.' (*Luther's Works* 53:36.)

Like the sonnets of Anne Lock, Pembroke's poetic forms were audacious. Apparently no one in English had written a sonnet sequence on any topic before Lock, nor had any English poet matched Pembroke's dazzling array of verse forms (Smith 269; Waller 190-211; Freer 72-108; Lifschutz 235-37; Woods 169-75, 290-302; Schleiner 58-60; Alexander 195-201; *Collected Works* 2:447-83). One seventeenth-century manuscript emphasizes this variety in its title: 'The Psalmes of David translated into divers and sundry kindes of verse, more rare, and excellent, for the method and varietie then ever yet hath bene don in English' (Bodleian MS Rawl. poet. 24). Yet these innovative forms were sanctified by the content. Anne Lock's considerable importance to the Protestant community was enhanced by her writing. Pembroke, by writing in the words of the Psalmist, became widely celebrated by her contemporaries, male and female, both for her poetry and for her virtue (*Collected Works* 1:45-53). The chorus of praise for her *Psalmes* may be contrasted with the negative response to her niece's boldly secular works. Sir Edward Denny, for example, who famously wrote after Pembroke's death to rebuke Wroth, praises Pembroke's translation of 'the holly psalmes of David' as an act of virtue that insures her place in the heavenly choir, where she 'now . . . sings . . . those devine meditations which shee so sweetly tuned heer belowe' (*Poems of Lady Mary Wroth* 239). Writing Petrarchan sonnets and a prose romance made a woman vulnerable to charges that she was unchaste, a monster, a hermaphrodite, as Denny termed Wroth. Writing Psalms made her a celebrated part of the community of 'the godly.' Thus when women turned to the Psalms to express themselves in poetic genres previously restricted to men, writing Psalms was both a mode of thought and a discursive strategy. The two strands were so entangled that Pembroke and Lock themselves might have been unaware how much of their decision to write metrical Psalms was an expression of faith and how much was circumvention of gender restrictions. Yet, despite the generational and class differences in their subject positions, both of these devout and accomplished women wrote metrical Psalms that articulated personal experience, instructed others in the godly life – and expanded the boundaries of English poetry.

Early modern women writers sought a tradition that would authorize their work. As the Countess of Pembroke was indebted to Anne Lock, so Aemilia Lanyer was indebted to Pembroke. Lanyer portrays Pembroke singing her *Psalmes* with a company of women – and so she was (*Poems* 27; see also Benson; Schleiner 139). Although the published poets who surrounded her as she worked were, to our knowledge, exclusively male, Pembroke did not stand alone. As she wrote she had before her the example of women such as Katherine Parr, Queen Elizabeth, Anne Askew, Lady Jane Grey, Elizabeth Fane, Elizabeth Tyrwhit, Frances Abergavennie, Dorcas Martin, and particularly Anne Lock, each of whom, in a variety of English literary modes and genres, had made the words of the Psalmist her own.

Notes

[1] I would like to thank Elaine Beilin, Gwynne Kennedy and other members of the 'Early Modern Women Writers and Genre' seminar at the 1998 Shakespeare Association of America conference for their helpful comments on an earlier version of this essay. Linda Austern, Michael Brennan, Victoria Burke, Noel Kinnamon, Paula Loscocco, Anne Prescott, Debra Rienstra, Betty Travitsky, Micheline White, and Georgianna Ziegler have engaged in lively discussions of this fascinating material.

[2] Psalm paraphrase is not part of the Jewish tradition, since the original Hebrew is used in worship. Psalm phrases could be incorporated into original prayers, however, usually by men but occasionally by women. Some of the *Tkhines*, Yiddish prayers for the private devotions of Ashkenazic Jewish women, were composed by women, including Sore bas Toyvim, a rabbi's

daughter who in the seventeenth century composed '*Tkhine* of Three Gates,' meditating on 'the three women's commandments' (Weissler 254; see also Klirs, Tarnor). Like prayers by and for Christian women, the *tkhines* focus on important elements of a woman's life and often incorporate passages from the Psalms. I am grateful to Betty S. Travitsky for these references. Parallels between the prayers by early modern Christian and Jewish women, a rich field for study, are beyond the scope of this essay, which focuses on the use of Psalms in writings by Protestant and Catholic English women.

[3] On the general context of early modern women and religious discourse, see Crawford 21-69; Ezell 170-225; Hannay, *Silent* 1-14; Hobby, *Virtue*; Jardine 37-67; Margaret King, *Women* 81-156; King, Dolan, and Hobby; Otten, *English Women's Voices* 277-392; Rowlands, 'Recusant Women' 149-80; Trill 30-55; Warnicke, *Women* 67-113; Wiesner 179-217; and Willen 140-165.

[4] STC 2689 Copy 1 *The Whole Booke of Psalmes* (1639); STC 2661 *The Whole Booke of Davids Psalmes* (1635); STC 2689 Copy 2 *The Whole Booke of Psalmes* (1639). Several of these bindings are reproduced in Bearman et al., eds. *Decorative and Historic Bookbindings*. I am grateful to Georgianna Ziegler for showing me these embroidered Psalters at the Folger Library.

[5] The sonnet sequence itself is anonymous, but it appears to have been written by Anne Vaughan Lock. See Hannay, 'Unlock' 20-22; Morin-Parsons 33-35; Felch, ed. *Collected Works of Anne Vaughan Lock* liii-iv; Roche 155-57; Greene, *Post-Petrarchism* 129-35.

[6] The Penshurst *Psalmes* MS is quoted with the kind permission of Viscount De L'Isle MBE from his collection at Penshurst Place.

Works Cited

Alexander, Gavin. 'Five Responses to Sir Philip Sidney 1586-1628'. Diss. U of Cambridge, 1996.

The Arundel Harington Manuscript of Tudor Poetry. ed. Ruth Hughey. Columbus: Ohio State UP, 1960. 1:338-41, nos.289 and 290.

Askew, Anne. *The Examinations of Anne Askew.* ed. Elaine V. Beilin. New York: Oxford UP, 1996.

Austern, Linda. '"For Music is the Handmaid of the Lord": The Psalm Tradition and Women's Musical Performance in Late Renaissance England,' paper read at RSA, March 1998.

Bearman, Frederick A., Nati H. Krivatsy, and J. Franklin Mowery, eds. *Decorative and Historic Bookbindings from the Folger Shakespeare Library.* Washington. DC: Folger, 1992.

Beilin, Elaine. *Redeeming Eve: Women Writers of the English Renaissance.* Princeton: Princeton UP, 1987.

Benson, Pamela. 'To Play the Man: Aemilia Lanyer and the Acquisition of Patronage'. *Opening the Borders: Inclusivity in Early Modern Studies.* ed. Peter Herman. Newark: U of Delaware P, 1999. 243-64.

Bentley, Thomas, ed. *The Monument of Matrones: conteining seven severall Lamps of Virginitie.* London, 1582.

Bèze, Théodore de. *The Psalmes of David.* Trans. Anthony Gilby. London: H. Denham, 1581.

The Bible and Holy Scriptures. Geneva, 1560. Facsimile. ed. Lloyd E. Berry. Madison: U of Wisconsin P, 1969.

Brown, Sylvia, ed. *The Mothers Legacies of Dorothy Leigh, Elizabeth Jocelin, and Elizabeth Richardson.* Forthcoming.

_____. '"Over Her Dead Body": Feminism, Postrstructuralism, and the Mother's Legacy.' *Discontinuities: New Essays on Renaissance Literature and Criticism.* eds. Comensoli, Viviana and Paul Stevens. Toronto: U of Toronto P, 1998. 3-26.

Burke, Victoria E. and Margaret P. Hannay. 'Elizabeth Ashburnham Richardson's Manuscripts.' *EMS.* Forthcoming.

Calvin, John. *The Psalms of David and others. With M. John Calvins Commentaries.* Trans. Arthur Golding. London: H. Middleton, 1571.

Clifford, Anne. *The Diaries of Lady Anne Clifford.* ed. D. J. H. Clifford. Phoenix Mill, Gloucestershire: Sutton, 1990.

Collins, An. *Divine Songs and Meditacions.* ed. Sidney Gottlieb. Tempe, AZ: MRTS, 1996.

Collinson, Patrick. 'The Role of Women in the English Reformation illustrated by the Life and Friendships of Anne Locke'. *Studies in Church History.* ed. G. J. Cuming. London: Thomas Nelson, 1965. 2:258-72.

Coverdale, Miles. *Remains of Bishop Coverdale.* ed. George Pearson. Cambridge: Cambridge UP, 1846.

Crawford, Patricia. *Women and Religion in England 1500-1720*. London: Routledge, 1993.

Crowley, Robert. *The Psalter of David Newely Translated into English metre*. London, 1549.

Diefendorf, Barbara B. 'The Huguenot Psalter and the Faith of French Protestants in the Sixteenth Century.' *Culture and Identity in Early Modern Europe (1500-1800): Essays in Honor of Natalie Zemon Davis*. ed. Barbara B. Diefendorf and Carla Hesse. Ann Arbor: U of Michigan P, 1993. 41-64.

Doelman, Jim. 'A Seventeenth-Century Publication of Three of Sir Philip Sidney's Psalms.' *N&Q* 38 (1991): 162-3.

Donawerth, Jane. 'Women's Poetry and the Tudor-Stuart System of Gift Exchange.' Donawerth, et al. Forthcoming.

Donawerth, Jane, et al., eds. *Women, Writing, and the Reproduction of Culture in Tudor and Stuart Britain*. Syracuse: Syracuse UP. Forthcoming.

Donne, John. *John Donne: The Divine Poems*. ed. Helen Gardner. Oxford: Clarendon P, 1952; rpt 1978.

Dubrow, Heather. *Echoes of Desire: English Petrarchism and its Counterdiscourses*. Ithaca: Cornell UP, 1995.

Elizabeth I. *A Godly Medytacyon of the christen sowle*. London, 1548.

_____. *Speeches, Letters, Verses, and Prayers of Elizabeth I*. eds. Leah S. Marcus, Janel Mueller, and Mary Beth Rose. Chicago: U of Chicago P. Forthcoming.

Ezell, Margaret. *The Patriarch's Wife: Literary Evidence and the History of the Family*. Chapel Hill: U of North Carolina P, 1987.

Felch, Susan M. 'Anne Lock.' *Teaching Tudor and Stuart Women Writers*. eds. Susanne Woods and Margaret Hannay. New York: MLA. Forthcoming.

Fisken, Beth Wynne. 'Mary Sidney's *Psalmes*: Education and Wisdom.' *Silent*, ed. Hannay. 166-83.

The forme of prayers and ministration of the sacraments . . . used in the Englishe congregation at Geneva: and approved, by John Calvyn. Geneva, 1556.

Foxe, John. *The Acts and Monuments of John Foxe*. ed. George Townsend. 8 vols. New York: AMS P, 1965.

Freer, Coburn. *Music for a King: George Herbert's Style and the Metrical Psalms*. Baltimore: Johns Hopkins UP, 1972.

Graham, Elspeth, Hilary Hinds, Elaine Hobby and Helen Wilcox, eds. *Her Own Life: Autobiographical writings by seventeenth-century Englishwomen*. London: Routledge, 1989.

Greenblatt, Stephen. *Renaissance Self-Fashioning: From More to Shakespeare*. Chicago: U of Chicago P, 1980.

Greene, Roland. *Post-Petrarchism: Origins and Innovations of the Western Lyric Sequence*. Princeton: Princeton UP, 1991.

_____. 'Sir Philip Sidney's Psalms, the Sixteenth-Century Psalter, and the Nature of Lyric.' *SEL* 30 (1990): 19-40.

Grymeston, Elizabeth Bernye. *Miscelanea. Meditations. Memoratives*. London, 1604.

Hannay, Margaret P. '"House-confined maids": The Presentation of Woman's Role in the *Psalmes* of the Countess of Pembroke.' *ELR* 24 (1994): 44-71.

_____. *Philip's Phoenix: Mary Sidney, Countess of Pembroke*. New York: Oxford UP, 1990.

_____, ed. *Silent but for the Word: Tudor Women as Patrons, Translators, and Writers of Religious Works*. Kent: Kent State UP, 1985.

_____. '"Unlock my lipps": the *Miserere mei Deus* of Anne Vaughan Locke and Mary Sidney Herbert, Countess of Pembroke'. *Privileging Gender in Early Modern England*. ed. Jean R. Brink. *Sixteenth-Century Essays and Studies* 23 (1993): 19-36.

Hobbs, R. Gerald. 'Hebraica Veritas *and* Traditio Apostolica: Saint Paul and the Interpretation of the Psalms in the Sixteenth Century.' *The Bible in the Sixteenth Century*. ed. David C. Steinmetz. Durham: Duke UP, 1990. 222-25.

Hobby, Elaine. *Virtue of Necessity: English Women's Writing 1649-88*. London: Virago P, 1988.

Hughey, Ruth and Philip Hereford. 'Elizabeth Grymeston and her *Miscelanea*.' *Library* 15 (1934): 61-91.

Hull, Dame Eleanor. *The Seven Psalms: A Commentary on the Penitential Psalms*. ed. Alexandra Barratt. Oxford: Clarendon UP, 1996.

Hunnis, William. *Seven Sobs of a Sorrowfull Soule for Sinn*. London, 1589.

James, Susan E. *Kateryn Parr: The Making of a Queen*. Brookfield, VT: Ashgate, 1999.

Jardine, Lisa. *Still Harping on Daughters: Women and Drama in the Age of Shakespeare*. New York: Columbia UP, 1989.

Jocelin, Elizabeth. *The Mother's Legacie, to her unborne Childe*. London, 1624.

Jones, Ann Rosalind. *The Currency of Eros*. Bloomington: Indiana UP, 1990.

[Joye, George], trans. *The Psalter of David in English . . . after Feline*. Antwerp, 1530.

Kennedy, William J. *Authorizing Petrarch*. Ithaca: Cornell UP, 1994.

King, John N. *English Reformation Literature: The Tudor Origins of the Protestant Tradition*. Princeton: Princeton UP, 1982.

_____. 'Patronage and Piety: The Influence of Catherine Parr.' *Silent*, ed. Hannay. 43-60.

_____. *Tudor Royal Iconography: Literature and Art in an Age of Religious Crisis*. Princeton: Princeton UP, 1989.

King, John N., Frances E. Dolan, and Elaine Hobby. 'Writing Religion'. *Teaching Tudor and Stuart Women Writers*. eds. Susanne Woods and Margaret Hannay. New York: MLA. Forthcoming.

King, Margaret L. 'Book-Lined Cells: Women and Humanism in the Early Italian Renaissance.' *Beyond Their Sex: Learned Women of the European Past*. ed. Patricia H. Labalme. New York: New York UP, 1980. 66-90.

_____. *Women of the Renaissance*. Chicago: U of Chicago P, 1991.

Klein, Lisa M. 'Your Humble Handmaid: Elizabethan Gifts of Needlework.' *RQ* 50 (1997): 459-93.

Klirs, Tracy Guren, et al., eds. *The Merit of Our Mothers: A Bilingual Anthology of Jewish Women's Prayers*. Cincinnati: Hebrew Union College P, 1992.

Kuin, Roger. *Chamber Music: Elizabethan Sonnet-Sequences and the Pleasure of Criticism*. Toronto: U of Toronto P, 1998.

Lanyer, Aemilia. *The Poems of Aemilia Lanyer*. ed. Susanne Woods. New York: Oxford UP, 1993.

Leaver, Robin. *'Ghoostly Psalmes and Spirituall Songes': English and Dutch Metrical Psalms from Coverdale to Utenhove 1535-1566.* Oxford: Clarendon P, 1991.

Leigh, Dorothy. THE MOTHERS BLESSING. London, 1640.

Lewalski, Barbara Kiefer. *Protestant Poetics and the Seventeenth-Century Religious Lyric.* Princeton: Princeton UP, 1979.

Lifschutz, Ellen St Sure. 'David's Lyre and the Renaissance Lyric: A Critical Consideration of the Psalms of Wyatt, Surrey and the Sidneys.' Diss. U of California, Berkeley, 1980.

Lock, Anne Vaughan [Prowse]. *The Collected Works of Anne Vaughan Lock.* ed. Susan M. Felch. Tempe, AZ: RETS/ MRTS, 1999.

_____, trans. Jean Taffin. *Of the marks of the children of God, and of their comforts in afflictions.* London: Thomas Man, 1590.

_____, trans. *Sermons of John Calvin, vpon the Songe that Ezechias made after he had bene sicke and afflicted by the hand of God.* London: John Day, 1560.

Loscocco, Paula. *'Wit's Now Feminine': Royalist Poetics in Republican England.* Forthcoming.

Love, Harold. *Scribal Publication in Seventeenth-Century England.* Oxford: Clarendon P, 1993.

Luther, Martin. *Luther's Works: American edition.* eds. U. S. Leupold and H. T. Lehmann. St Louis, 1955-86.

Marot, Clément and Théodore de Bèze. *Les Pseaumes de David.* Geneva: P. Dauntes, 1562.

Martin, Randall. 'The Autobiography of Grace, Lady Mildmay.' *Renaissance and Reformation* 18 (1994): 33-82.

Mildmay, Grace Sherrington. *Autobiography. Women Writers in Renaissance England.* ed. Randall Martin. London: Longman, 1997. 208-27.

Morin-Parsons, Kel, ed. *'A Meditation of a Penitent Sinner: Written in Maner of a Paraphrase upon the 51. Psalme of David.'* Waterloo, Ontario: North Waterloo Academic P, 1997.

Mueller, Janel. 'Complications of Intertextuality: John Fisher, Katherine Parr, and "The Book of the Crucifix."' *Representing Women in Renaissance England.* Summers and Pebworth, eds. 24-41.

Otten, Charlotte F., ed. *English Women's voices, 1540-1700.* Miami: Florida International UP, 1992.

_____. 'Women's Prayers in Childbirth in Sixteenth-Century England.' *Women and Language* 16 (1993): 18-21.

Parker, Matthew. *The Whole Psalter translated into English metre.* London: John Daye, 1567.

Pisan, Christine de. *Les Sept Psaumes allegorisés of Christine de Pisan, a Critical Edition from the Brussels and Paris Manuscripts.* ed. Ruth Ringland Rains. Washington, DC: Catholic U of America P, 1967.

Pollock, Linda. *With Faith and Physic: The Life of a Tudor Gentlewoman: Lady Grace Mildmay 1552-1620.* London: Collins and Brown, 1993.

Prescott, Anne Lake. 'Evil tongues at the court of Saul: The Renaissance David as a slandered courtier.' *JMRS* 21 (1991): 163-86.

_____. 'King David as a "Right Poet": Sidney and the Psalmist'. *ELR* 19 (1989): 131-51.

Reid, W. Stanford. 'The Battle Hymns of the Lord: Calvinist Psalmody of the Sixteenth Century.' *Sixteenth Century Essays and Studies* 2 (1971): 36-54.

Rienstra, Debra. 'Aspiring to Praise: The Sidney-Pembroke Psalter and the English Religious Lyric'. Diss. Rutgers U, 1995.

Rienstra, Debra and Noel Kinnamon. 'Revisioning the Sacred Text'. *Sidney Journal* 17 (1999): 53-77.

Roche, Thomas P., Jr. *Petrarch and the English Sonnet Sequences.* New York: AMS P, 1989.

Rohr-Sauer, Philipp von. *English Metrical Psalms from 1600 to 1660.* Freiburg: Poppen and Ortmann, 1938.

Rowlands, Marie B. 'Recusant Women, 1560-1640.' *Women in English Society, 1500-1800.* ed. Mary Prior. London: Methuen, 1985. 149-80.

Schleiner, Louise. *Tudor and Stuart Women Writers.* Bloomington: Indiana UP, 1994.

Shuger, Deborah Kuller. *The Renaissance Bible: Scholarship, Sacrifice, and Subjectivity.* Berkeley: U of California P, 1994.

Sidney, Mary. *The Collected Works of Mary Sidney Herbert, Countess of Pembroke.* eds. Margaret P. Hannay, Noel J. Kinnamon and Michael G. Brennan. 2 vols. Oxford: Clarendon P, 1998.

Sidney, Philip. *The Countesse of Pembrokes Arcadia. Written by Sir Philip Sidney Knight. Now since the first edition augmented and ended.* London, 1593.

_____. 'Defence of Poetry.' *Miscellaneous Prose of Sir Philip Sidney.* ed. Katherine Duncan-Jones and Jan van Dorsten. Oxford: Clarendon P, 1973.

Sinfield, Alan. *Faultlines: Cultural Materialism and the Politics of Dissident Reading.* Berkeley: U of California P, 1992.

Smith, Hallett. 'English Metrical Psalms in the Sixteenth Century and their Literary Significance.' *HLQ* 9 (1946): 249-71.

Southwell, Robert. *The Poems of Robert Southwell, S. J.* eds. James H. McDonald and Nancy Pollard Brown. Oxford: Clarendon P, 1967.

Spiller, Michael. *The Development of the Sonnet.* London: Routledge, 1992.

Steinberg, Theodore. 'The Sidneys and the Psalms.' *SP* 92 (1995): 1-17.

Sternhold, Thomas. *The whole booke of psalmes collected into English meter by Thomas Sternhold, J. Hopkins and others.* Geneva: J. Crespin, 1569.

Stortoni, Laura Anna, ed. *Poets of the Italian Renaissance: Courtly Ladies and Courtesans.* Trans. Laura Anna Stortoni and Mary Prentice Lillie. New York: Italica P, 1997.

Summers, Claude J. and Ted-Larry Pebworth, eds. *Representing Women in Renaissance England.* Columbia: U of Missouri P, 1997.

Swaim, Kathleen. 'Contextualizing Mary Sidney's Psalms.' *Christianity and Literature* 48 (1999): 253-73.

Tarnor, Norman. 'Three Gates Tehino: A 17th century Yiddish Prayer by Sara Bas Tova.' *Judaism* 40 (1981): 354-367.

Thornton, Alice. 'A Book of Remembrances.' *Her Own Life.* Graham, et al., eds. 147-64.

Todd, Richard. "'So Well Atyr'd Abroad": A Background to the Sidney-Pembroke Psalter and Its Implications for the Seventeenth-Century Religious Lyric.' *Texas Studies in Literature and Language* 29 (1987): 74-93.

Travitsky, Betty, ed. *The Paradise of Women: Writings by English Women of The Renaissance.* Westport: Greenwood P, 1981.

Trill, Suzanne. 'Religion and the construction of femininity.' *Women and Literature in Britain 1500-1700.* ed. Helen Wilcox. Cambridge: Cambridge UP, 1996. 30-55.

Tyrwhit, Elizabeth. *Works.* ed. Susan Felch. Forthcoming.

Verstegan, Richard. [Richard Rowlands]. *Odes. In Imitation of the Seaven Penitential Psalmes.* Amsterdam, 1601.

Victoria and Albert Museum. *Princely magnificence: court jewels of the Renaissance, 1500-1630.* London: Debrett's Peerage in association with the Victoria and Albert Museum, c. 1980.

Wall, Wendy. *The Imprint of Gender: Authorship and Publication in the English Renaissance.* Ithaca: Cornell UP, 1993.

Waller, Gary. *Mary Sidney, Countess of Pembroke: A Critical Study of Her Writings and Literary Milieu.* Salzburg: Institut für Anglistik und Amerikanistik, Universität Salzburg, 1979.

Warnicke, Retha M. 'Lady Mildmay's Journal: A Study in Autobiography and Meditation in Reformation England.' *Sixteenth Century Journal* 20 (1989): 55-68.

_____. *Women of the English Renaissance and Reformation.* Westport: Greenwood P, 1983.

Wayne, Valerie. 'Advice for women from mothers and patriarchs.' *Women and Literature in Britain, 1500-1700.* ed. Helen Wilcox. Cambridge: Cambridge UP, 1996. 56-79.

Weigall, Rachel. 'An Elizabethan Gentlewoman. The Journal of Lady Mildmay, circa 1570-1617.' *Quarterly Review* 215 (1911): 119-38.

Weiner, Seth. 'Sidney and the Rabbis: A Note on the Psalms of David and Renaissance Hebraica'. *Sir Philip Sidney's Achievements.* eds. M. J. B. Allen et al. New York: AMS P, 1990. 157-62.

Weissler, Chava. 'The Traditional Piety of Ashkenazic Women.' *Jewish Spirituality from the Sixteenth-Century Revival to the Present.* ed. Arhur Green. New York: Crossroad, 1987. 245-83.

White, Micheline. 'A Biographical Sketch of Dorcas Martin: Elizabethan Translator, Stationer, and Godly Matron.' *Sixteenth Century Journal* 30 (1999): 775-92.

_____. '"Cunning in Controversies": English Protestant Women Writers and Religious and Literary Debates, 1580-1616.' Diss. Loyola U, 1998.

Whitehead, Lydia. 'A *poena et culpa*: penitence, confidence and the *Miserere* in Foxe's *Actes and Monuments.'* *RS* 4 (1990): 287-97.

Wiesner, Merry E. *Women and Gender in Early Modern Europe.* Cambridge: Cambridge UP, 1993.

Wilcox, Helen. '"My Soule in Silence"?: Devotional Presentations of Renaissance Englishwomen.' *Representing Women in Renaissance England.* Summers and Pebworth, eds. 9-23.

Willard, Charity Cannon. 'Christine de Pizan's Allegorized Psalms.' *Une femme de Lettres au*

Moyen Age: Études autour de Christine de Pizan. eds. L. Dulac and B. Ribémont. Orleans: Paradigme, 1995. 316-24.

Willen, Diane. 'Women and Religion in Early Modern England.' *Women in Reformation and Counter-Reformation Europe: Private and Public Worlds.* ed. Sherrin Marshall. Bloomington: Indiana UP, 1989. 140-65.

Wilson, Katharina M., ed. *Women Writers of the Renaissance and Reformation.* Athens: U of Georgia P, 1987.

Woods, Suzanne. *Natural Emphasis: English Versification from Chaucer to Dryden.* San Marino: Huntington Library, 1984.

Wroth, Lady Mary. *The Poems of Lady Mary Wroth.* ed. Josephine A. Roberts. Baton Rouge: Louisiana State UP, 1983.

Wyatt, Thomas. *Certayne psalmes chosen out of the psalter of David.* London, 1549.

Ziegler, Georgianna. 'Jewels for the Soul: The Psalm Books of Esther Inglis,' paper read at RSA, March 1998.

_____. '"More Than Feminine Boldness": the Gift Books of Esther Inglis.' Donawerth et al.

Zim, Rivkah. *English Metrical Psalms Poetry as Praise and Prayer, 1535-1601.* Cambridge: Cambridge UP, 1987.

PART III

Negotiating Power and Politics

7

The Plural Voices of Anne Askew

Joan Pong Linton

Apart from the *Examinations* which recount her two trials for heresy, Anne Askew's name has been connected with three works in verse: a paraphrase of Psalm 54, the Newgate ballad, and 'A Ballad of *Anne Askew, intitled I am a Woman poore and Blind.*' The first two poems appeared respectively in John Bale's editions of Askew's *First* and *Lattre Examinations* (1546, 1547), but were omitted from the section on Askew in John Foxe's *Acts and Monuments.* 'The Ballad of *Anne Askew*' was entered into the Stationer's Register in 1624 and printed the same year, although it was certainly in circulation before then, since Thomas Nashe referred to the ballad in 1596 in *Have With You to Saffron-Waldron* (113). Although Bale attributed the paraphrase of Psalm 54 and the Newgate ballad to Askew, the authorship of the three verses has never been ascertained, nor am I concerned to do so here. What interests me about these verses is the way they position Askew between writer and written, speaker and spoken, thereby foregrounding the structures of appropriations through which we inevitably read the story of the martyr, whether in her own words or in the words of others.

Such ambiguous position Askew already occupies in the *Examinations,* if we consider the interpretive frameworks of the martyrologies in which she is enshrined. Especially in the case of her first two editors, John Bale and John Foxe, scholars have noted silent emendations, glosses, and even editorial intrusions that frame her story for the reformist cause.[1] At the same time, Askew herself appropriates scripture in her verbal exchanges with examiners as a way of testifying to her faith in voices other than her own. This plural voicing, I would argue, is more than just a strategy of evasion, but bespeaks her own sense of participation, through the interweaving of voices, in a communal text of faith (Beilin 32). In dying for her beliefs, the martyr also projects an ideal community beyond the present, a motive that finds further expression in the paraphrase of Psalm 54 and the ballads. Within this intertextual framework, I hope to show how the scriptural community of the *Examinations* increasingly gives way to an imagined community in the making, even as the participatory motive overtakes the exemplary. I will explore specifically the textual production of Askew's plural voice and self in these verses as the vehicle that renders her personal agency socially transforming.

My analysis locates the verses in question within traditions of literary and devotional practice. As Helen White wisely notes, while English reformers attacked Catholic beliefs and sacraments, they were also conservative of traditional devotional practices that were widely popular, adapting them to their own purposes (63). Such adaptation constituted, in Stuart Hall's terms of cultural politics, a form of 'negotiation' with tradition in order to redefine the terms of religious and narrative authority (Jones 2-4). The paraphrase of Psalm 54 and the Newgate ballad appropriate scriptural sources to the martyr's situation and perspective, and invite other subjects to participate in them. Indeed, as popular genres both written and oral, the psalm and ballad render accessible these authorial negotiations to literate and illiterate audiences alike. The process culminates in 'The Ballad of *Anne Askew*,' the title designating Askew at once as speaker and spoken, despite her indeterminate position between writer and written.[2] By locating Askew's story beyond print in venues of oral transmission, these verses extend the martyr's plural voices in retelling aspects of her life, producing in the process the plural articulations of a martyr's story that escape the canonical image of Askew perpetuated in the martyrologies.

To conceptualize the exemplary and the participatory self, I draw on the distinction Doris Sommer makes between autobiography and testimonial as narrative forms structured respectively by the tropes of metaphor and metonymy. In her words, there is a

> fundamental difference between the metaphor or autobiography
> and heroic narrative in general, which assumes an identity by
> substituting one (superior) signifier for another (I for we, leader
> for follower, Christ for the faithful) and metonymy, a lateral
> identification through relationship, which acknowledges the
> possible differences among 'us' as components of the whole.

While the metaphoric operation projects a self as an exemplary model for the community, the metonymic operation enacts a self as a participant and extension of a community based on 'particular shared objectives rather than interchangeability among its members.' Sommer aligns autobiography with the assumption of 'universal or essential human experience' as the basis of individual identity in Augustine's *Confessions,* and the testimonial with motives of resistance in accounts written by Latin American women of their participation in popular struggles. The two kinds of narrative are further differentiated by their medium: 'unlike the private and even lonely moment of autobiographical writing, testimonies are public events' in which 'the orality [of exchanges] helps to account for the testimonials' construction of a collective self' (108-9, 118).

Sommer's formulation can be extended to an analysis of life narratives from the English Reformation with two complications. First, the distinction between oral and written is often blurred when the life narratives of martyrs include reconstructed oral exchanges from ongoing religious struggles. As well, martyrologists often draw from diverse oral and written sources in a variety of genres in presenting a compelling story of the martyr's life and actions. Second, the 'I's specific to autobiography and testimonial can and do at times coexist in a martyr's life narrative. While the martyrology celebrates the exemplary status of the martyr with respect to the community, the martyr's projected self is often *also* the 'I' of the testimonial, aligned with fellow dissenters in their resistance to religious persecution.

Both exemplary and participatory motives operate in Askew's *Examinations.* Described by Elaine Beilin as 'spiritual autobiogaphy' (30-32), Askew's text reveals her self-awareness as a model for the reformist faith. Especially in her use of scriptural citations, Askew models Bible reading as a means by which a dissenter may both speak her conscience and avoid condemnation for heresy. It is hard to tell how faithfully these written accounts render the oral proceedings, but in one sense Askew is already enacting a script of an ideal self. As Diane Watt writes, 'Askew seems to follow the example Christ himself set when he was brought before his accusers, by questioning her examiners, remaining silent or answering indirectly, and again like Christ she was rebuked for her insolence and accused of speaking in parables' (98). In imitating Christ Askew addresses a community of faith. In the *First Examination,* she claims to have written her account of her trial 'to satisfy your expectation, good people' (165, l. 12). In the *Latter Examination,* she exhorts a 'dere frend in the Lord' (179, l. 6) to cling to a spiritual understanding of the host as a sign and commemoration of

Christ's passion and a promise of spiritual fellowship. However formulaic, these addresses locate a retrospective position in the narrative from which she measures her own performance in the eyes of her intended readers.

Much of Askew's wit comes from the ability to cite scripture in response to questions on doctrinal issues, referring the questioner to an unquestionable source. She is so successful that, at one point, an exasperated Stephen Gardiner, bishop of Winchester, calls her 'a parate' (180, l. 56). Beyond her personal conscience, the citations project an ideal community of biblical figures, including David, Moses, Job, the prophets Daniel, Amos, Isaiah, Hosea from the Old Testament, and the evangelists, Stephen, and Paul from the New Testament. Their words and actions provide commentary for her personal struggle and thus give it a history. By interweaving her voice with theirs, she enters a scriptural community, one that prefigures her present community of dissenters. This present community is not localized; rather, it is scripted into action by a reformist agenda through the practice of Bible reading, a shared practice in which men and women alike are authorized to prophesy or interpret scripture. In citing scripture, Askew enacts the agency that literacy affords her not only in defense of a Bible-centered faith, but also to produce textually the community in which she participates.

The scriptural citations in the *Examinations* prepare us for the plural voicing in the verses written by or attributed to her. These verses continue the participatory motive already present in the *Examination,* while at the same time locating her story in everyday practices of popular piety. Askew's version of Psalm 54 has its context in the reading and singing, as well as paraphrase and translation of psalms, practices undertaken by men and women, often with the aid of psalters and primers. Of particular relevance here is the Book of Hours, a section of the primer which contains selected prayers and psalms to be read at set 'hours' of the day (Prime, Terce, Sext, and None, or 6 a.m., 9 a.m., noon, and 3 p.m.). While such practice dated from the Middle Ages as a form of 'corporate prayer' among the clergy, the production of printed primers helped to popularize the use of psalms in devotion, in both private and public worship (White 54, 149). The singing and paraphrase of psalms became increasingly politicized as the religious struggles of the Reformation intensified. As Hannay, Kinnamon, and Brennan point out, the words of the psalmists 'serv[ed] both as "battle hymns" in the Continental religious wars and a personal consolation in times of persecution.' In England, 'even reciting vernacular Psalms could become a political statement,' as seen in Foxe's accounts of Dr Rowland Taylor who for reciting Psalm 51 in English was struck by the sheriff, and of Lady Jane Grey who, 'awaiting execution, recited the Psalm of "*Miserere mei Deus*" in English.' In private devotion as well, 'psalm meditation became almost de rigueur for sixteenth-century prisoners, particularly those who believed that they were persecuted for their religious beliefs' (5-6, 7).

In Askew's case, her choice of Psalm 54 is noteworthy as it is the first psalm in the Book of Hours in four of the five primers from her day – from the Catholic Sarum Primer to the reformist Joye and Marshall Primers and the more conservative Hilsey Primer (Butterworth 288). A psalm that transcends religious difference is thus her vehicle for expression, suggesting a broader audience than the one intended for the *Examinations*. In appropriating scripture to her own situation, Askew locates a reformist reading of the Bible in popular devotional practice. The psalm's title, *Deus in nomine tuo,* is glossed in the first two lines of the paraphrase: 'For thy names sake, be my refuge, / And in thy truth, my quarell judge,' the parallel construction equating God's name with his truth. The speaker's quarrel, it turns out, is with 'faithless men' who 'for thy sake, my deathe practyse.' In turn, she urges God to 'revenge my wronge, / And vysyte them, ere it be longe.' The restraint in these words is remarkable, and it anticipates the kind of justice she desires in the closing lines: 'From evyll thu hast delyvered me, / Declarynge what myne enmyes be. / Prayse to God' (72, ll. 1-2, 15-17).

This emphasis on truth acquires a personal ring if we compare the paraphrase with the official translation from *The Great Bible,* in which the speaker wants God to 'auenge me in thy strength' (Fol. xi), or from the Joye primer, in which the speaker asks God to 'delyvre me by thy power' (n.p). Aside from their emphasis on God's strength and power, both these versions lack the specificity of Askew's insistence that God judge her 'quarell.' Her words underscore the urgency of a struggle in which both sides – even her persecutors – are claiming to act in God's name. The description of her persecutors as 'faithless men' emphasizes faith as the issue at stake, in contrast with the 'straungers and tirauntes (whych haue not God before their eyes)' who oppress the supplicant of *The Great Bible.* In this struggle, moreover, the martyr must fight alone: her 'Yet helpest thu me, in thys dystresse, / Savynge my sowle, from cruelnesse' (ll. 9-10) departs again from the official version: 'Beholde, God is my helper: the Lorde is w[ith] them that vpholde my soule.' And if Askew's paraphrase may have provided a model

for Mary Sidney Herbert's (Hannay et al. 8), Askew's sense of being utterly
alone is not replicated in Sidney's 'but god, thou art my helper in my right, /
thou succour send'st to such as succour me.' For Sidney, the double succor
makes for a liberatory ending:

> praising thy name which thus hast sett me free:
> giving me scope to soare with happie flight
> above my evills: and on my enemy
> making me see, what I to see delight. (54, ll. 9-10, 13-16)

Sidney's metaphorical flight brings home by contrast the martyr's
predicament, confronting a death from which no escape is possible.

Such finality may explain Askew's insistence on truth – 'declarynge
what, myne enmyes be' – as the ultimate justice. She would be justified in the
eyes of God, a position fully consistent with that in the *Examinations*. In the
Latter Examination, for example, Askew addresses Sir Thomas Wriothesley,
Lord Chancellor and one of her torturers, in a letter: 'I think his grace shall
wel perceive me to be waged in an uneven pair of balaunces. But I remit my
matter and cause to almightye God, whyche rightlye judgeth all seacreates'
(185, ll. 177-79). Askew's faith in the truth revealed is foregrounded in the
woodcut on the title page to Bale's editions of the *First* and *Latter
Examinations.* The woodcut presents her as a figure of Truth: 'Anne Askewe
stode fast by thys veryte of God to the ende,' along with a citation from Psalm
116, 'The veryte of the lorde endureth for euer' (1, 73). As Diane Watt
surmises, Bale was responsible for the details in the woodcut, with its
iconographic evocation of Revelation that links Askew's truth to the reformist
tradition of female prophecy (104). While Bale is interested in presenting the
martyr as the exemplar of truth, it is not a position which the Askew in the
psalm can occupy. Because 'the ambiguous "I" of the Psalms leaves a space
for the reader to insert a personal voice' (Hannay et al. 8), David's Psalm
becomes the shared theme in which readers may participate and relate to their
own situations. Indeed, the comparative analysis above has indicated the
diverse voices in which, and positions from which, such appropriation can
occur, each bringing a new testimonial 'I' to an evolving, textually constituted
community.

From the quarrel in the paraphrase of Psalm 54 we now turn to combat
in the Newgate ballad, which likens the martyr to 'the armed Knyght /

Appoynted to the fielde' (149, ll. 1-2). The similitude evokes the topos of *miles Christianus,* a 'popular form of allegoresis [which] developed in early Christian literature and flourished in the Middle Ages' (Newhauser 325), and remained popular during the sixteenth and seventeenth centuries (Wang 231). Drawing on metaphors of combat in Job 7.1, the topos compares life to a continual battle against evil for which the Christian must be spiritually armed. The description of spiritual armor derives from Paul's epistle to the Ephesians 6.10-17, namely, the loincloth of truth, breastplate of righteousness, shoes of the gospel, shield of faith, helmet of salvation, and sword of the word of God. In the practice of everyday piety the shield of faith borne by the Christian knight was 'a set-piece on *memoria mortis.*' In death rituals the shield's four corners were inscribed with religious lyrics marking the stages of the body's decomposition, a reminder for virtuous living as preparation for death (Newhauser 327-29). The allegory of warfare had specific relevance not only for the medieval culture of knighthood and the Crusades, but also for the religious politics of the Reformation.

Within this tradition, Erasmus's *Enchiridion Militus Christiani* (1503/4) is a pivotal work because it appeals to reformist values in some respects and to traditional values in others, and because of its cultural influence. Over fifty editions of the Latin original were printed during Erasmus' life time, while the 1534 English translation by the reformer William Tyndale, entitled *The hansome weapon of a christian knight,* numbered ten editions during the sixteenth century, six during the reign of Henry VIII (O'Donnell xvi). In Tyndale's translation, Erasmus stresses arming the mind as the Christian's 'first care,' advocating the 'weapons' of 'prayer and knowledge / otherwyse called lernynge. . . . The one maketh intercessyon and prayeth. The other sheweth what is to be desyred, and what thou oughtest to pray. To pray feruently / and (as Iames exhorteth vs) without doutyng or mystrustyng, faith and hope bringeth to passe' (B1v; O'Donnell 42-43). This emphasis on faith and learning in Erasmus's spiritual defense provides a context for understanding Askew's struggle.

The ballad explicitly invokes the Christian knight topos, aligning the martyr's performance with the reformist emphasis on faith. Contemporary audiences, aware of Askew's torture in the tower and her burning in Smithfield, would notice the understatement in the opening lines:

Lyke as the armed knyght

> Appoynted to the fielde
> With thys world wyll I fyght
> And fayth shall be my shielde,
>   Faythe is that weapon stronge
> Whych wyll not fayle at nede
> My foes therfor amonge
> Therwith wyll I procede. (149, ll. 1-8)

In this generalized portrait, what comes through is the martyr's unequal fight with worldly evil. Even the simile, 'lyke as the armed knyght,' distances the audience from the martyr's suffering, foregrounding the knight as an idealized figure through which readers and listeners may individually participate in a collective making of faith.

This participatory dynamics in turn helps propel a dual temporality in the ballad, one set in motion by the future tense 'wyll.' Most immediately, the verb captures that short space before the execution in which the martyr prepares for death as a final fight. As the speaker intimates, while faith enables her 'to feare no worldes dystresse,' hope bids her to 'rejoyce in hart' knowing that 'Christ wyll take [her] part' (149, ll. 17-19). In longer view, the future tense indicates the textual survival of her fighting spirit in readers and listeners, inspiring them in their ongoing struggle with evil in the world. Both in its muted violence and its orientation to the future, the ballad can be said to give textual life – not afterlife – to the martyr's fight even as it mediates a new faith to her imagined community.

Yet there is finality to the martyr's fight that engenders a visionary moment, to which Askew's ship of the soul – 'my shyppe substancyall' (50, l. 36) – serves as a figure of transport. Scholars have noted that the vision itself is adapted from Surrey's translation of Ecclesiastes, chapter three (Mason 243-44; Beilin xxxii), possibly written in 1546 while he was imprisoned in the Tower awaiting execution. The inclusion of a contemporary source raises for some the question of 'the ballad's originality' (Diane Watt 95), but it also adds to the complexity of the plural voice and self that emerges.   In envisioning the royal throne of justice usurped by one of cruel wit, Surrey in effect gives voice to a complaint that otherwise remains implicit in the ballad, a complaint that Askew explicitly voices in the *Examinations* and the paraphrase of Psalm 54.

In this interplay of voices, the voice of Surrey provides a medium through which the martyr's fears are at once refracted and externalized, allowing her to continue in the voice of the Christian knight as she addresses her own perilous situation:

> More enmyes now I have,
> Than heeres upon my heed
> Lete them not me deprave
> But fyght thu in my steed.
>   On the my care I cast
> For all their cruell spyght
> I sett not by their hast
> For thu art my delyght. (149-50, ll. 25-32)

These lines become especially poignant if we realize that the reference to hairs repeats a statement, at times verbatim, from the confession of faith Askew made in Newgate (and committed to writing in the *Latter Examination*) shortly before her execution:

> O Lorde, I have mo enemies nowe then there be heeres on my
> head. Yet Lorde, let them never overcome me with vayn words,
> but fyght thou Lorde in my stede, for on the cast I my care. With
> all the spight they can imagine, they fall upon me, whiche am thy
> poore creature. Yet swete Lorde, lett me not sett by them whiche
> are against thee. For in thee is my whole delyght. (190-91, ll.
> 317-24)

The verbal echo, which gathers the generality of the knight figure into the particularity of Askew's life, functions as a 'signature,' metaphorically speaking, that authorizes the voice in the ballad through autobiography. In turn autobiography has its authorizing moment, for the reference to hairs on her head recalls Christ's words to his disciples in preparing them for their role as preachers of a new faith. In Luke 21, Christ warns of the persecutions they would suffer on his account:

> Ye shalbe betrayd of youre fathers a[n]d mothers & brethre[n],
> & kinfolke & fre[n]des, & some of you shall they put to deeth.
> And hated shall ye be of all men for my names sake, a[n]d ther
> shall not one herre of youre head peryshshe. Possesse ye youre
> soule by pacience. (*The Great Bible* xxxv)

Matthew 10 provides another version of the story, which includes Christ's instruction to guard against killers of souls, and his assurance that God cares even for sparrows, let alone the hairs on the disciples' heads.

Scriptural citation thus metonymically authorizes Askew's voice as a performative agency: in response to Christ's promise in the Gospels, on the hope that faith makes possible. By the end of the ballad, she is already pleading for divine mercy on behalf of her oppressors: 'Lete them not tast the hyre / Of their inqyuyte' (ll. 55-56). The implied sense of an eventual reversal of power is confirmed by the citation immediately following: 'God hath chosen the weake thynges of the worlde, to confounde thynges whych are myghtye. Yea, and thynges of no reputacyon, for to brynge to nought thynges of reputacyon, that no fleshe shuld presume in hys sight.1.Corinth.1' (ll. 59-62). In listening to the voices in the ballad, one begins to realize that the voice of Askew is in fact the interplay of their resonances. As such, Askew's voice cannot be localized but resides instead in the relation between voices. One effect of the interplay is to revise the figure of the Christian knight in the course of the ballad, as the masculine armor in Ephesians cited at the beginning gives way to the hair on the disciples' heads entrusted to God's care. Insignificant as sparrows, such hair is a far cry as well from the Old Testament warrior whose hair is the essence of his strength (Samson) or beauty (Absolom). By the same token, the knight has become a community of disciples into which Askew has inserted herself. The revised, Christo-centric image of the knight thus instances Askew's negotiated agency with respect to scriptural authority and allegorical tradition.

The authorizing maneuver in the Newgate ballad recalls Askew's concern in the *Examinations* to authenticate her writing in transmission with her signature. Yet the participatory openness of both the ballad and the psalm paraphrase renders Askew's authorship open to question. This may explain the exclusion of the unsigned verses from Foxe's martyrology, which elsewhere includes ballads and psalms among its variety of materials. By contrast, Bale's inclusion of the verses indicates a different editorial outlook on authorship. His titling of the verses – 'The voyce of Anne Askewe out of the 54. Psalme of David, called, Deus in nomine tuo' and 'The Balade whych Anne Askewe made and sange whan she was in Newgate' – is telling in this connection (72, 149). The titles point to another textual tradition coexisting with the productions of print – that of storytelling in which the narrative voice is presumed plural and authorship is participatory.

As Walter Benjamin explains, oral or written, the essence of storytelling is the art of retelling; its truth lies not in verifiability but in the use or 'counsel' tellers and audiences derive from the tellings and retellings (86). In a largely oral society such as Askew's, Bruce Smith observes, tellers and listeners are active participants in oral performances which offer 'the possibility of becoming many subjects by internalizing the sounds and rhythms of those subjects' voices' (201). Even as 'Askew' tells her story of persecution in retelling David's, or pojects a polyvocal Christian warrior, the community of listeners and retellers is already 'imagined' in the telling. Thus while the *Examinations* remained available to a popular audience – in 1571 the Privy Council ordered copies of *Acts and Monuments* distributed to every cathedral church (King 435) – Askew's story also flourished outside official channels. We have no record of how the Psalm paraphrase and the Newgate ballad were received, but Nashe's 1596 allusion suggests that another ballad featuring Askew as speaker was widely current half a century after her death. Still in circulation in 1675, 'The Ballad of *Anne Askew*' testifies to the enduring appeal of Askew's story (Tessa Watt 83-85).

In 'The Ballad of *Anne Askew,*' the speaker tells of a garden 'unknowne' given her by God which in her ignorance she mistook to be 'my owne body.' She sought spiritual cultivation from a 'proud Gardner' who 'flattered me with words so kind / to have me continue in blindnesse still' (195, ll. 5-7, 21, 23-24). It was only in reading the Bible that she found truth in a new faith. The 'Gardner' mentioned is a pun on the name of Bishop Gardiner, chief among Askew's persecutors and an instigator of the plot to implicate her supporters in high places. Besides this detail relating to her life, the ballad also invokes literary, devotional, and polemical traditions that were the sites of struggle between the old and new faiths. The ballad thus recapitulates the politics of the Reformation in the narrative of a woman's conversion.

Specifically, the before-and-after structure of the conversion narrative lends itself respectively to tropes of the garden as a woman's body and as an allegory of the soul. In particular, the latter had a basis in popular piety relating to the education of the laity, especially children, through the use of manuals called *Hortulus Animae*. According to Charles Butterworth, 'the traditional Hortulus was a compilation or anthology of miscellaneous prayers, strongly imbued with Catholic dogma. It was current especially in Germany, where the followers of Luther repudiated it as superstitious.' The first English Hortulus, attributed to George Joye, appeared in 1530 and continued the tradition of 'fruitful instruction' of children and the laity in general. The contents of Joye's Hortulus were strongly Protestant, however, and 'virtually [its] entire contents' were reproduced in the first English Primer, the Marshall Primer printed in 1534, 'Cum priuilegio Regali' (20, 34, 59). Subsequent early English Primers (1534-1545), some more reformist than others, remained popular, surviving censorship in 1542.

The reformist *hortulus* inspired private devotional practice as well, notably writings by Katherine Parr, Askew's patron, later published as *The Lamentacion of a synner* (1547). The lives of the two women thus intersected not only in the intricate politics of the Henrician Reformation, but also in the cultural idiom that rendered their experiences intelligible to readers. In the *Lamentacion,* Parr writes:

> For I am so ignoraunt blynde, weak, and feble that I can not bring myselfe out of this intangled & waywarde maze: but the more I seeke meanes and wayes to wynde my selfe out, the more I am wrapped and tangled therein.
>
> So that I perceyue my striuing therin to be hinderance, my trauail to be labour spent in going backe. It is [th]e hand of the lorde that can and wyl bring me oute of this endeles mase of death: for w[ith]out I be preue[n]ted by [th]e grace of [th]e lord, I can not ask forgeuenes nor be repentant or sory for them. (Biir-Biiv)

The parallels with Askew's ballad are clear. Parr's self-image recalls that of Askew the speaker; and Askew's garden 'unknowne' has its counterpart in Parr's 'maze.' Whether a private garden or the classical labyrinth, the 'maze' suggests the work of human artifice. The passage thus describes a conversion experience in which God alone delivers Parr from error of her own making into the truth of a reformed faith. Both God's prevenient grace in her delivery and the priority of faith over works elsewhere in the narrative bespeak a Protestant emphasis on the individual's direct relationship with God. Her doctrinal position redefines confession as an 'open declaracion' (A8v), a rejection of the Catholic sacrament of auricular confession which subverts the Christian's relationship with God.

Closer examination also discloses a crucial difference between the two works. Praised as a model from whom the reader 'may learn to knowe thy selfe' (see preface, n.p), Parr's spiritual sense of the maze contrasts strongly with Askew's carnal understanding of her garden. While Parr enacts spiritual reform through a textual reform of the Hortulus tradition, Askew's persistent ignorance sets the stage for a Protestant satire on the carnality of Catholic sacraments. First, the speaker was fed 'stinking meate, / for to keepe me from my salvation,' a reference to the Catholic belief in the corporeal presence of the host. Then come 'Popish ceremonies many a one': the 'tren-talies of Masse, and Buls of lead' that allowed 'not one word spoken of Christs passion'; the 'Masses of Requiem with other Jugling deeds' that aggravate her soul 'till Gods spirit out of my garden was gone'; and the building of 'some Chappell, or some Chauntry' for praryers for the dead, a practice rejected by the Protestants (196, ll. 29-30, 34, 31-32, 35-36, 39).

In its attack on Catholic sacraments, the ballad participates in the reformist tradition of the ploughman, which derived from William Langland's *Piers Plowman,* especially its development of *cor hominis,* the Christian idea 'that the path to spiritual salvation lies through the heart of the individual' (Donaldson 110). As Barbara Johnson notes, the ploughman figure owed its popularity to apocrypha that appeared well before the first Renaissance publication of Langland's poem in 1550. Over time, the figure came to represent not only 'the ideal Christian who knew the way to truth' but also 'strong anticlericalism,' 'Lollard issues,' 'an antique figure who could lend authority to [reformist] claims,' and a voice 'for the poor' (75, 87). In his famous *Sermon of the Plow* (1548), Bishop Latimer specifically links 'ploughers' to preaching: 'for God's word is a seed to be sown in God's field, that is, the faithful congregation, and the preacher is the sower' (59).

The language of the ploughman tradition resonates in the ballad both in the speaker's desire to 'have sowne' in her garden 'the seede of Christs true veritie' and in her subsequent distress that 'in me was sowne all kinde of fained seedes.' The tradition's anticlericalism finds its target in the 'proud Gardner' who is aligned with the devil, and who warns against 'new learning,' enjoining the speaker 'to doe as your fathers have done before' (195-96, ll. 7-8, 33, 45, 49-52, 28, 44). Yet this new learning is what she 'findes written in [the Lord's] Testament,' which she 'will not deny, / for Prison, fire, Faggot, nor firce sword' (197, ll. 55, 59-60). As Allan Chester explains, 'new learning' was 'a term of opprobrium used by the religious conservatives against the teachings of Martin Luther and his English disciples' (qtd. in Johnson 179). For reformists, however, the term sounds the populist appeal of the lay ploughman, as seen in the 1531 printing of *The Praier and complaynte of the plowman unto Christe,* a prose tract 'probably dat[ing] from the early fifteenth century.' In its attack on the abuses of the church, the tract embodies 'the newfound voice of the layman' who resists priestly mediation in his relationship with God. The Preface claims that Christ's message 'was "new leringe," and Christ and his disciples were "men nother of authorite nor reputation / but laye men / ydiotes fyschers, / carpenters and other of the sort".' Finally, Foxe includes the tract in his *Acts and Monuments,* and the figure of the lay ploughman is enshrined in Protestant martyrology (Johnson 76, 78). In testifying to 'new learning' Askew the speaker thus performs the socially transforming agency of the lay ploughman.

Of course, religious polemic does not guarantee doctrinal rigor, nor does the ballad's rhyme scheme help matters. In the lines following, reference to God's grace comes as almost an afterthought, by way of rhyming with 'no space' to tell the whole story:

> Because that now I have no space,
> the cause of my death truely to show:
> I trust hereafter by Gods holy grace,
> that all faithfull men shall it plainely know. (198, ll. 77-80)

But true to form the ballad assumes the audience's familiarity with Askew's story and imagines the audience as a community in which this story will continue to be valued. This imagined community would be populist in its religious sympathies, given the evocation of the ballad's lay ploughman. Nor is it hard to imagine her story transcending social divisions. In the *Latter Examination,* Askew writes that while a prisoner in Newgate she received financial help not only from friends in high places but also from apprentices through her maid: 'For as she went abrode in the streates, she made mone to the prentises, and they by her did send ne monye' (187, ll. 218-19). By its 1624 printing, the Bible-centered faith for which she gave her life had become official religion, even as the growth of popular literacy enabled a growing number of the laity to take an active role in interpreting scripture for themselves.

Despite its populist appeal, the ballad has been criticized for its stereotypical representation of Askew as a weak woman and a victim of miseducation. Such criticism overlooks, however, the stereotype's transformation from weak woman into lay ploughman, in the process asserting female participation in the allegorical figure. If in Parr's *Lamentacion* the figure of the spiritually blind woman functions as a persona for religious instruction, in the ballad the persona transvalues religious authority. Significantly, in modeling the practice of Bible reading, the ballad does not cite scripture in its plural voicing, as do the other two poems and the *Examinations*. Instead, the use of a persona marks a space of absence that individual subjects may inhabit. Just as the Bible mediates in the speaker's conversion, so the ballad narrates the self-transformation in which performers, listeners, and readers participate, from their own anonymous circumstances.

The contemporary perception of Askew's verses as 'made' and 'sung' draws attention to the practices of orality and literacy that constitute the sociality of storytelling and that extend Askew's own participatory sense of community. Specifically, the roles the speakers assume in these verses – from supplicant to armed knight to woman poor and blind – mark the range of voices, gender-specific and gender-neutral, from which a transformative agency may emerge. The uncertain authorship of Askew's verses (from the propriety perspective of print) also authorizes, within living memory, open-ended retellings of her story.

Notes

[1] Beilin (29-47) and Diane Watt (88-115, especially 94-95) provide the fullest analysis of editorial handling of Askew by Bale and Foxe.
[2] Beilin discusses Askew's possible authorship of the ballad (Askew xxxix), while others see it as a ballad about Askew (King 444; Tessa Watt 94).

Works Cited

Askew, Anne. *The Examinations Of Anne Askew.* ed. Elaine V. Beilin. New York: Oxford UP, 1996.

Beilin, Elaine V. *Redeeming Eve: Women Writers of the English Renaissance.* Princeton: Princeton UP, 1987.

Benjamin, Walter. *Illuminations.* New York: Harcourt, 1955.

Butterworth, Charles C. *The English Primers (1529-1545): Their Publication and Connection with the English Bible and the Reformation in England.* Philadelphia: U of Pennsylvania P, 1953.

Donaldson, E. Talbot. *Piers Plowman: The C-Text and Its Poet.* New Haven: Yale UP, 1949.

Erasmus, Desiderius. *Enchiridion militis christiani / whiche may be called in englysshe, the hansome weapon of a christen knyght / replenysshed with many goodly and godly preceptes: made by the famous clerke Erasmus of Rotterdame, and newly corrected and imprinted.. Cum priuilegio regali.* Trans. William Tyndale. London: Wynken de Worde for Iohn Byddell, 1534. *Enchiridion Militis Christiani: An English Version.* ed. Anne M. O'Donnell. Oxford: Oxford UP, 1981.

The Great Bible: a facsimile of the 1539 edition. Tokyo, Japan: Elpis, 1991.

Johnson, Barbara A. *Reading Piers Plowman and The Pilgrim's Progress: Reception and the Protestant Reader.* Carbondale: Southern Illinois UP, 1992.

Jones, Anne Rosalind. *The Currency of Eros: Women's Lyric in Europe 1540-1620.* Bloomington: Indiana UP, 1990

[Joye, George.] *Ortulus anime the garden of the soule.* Emprinted at Argentine [i.e.Antwerp]: by me Francis Foxe [i.e., M. de Keyser], in the yeare of ower Lorde 1530.

King, John N. *English Reformation Literature: The Tudor Origins of the Protestant Tradition.* Princeton: Princeton UP, 1982.

Latimer, Hugh. *Sermons By Hugh Latimer.* ed. Rev George Elwes Corrie. 3 vols. Cambridge: Cambridge UP, 1844. Vol 1.

Mason, H. A. *Humanism and Poetry in the Early Tudor Period.* London: Routledge, 1959.

Nashe, Thomas. *The Works of Thomas Nashe.* ed. Ronald B. McKerrow. 4 vols. Oxford: Basil Blackwell, 1958. Vol. 3.

Newhauser, Richard. '"Strong is it to flitte" – A Middle English Poem on Death and Its Pastoral Context.' *Literature and Religion in the Later Middle Ages: Philological Studies in Honor of Siegfried Wenzel.* eds. Richard G. Newhauser and John A. Alford. Binghamton: MRTS, 1995. 319-36.

Parr, Katherine. *The Lamentacion of a synner. The Early Modern Englishwoman: A Facsimile Library of Essential Works.* Part 1, vol. 3, *Katherine Parr.* eds. Betty S. Travitsky and Patrick Cullen. Aldershot: Scolar P, 1996.

Sidney, Mary, Countess of Pembroke. *The Psalmes of David. The Collected Works of Mary Sidney Herbert, Countess of Pembroke.* 2 vols. eds. Margaret P. Hannay, Noel J. Kinnamon, and Michael G. Brennan. Oxford: Clarendon P, 1998. Vol. 2.

Smith, Bruce R. *The Acoustic World of Early Modern England: Attending to the O-Factor.*

Chicago: U of Chicago P, 1999.

Sommer, Doris. '"Not Just a Personal Story": Women's Testimonios and the Plural Self.' *Life/Lines: Theorizing Women's Autobiography.* eds. Bella Brodzki and Celeste Schenck. Ithaca: Cornell UP, 1988. 107-30.

Wang, Andreas. *Der 'miles christianus' im 16 .und 17. Jahrhundert und seine mittelalterliche Tradition.* Frankfurt: Peter Lang, 1975.

Watt, Diane. *Secretaries of God: Women Prophets in Late medieval and Early Modern England.* Cambridge: D. S. Brewer, 1997.

Watt, Tessa. *Cheap Print and Popular Piety, 1550-1640.* Cambridge: Cambridge UP, 1991.

White, Helen C. *The Tudor Books of Private Devotion.* Madison: U of Wisconsin P, 1951.

8

Mary Sidney and Gendered Strategies for the Writing of Poetry

Shannon Miller

Recent work on Mary Sidney has emphasized her role as translator, as patron, and as an original poet. Yet, from Mary Ellen Lamb's study of the Sidney circle to Margaret Hannay's rich biographical work to Wendy Wall's analysis of Sidney's dedicatory poem 'To the Angell Spirit,' most of this criticism has stressed Sidney's biography, especially her identity as the sister of Philip Sidney, his influences on her literary career, and the consequences of his death for her writing. In this essay, I wish to reorient the conversation to address Mary Sidney's own literary production, in particular the strategies she employs in her four original poems: the two dedicatory poems written to accompany a presentation copy of the psalms; the 'Dialogue between two shepherds, Thenot and Piers' written for Queen Elizabeth's planned 1599 state visit to Wilton; and Sidney's elegy on her brother Philip, 'The Dolefull Lay of Clorinda.'[1] While I will not be addressing Sidney's artistic choices in her translations of the psalms, the *Tragedy of Antonie*, the *Discourse of Life and Death*, and the *Triumph of Death*, this sustained focus on the four poems – all engaging issues of audience, the sufficiency of language, and the deployment of generic conventions – allow us to interrogate Mary Sidney's poetic strategies. Because of the period's cultural restrictions on women's speech, these strategies are cognizant of, and the consequence of, gender as her poetry must work specifically to offset resistance to women as producers of poetic texts.

Within the two dedicatory poems to her and Philip's translations of the psalms, Mary Sidney turns to an elaborate re-working of the patron-client system. This reconfiguration of patronage is highlighted by reading 'Even now that Care' in dialogue with the seemingly more personal elegy for her brother, 'To the Angell Spirit.' Mary Sidney's language in each dedication initially seems to distinguish 'private' from 'public' forms of expression. But when read in conjuction, we observe instead the strategic deployment of patronage conventions as she creates a new position: that of female courtier. In the dedicatory poem to the Queen, 'Even now that Care,' Mary Sidney enters into the highly political realm of patronage as she assumes the position of client appealing to monarch. Yet the position of the usually male client requires Mary Sidney to expose and re-imagine certain conventions in patronage. Strangely enough, Mary Sidney achieves this by resurrecting the difficult court interactions of Philip and Queen Elizabeth in order to establish a new relationship between the monarch and her former lady-in-waiting. When viewed in conjunction with the dedicatory poem to Elizabeth, we see how 'To the Angell Spirit' and the 'Dialogue between two shepherds' function as a trio to reconstruct a relationship between Queen and female courtier.

Mary Sidney's use of such strategies also draws us away from an over-emphasis on her emotions for her brother and what have come to be assumptions of the sincerity of her expression of grief over his loss; these assumptions have blinded readers to Mary Sidney's active manipulation of audience and the forms she employs to create space for a female writer's voice.[2] Thus, my readings will also challenge what has come to be the accepted critical view about writing by women: that women's writing is focused on issues of or representations of the 'private' or the internal while men's is oriented toward 'public' subjects and audiences. Despite the post-Lockean evolution of the public versus the private sphere,[3] this anachronistic view of men's and women's language and literary choices as determined by a public/private split has shaped much of the literary criticism on early women writers produced in the last ten years. The emphasis on biography as a tool for reading early women's texts – a strategy that has opened up both many texts and much historical knowledge about women's lives – has fueled this implied opposition in discussions of men's and women's writing.[4] While new historicist criticism has located the production of men's texts within broader cultural issues, historical developments, and 'ideology,' the focus within work on women's writing has been on reading through biographical details or the cultural treatment of women.[5]

Mary Sidney's poetry highlights the difficulty of categorizing women's poetry as more focused on 'private' issues, and the problems of stressing biographical material over, or without a proper balance with, literary techniques and strategies. The 'Dolefull Lay of Clorinda' illustrates how 'private' some of her work appeared to be, while the 'Dialogue between two shepherds' suggests how 'publicly' oriented other poems are. This opposition is in part maintained by the generic identity of these poems – elegy versus pastoral entertainment. Such divisions, of personal grief and of court patronage, are initially sustained within the pair of poems written to accompany her translations of David's psalms. But we will see the lack of efficacy of such categories for both classifying and interpreting these poems once we shift our attention to Sidney's literary choices.

Her literary strategies are highlighted by the occasional situations which prompted Sidney's original authorship of poetry. Three of the poems were produced for Queen Elizabeth's planned visit to Wilton in 1599, though Elizabeth was ultimately unable to visit Wilton as arranged.[6] For the royal visit, Mary Sidney penned the 'Dialogue between two shepherds,' a pastoral entertainment that – if the visit had occurred – would have been performed for the Queen and her court entourage. Mary Sidney also wrote two poems for the occasion which were to accompany the presentation copy of her completed translation of David's psalms.[7] All of these poems, then, work to produce a receptive audience in the Queen herself. Because of the conditions of their production, their integrated purpose in welcoming but also – as we will see – directing Elizabeth's actions, I will be considering them as a unit since they were composed for a particular moment and audience. My attention to the material conditions of presentation and audience thus exposes the problems – and historical inaccuracy – of viewing women's literary production as an isolated, private event.

Private versus Public Poetry: Mary Sidney in Print and in Performance

The 'Dolefull Lay of Clorinda' stands outside this trio of poems, composed most likely for the volume of elegies to celebrate Philip Sidney, *Astrophel*;[8] yet it too complicates any simple classifications of 'privately' versus 'publicly' directed poetry. Positioned in genre and in subject as a private poetic production, from its opening the 'Lay' discusses the problem of finding an audience: 'Ay me, to whom shall I my case complaine / That may compassion my impatient griefe?' (1-2). In her search for an audience, and consequently the production of this poem, Clorinda rejects the 'heavens' who have been 'the authors' of her 'unremedied wo,' and finds 'my selfe' one of her few possible auditors because only she can understand the pain and the loss she has experienced: 'Sith none alive like sorrowfull remaines' (19-20). The 'Dolefull Lay' continues to reject a possible, public audience until the focus of the poem shifts onto the body of Astrophel/Philip Sidney. The conventional elegiac apotheosis of Astrophel/Philip may or may not offer emotional consolation for his loss, but the highlighting of Sidney's 'Phoenix' traits become part of the political process of producing a Protestant martyr in Philip, a process that is repeated in most of Mary Sidney's poems. The language of rebirth, 'Ah no: it is not dead, ne can it die, / But lives for aie, in blisfull Paradise' (67-8), is a dominant trope through the poem to its end as Philip is transformed into 'a new-borne babe' who lives in this Paradisical space 'in everlasting blis' (69, 85).

A tension between the public or political purpose of the poem and its effectiveness as a conventional elegy plays out this issue of public versus private in a slightly modified form. Mary Sidney produces this elegy through an invocation of personal grief – a particularly authorizing emotion for women's production of poetry – that she combines with a purposeful rejection of audience.[9] The poem highlights the private nature of Clorinda's, the narrator's, grief through the images of intense physical pain which punctuate the poem: 'where shall I unfold my *inward* pain / That my *enriven* heart may find reliefe?' (3-4; my emphasis). Clorinda can find no audience for her 'inward' grief which underscores her pain, 'enriven' into her heart. Sidney constructs the poem as an 'inward' expression that never achieves, or requires, an external audience. This can offset some of the cultural resistance to a woman publishing as she is abdicating the 'public' component of publication. The purposeful 'privatizing' of her emotion and her poem can allow for its production, though the cost seems to be the physicalized pain of grief that propels this 'private' poem forward.

As a result, this poem cannot be said to do the 'work' of an elegy that Peter Sacks has outlined in *The English Elegy*. Though the final two stanzas of the poem 'shift [the] focus back to the mourner, who, no longer isolated, speaks from within a community' (Sacks 62), these framing stanzas seem very likely to have been composed by Spenser as he laced the various elegies together to form the elegiac narrative of *Astrophel*. As the Oxford edition of Mary Sidney Herbert's poems suggests, Spenser 'certainly does supply verses that set up a pastoral framework for the other elegies, thus providing an unusually coherent volume' (124). This suggests that Mary Sidney's composition of the poem ends at line 96, and that Spenser's framing verse begins with 'Which when she ended had, another swaine / Of gentle wit and daintie sweet device' (l. 97). The editors of the Oxford edition buttress their editorial selection of line 96 as Mary Sidney's conclusion for the poem by examining the physical layout of the *Astrophel* volume. The page facing 'The Lay' contains the two final stanzas which introduce Lodowick Bryskett's poem, thus visually these introductory lines are divided from the voice of Clorinda in the 'Lay.' Once we read the poem as concluding at line 96, we see that the apotheosis of Sidney may praise him and elevate him spiritually, but it does nothing for the chief mourner: 'But our owne selves that here in dole are drent. / Thus do we weep and wail, and wear our eies, / Mourning in others, our owne miseries' (94-6).[10] Her emotional experience is as filled with 'inward pain' at the poem's conclusion as it was at the elegy's beginning (3).

Yet the poem's sustained recording of private grief is occurring in print; this 'publishing' of Mary Sidney's loss has a significant political goal as it works with the other elegies within *Astrophel* to construct the posthumous figure of Philip Sidney, martyred Protestant hero. Identifying Philip as a 'Phoenix' positions him as both a Christ-like figure, making way for his identity as a Protestant martyr, but it also positions him in a competitive relationship to Elizabeth's encomistic machine. Mary Sidney re-figures the Queen's popular Phoenix image in a much more literal application of the re-birth motif as he reappears to us as a 'new-borne babe' 'in blissful Paradise' (69, 68). The emphasis on the privative nature of her emotion continually gives way, even prompts the move to, the political identity of her brother and the exigencies of the patronage system that marked her brother's relationship with the Queen.

The 'Dialogue between two shepherds, Thenot and Piers' sustains this focus on a system of praise and patronage, allowing us a first glimpse of Mary Sidney's unique experience as a powerful female patroness whose power at Wilton could at least compete with, if never overshadow, Elizabeth's position as the land's most powerful patron. The 'Dialogue' draws explicitly upon the Queen's conventional imagery of praise: she is 'Astrea,' the figure of divine justice who has returned to earth during the reign of Elizabeth. The poem, invoking many of the fears that mark Spenser's proem to Book 3 of the *Faerie Queene*, emphasizes the threat of language's inadequacy to convey the divinity that is Astrea/ Queen Elizabeth.[11] Thenot offers conventional praise as influenced by Neo-Platonic thought in his opening three lines[12]: 'I sing divine ASTREA's praise, / O Muses! help my wits to raise, / And heave my Verses higher' (1-3). This language of praise will be, throughout the dialogue, countered by Piers's expression of a purer, non-hyperbolic expression of virtue: 'Thou need'st the truth but plainly tell, / Which much I doubt thou canst not well / Thou art so oft a lier' (4-6). This debate over the insufficiency of language and the misleading elements of conventional court praise structures the 'Dialogue' which then ends with 'silence'[13]:

> Thenot: Then Piers, of friendship tell me why,
> My meaning true, my words should lye,
> And strive in vain to raise her?
> Piers: Words from conceit do only rise,
> Above conceit her honor flies,
> But silence, nought can praise her. (55-60)

This exchange, throughout the 'Dialogue,' positions the Protestant simple style against the elements of Elizabeth's court-generated panegyrics.   The 'Dialogue' presents a conventional Protestant resistance to the use of imagery, metaphor, and other tropes to attempt a description of divinity. And within such statements about poetics are embedded the highly politicized issues of proper Protestant worship. As Barbara Lewalski helpfully glosses the final line of Herbert's 'Jordan I,' 'the poetics implied [here] . . . poses instead a direct recourse to the Bible as repository of truth: the speaker calls upon biblical models and biblical poetic resources . . . and associates himself straightforwardly with the Psalmist in heartfelt and uncontrived (plain) utterance' (4). As Lewalski outlines in *Protestant Poetics*, the psalmist is the purest conveyer of God's truth. A translator of the psalms – whose completed project was to be presented to the Queen on this same visit to Wilton – Mary Sidney could be considered a figure for Piers, the voice of resistance to hyperbolic language. Within the 'Dialogue,' it is the Protestant language-theorist, Piers, who is given both the final word and the winning position which 'silences' such 'praise.'

Yet this is a somewhat odd position for Mary Sidney to take up given both the literary production of her brother and, more significantly, the tenor and style of the Sidney-Pembroke Psalter. Since the performance of this court pastoral was to accompany Elizabeth's receipt of the psalms, the pastoral entertainment ideally should be read in conjunction with Mary Sidney's identity as a psalmist. Lewalski argues that these are not translations that present an unadorned rendering of David's psalms. These 'extremely artful poems, with their intricate and almost infinite varieties of stanzaic forms and metrical patterns, and their fine adjustment of contemporary poetic forms and metaphors . . . create a new persona for the Psalmist. He is transfigured as an Elizabethan poet' (241). As such, these psalms resemble the poetry more of a Thenot than a Piers. In this light, the 'Dialogue's' status as a critique of non-Christian, non-Protestant language theory gives way to commentary about Elizabeth's praise machine.

We see a gradual undermining, within the 'Dialogue,' of the language of the Cult of Elizabeth encapsulated in references to Astrea. Piers argues convincingly for the inadequacy of language which describes Astrea as 'A manly Palm, a maiden Bay, / Her verdure never dying' (50-51). The imagery seems initially contradictory as it invokes the male and female elements of the 'Phoenix' so common within the imagery of Elizabeth. But Thenot's praise seems at best clumsy, at worst quite insulting. Piers highlights this in his response: 'Palm oft is crooked, Bay is low / She still upright, still high doth grow' (52-3). This final exchange between them, in which Thenot's description becomes laughably, as well as ineffectually, grounded in the physical, prompts Thenot's concession to Piers' challenge: he admits that though 'my meaning . . . is true,' 'my words . . . lye,' and consequently he 'strive[s] in vain to raise her' (56-7). Piers offers no actual solution to this quandary of language: except for 'silence, nought can praise her' (60). Yet what we will see silenced is not poetic production but the form of court praise of which this 'Dialogue' initially appeared to be a part. The structure of court patronage – centered around Elizabeth and expressed through a conventional set of panegyrics which are questioned here – receives a critical reworking in this poem. This embedded critique of a certain form of patronage initiates a pattern that resonates through Mary Sidney's other addresses to Elizabeth.

As Margaret Hannay has remarked, the dedicatory poem to Queen Elizabeth, 'Even now that Care,' functions as a pair with the elegy to Philip, 'To the Angell Spirit.' Yet we can observe an active interaction between the two poems: they play off of each other in order to highlight the issues of Protestant identity, political hierarchy, and patronage. While Mary Sidney is clearly attempting to validate her own voice as a writer through the figure of, and the death of, her brother, she combines this purpose with an explicitly political presentation of self and of the Sidney family. Hannay describes the

political purpose of Mary Sidney's poetic choices: 'As the last strong voice of
the Dudley/Sidney alliance left in Elizabethan England, the countess . . .
supported the Protestant cause . . . through her establishment of a hagiography
which elevated her brother to the status of Protestant martyr' ('Dedication'
165). Yet while most critics have emphasized the private nature of Mary
Sidney's grief in 'To the Angell Spirit,' the language describing Philip
Sidney's loss, even martyrdom, throughout the poem consistently pushes
beyond the boundaries of the 'private' or the 'personal.' The ostensible
'private' elegy does political work. Mary Sidney is always aware of the
audience of the Queen, and of the public role of her grief in the elegy;
consistently, 'Even now that Care' and 'To the Angell Spirit' record within
themselves their planned 'publication' to the Queen. Mary Sidney constructs
both of these dedicatory poems to address each other, and to redefine each
poem's message because of the pairing. As we will see, the appeal for the
Queen's readership within 'Even now that Care' invokes the memory of
Philip throughout, a fusion of elegy with a political dedicatory poem that
makes this poem every bit as much of a public performance as the 'Dialogue'
would have been.

Mary Sidney as Female Courtier: Rethinking Patronage

From the beginning of 'Even now that Care,' Mary Sidney stresses the
political identity of the Queen, reminding her 'that the fate of Europe rests in
her hands' (Hannay, 'Dedication' 152). The opening stanza of this poem
declares Elizabeth's political cares, ones which appear to leave no space for
the private nature of poetry writing.

> Even now that Care which on thy Crowne attends
> and with thy happy greatnes dayly growes
> Tells me thrise sacred Queene my Muse offends,
> and of respect to thee the line out goes,
> One instant will, or willing can shee lose
> I say not reading, but receiving Rimes,
> On whom in chiefe dependeth to dispose
> what Europe acts in theise most active times? (1-8)

The poem continues to describe the Queen's active political role,[14] but also to suggest the possibility that she might have time for this gift of the psalms: 'Business m[u]st ebb, though Leasure never flowe' (18); when this 'ebb' occurs, the Queen will have a moment for these 'Postes of Dutie and Goodwill' (19). But Mary Sidney also imagines, within this political portrait, the Queen's receipt of this gift and her reading of the psalms. The Queen is obviously constructed as an audience through these opening stanzas, one of many immediate contrasts with the opening of 'To the Angell spirit.' There, Mary Sidney engages Philip as a muse figure, and the opening stanzas stress the production of these elegiac verses. The address is highly personal, reflecting the physical pain of both his death, 'Deepe wounds enlarg'd, long festred in their gall / fresh bleeding smart' (19-20), as well as Mary Sidney's grief: 'not eie but hart teares fall. / Ah memorie what needs this new arrest?' (20-1).

Such immediately apparent distinctions between the two poems break down as we turn to Mary Sidney's strategies in this poem to gain a patron for her poetry as well as for her religious and political purposes. We see two poems that work as a pair to promote the larger Sidney goals. Mary Sidney turns back to the figure of Philip in 'To the Angell spirit,' invoking his own poetry, his role as her muse, and his client-patron relationship with Queen Elizabeth in order to explore the conflicts in the patronage structure. Mary Sidney's invocation of her 'Muse' as Philip highlights the contested patronage relationship that had existed between Philip and Elizabeth, a mode of interaction she reconstructs to model a new form of patronage which stresses spiritual over material rewards. This process of redefining a patronage relationship with the Queen occurs through Mary Sidney's exploration of types of bonds – spiritual and material – that will culminate in her spiritual union of Queen Elizabeth and King David. Besides acknowledging the relationship between the Queen and her brother, Mary Sidney can offer a match that takes account of the highly unusual role of the female courtier, one unsuited to the normal exchanges of the court patronage system.

In the first step of her multi-pronged strategy for acquiring patronage, Mary Sidney draws Elizabeth into accepting the psalms through a series of echoes to Philip's own poetry. In the first poem of Philip Sidney's *Astrophel and Stella*, the narrator faces a similar problem in his need to create an audience. He attempts to lure Stella in as a reader, and then as a lover: 'Pleasure might cause her read, reading might make her know / Knowledge might pity win, and pity grace obtain' (*A&S* 1.3-4). Mary Sidney pursues this same pattern to elicit gradual acceptance from the Queen; first she will prompt the queen to accept the poems in the 'One instant' that she will 'willing . . . lose.' Initially, the poem models the moment when the Queen accepts the Rimes – but doesn't read them: 'I say not reading, but receiving Rimes.' Once received from Mary Sidney, the poet will 'cherish some hope they shall acceptance finde' (10). And knowing the queen's 'grace' and her 'abler . . . mind' (12), she will be prompted to the enjoyable 'Exercise' of reading the poems, an undertaking others would consider 'toile' (16). These 'Postes of Dutie and Goodwill' will 'presse' Queen Elizabeth to allow them to 'offer' what they 'owe': these poems, then, will influence her – with some implication of coercion – to read them.

While the poem parallels the opening to *Astrophel and Stella*, it also invokes its author. The opening lines of the poem to Elizabeth, 'thrise sacred Queene my Muse offends / and of respects to thee the line out goes' (3-4) contradict the opening claim in 'To the Angell spirit.' If the psalms are, as Mary Sidney states within 'To the Angell spirit,' 'To thee pure sprite, to thee along addres't' (1), the need for a poem dedicating her and Philip's translation of the psalms to Elizabeth is entirely negated; the 'lines' of the psalms cannot both go out to the Queen and also be 'to thee alone . . . addres't.' What Mary Sidney's two opening dedications do is place Philip and Queen Elizabeth in competition, a situation Mary Sidney generates at the beginning of both poems. What emerges is a portrait of the contestation, even competition, that had marked Elizabeth's relationship with Philip.[15] While it was common for writers to dedicate to multiple patrons, this did not apply to dedicating work to the Queen. Her position as monarch demanded, and conventionally received, the singular attention that these two openings deny.

Mary Sidney furthers this sense of competition through her re-invocation of the Muse figure. In 'Even now that Care,' her 'muse' has offered offense to Elizabeth.[16] Yet Mary Sidney's 'muse' in both poems is the spirit of her dead brother. Certainly there is no question of his identity within the first stanza of 'To the Angell spirit':

> To thee pure sprite, to thee alone's addres't
>   this coupled worke, by double int'rest thine:
>   First rais'de by thy blest hand, and what is mine
> inspired by thee, thy secrett power imprest.
>   So dar'd *my Muse* with thine it selfe combine,
>   as mortall stufe with that which is divine,

Thy lightning beames give lustre to the rest . . . (1-7; my emphasis)

The opening lines, after establishing that Philip is the only person to whom the poems are addressed, fuse Philip with the conventional figure of the muse: she is 'inspired' by him and 'imprest' by his secret power. Philip becomes the artistic inspiration that drives her forward in her completion of the psalms, 'First rais'de by thy blest hand, and what is mine / *inspird* by thee, thy secret power *imprest*' (3-4; my emphasis).

When Mary Sidney then says in her complementary poem to Elizabeth that 'my Muse offends,' the meaning becomes grounded in the specifics of the patronage relationship between Philip Sidney and Queen Elizabeth. Philip Sidney constantly offended the Queen, resulting in his forestalled hopes at court as well as stymieing the Protestant alliance's plans. Mary Sidney will recall this conflict within the poems in order to provide a critique of an overly material view of patronage and alliance. She offers the figure of Philip as an ideal for a spiritual form of exchange and obligation because of his transcendent state. Elizabeth and the reader are thus directed to prefer other, less materially-based forms of alliance: Elizabeth's protection of these psalms, of Protestant verse as a form, and the spiritual union with King David that symbolizes the Queen's union both with these verses and their political and religious values. The apotheosis of Philip, his martyrdom and affiliation with Christ, establishes an 'other worldly' resonance in 'To the Angell Spirit' that Mary Sidney employs to address the practices of patronage in 'Even now that Care.'

What Mary Sidney will suggest within this poem is a break from certain conventions of patronage. She initiates this by highlighting property, ownership, and debt in 'Even now that Care.' The language of debt and ownership that runs through the dedication to Elizabeth highlights issues of gifts, claims, responsibility, but also exchange. The convention of patronage – a highly-organized system of gift-giving – is that a client will always owe a 'debt of Infinits.' One cannot pay back a patron such as the Queen. Nor can Mary Sidney ever repay the figure of Philip to whom she owes this oxymoron of a 'debt of Infinits' in 'To the Angell spirit' (35). She turns to heavily mercantile language in the seventh stanza of this poem to illustrate the contraction of and in such debts:

Oh, when to this Accompt, this cast upp Summe,

> this Reckoning made, this Audit of my woe,
> I call my thoughts, whence so strange passions flowe;
> How workes my hart, my sences striken dumbe?
> that would thee more, then ever hart could showe,
> and all too short who knewe thee best doth knowe
> There lives no witt that may thy praise become. (43-9)

In this account of her artistic and personal relationship with Philip, she invokes accounting language four different times to emphasize her inability to make an 'accompt,' 'cast upp Summe,' provide a 'Reckoning,' or survive an 'Audit.' The very repetition of the language illustrates the incommensurable nature of her debt.[17] The more she tries to account for it, the more infinite its traits are revealed to be.

Such language of debt, in contrast, is constantly accounted for within the poem to Elizabeth. Mary repeatedly describes the debt she and Philip owe:

> Then these the Postes of Dutie and Goodwill
> shall presse to *offer* what their Senders *owe*;
> Which once in two, now in one Subject goe,
> the poorer left, the richer reft awaye:
> Who better might (O might ah word of woe,)
> haue giv'n for mee what I for him *defraye*. (19-24; my emphasis)

In this passage, they 'owe' Elizabeth poems which are offered to 'defraye' the debt that has been incurred. The patronage relationship in its ideal form – one observed within conventional addresses to Elizabeth and for her patronage – cannot have its gifts, which establish ownership and then require payment or the 'defraying' of an old debt, detailed.

Not so here. These poems are

> small parcell of that undischarged rent,
> from which nor paines, nor paiments can us free.
> And yet enough to cause our neighbours see
> wee will our best, though scanted in our will:
> and those nighe feelds where sow'n thy favors bee
> unwalthy doo, not elce unworthie till. (35-40)

Though Mary Sidney acknowledges that no 'paines, nor paiments can us free' from the abstract, unrepayable debt they owe Elizabeth, she continues in this stanza to ground their connection to the Queen through reference to gifts of land. Instead of gesturing toward the abstract nature of the debt she owes to Philip, Mary Sidney 'accompts' for the gifts from Elizabeth: land which the Sidney family had received from the crown. This stanza further stresses the physicality of the land: they owe 'rent' on it; 'our neighbours' look onto their act of (artistic) husbandry; and they try to 'sow' her favors from the 'nighe feelds.' By grounding the issue of favor so explicitly within the language of land grants – the primary wealth which the nobility held at the pleasure of the monarch – Elizabeth's material awarding of favors is highlighted. And by gesturing to the feudal exchange process by which subjects till the land to pay the lord an agreed-upon tribute or rent, Sidney describes an explicitly contractual form of obligation. Through such imagery, Mary Sidney offers a 'Reckoning' for the abstract, unaccountable debt a client, and subject, are expected to 'owe' to their monarch. This detailing of the exchange that is patronage exposes its material, literal identity, and simultaneously offers an ideal vision of an abstract, non-material form of obligation and exchange. In part, Mary Sidney appears to be critiquing the form of court patronage that is grounded on the exchanges of such literal forms of favor: the distribution of lands and favors from which her family would have at times profited and at others would have suffered.

Mary Sidney now moves from detailing the debt to offering a substitution – within and between the poems – for the figure who embodies this ideal of the 'Infinit'; the portrait that emerges of her brother both sustains praise of him while offering an alternate model of obligation and alliance. The poem to Elizabeth explicitly challenges the Queen's identity as a sign for ultimate sufficiency. When Mary Sidney poses the question, 'For in our worke what bring wee but thine own' (41), the question resonates with us: Is it her own? Mary Sidney has already granted to Philip the most complete image of patronage in describing him as the source from which all acts of tribute flow:

> And sithe it hath no further scope to goe,
>   nor other purpose but to honor thee,
>   Thee in thy workes where all the Graces bee,
> As little streames with all their all doe flowe
>   to their great sea, due tribute's gratefull see:
>   so press my thoughts my burthened thoughts in mee,

To pay the debt of Infinits I owe (29-35)

As Margaret Hannay has stated, the dedicatory poem to the Queen 'does not contain the fulsome praise of Elizabeth one would expect from the title, from her obsequious 1601 letter to the queen, and from the decorum of the cult of the *Faerie Queene*' (152). But Mary Sidney does much more than not praise the queen; she makes Philip the image of an all-dispensing fount of grace and tribute. As such, Mary Sidney grants to her brother what another client – Edmund Spenser – grants to the Queen herself in the proem to Book 6 of the *Faerie Queene*. There, his 'most dreaded Soueraine / That from your selfe I doe this vertue bring / And to your selfe doe it returne againe: / So from the Ocean all riuers spring / And tribute backe repay as to their King' (6, Proem, 7, 1-5). In both of these images, the expansiveness of the ocean combines with its resonance as the source of all to testify to a completeness in Philip usually only granted to the monarch: all comes from the ruler such that any gift to the monarch is simply an acknowledgment of his/her infinite value. Where other clients award this imagery of the ultimate patron only to the Queen, Mary Sidney grants it to Philip.

This language of sufficiency in the poem to and about Philip Sidney is continued with the reference to his 'great worth,' praise which ends in awarding him the title of 'Phoenix' (36; 38). In another displacement of Elizabeth, who has already been displaced as the psalms' patron and as the ideal patron, Mary Sidney now grants to her brother the language of the Cult of Elizabeth. This moment resonates with the 'Dialogue' between Thenot and Piers. In ending the dialogue by validating Piers's position, and his consequent 'silencing' of the language of praise encorporating the figure of Astrea as well as of the figure of the Phoenix, Mary Sidney usurps praise conventionally offered to Elizabeth for her production of Philip's image. And we have already seen her make similar use of Elizabeth's conventional imagery; in the 'Dolefull Lay,' Mary Sidney transformed the dead body of Philip Sidney into a Phoenix-like figure who 'lives' again in 'blisfull Paradise . . . like a new-borne babe' (67-8). All four poems work as a unit as they elaborate on this specific image, constructing and re-enforcing meaning between as well as within each work. The pairing with 'Angell Spirit' provides the context for this sustained attack on Elizabethan patronage conventions: the abstract form of the exchange described between Mary and Philip offers an alternate spiritual model of obligation. This will set the stage for a new connection between Elizabeth, these poems, and the figure with whom the Queen is to enter into a new relationship: King David.

After delineating, through these various poems, a portrait of the traditional practices of patronage, Mary Sidney begins to construct the patroness that Elizabeth should be, both to these poems and to the Protestant alliance that they promote. At line 42, she begins detailing the kind of place Elizabeth should construct for this translation:

> What English is, by many names is thine.
> There humble Lawrells in thy shadowes growne
> To garland others woorld, themselves repine.
> Thy brest the Cabinet, thy seat the shrine,
> Where Muses hang their vowed memories:
> Where Wit, where Art, where all that is divine
> Conceived best, and best defended lies. (42-8)

While the opening of the poem emphasizes Elizabeth's political obligations and concerns, Mary Sidney now turns the dedication into an assertion about the need for the protection of national poetry. Elizabeth needs to serve as protection for such 'humble Lawrells' that will grow in the 'shadowes' of her protection. Elizabeth needs to make her 'brest' the Cabinet in which they will be held, valued, and loved. Her 'seat' or throne must create a space for honor, thus prompting the necessary tribute from others. The threat of not providing protection for a national poetry is the rejection by other nations of such artistic production. Mary Sidney expresses this concern within the oddly constructed sentence that opens stanza 7:

> Which if men did not (as they doe) confesse,
> and wronging worlds woold otherwise consent:
> Yet here who mynds so meet a Patrones
> for Authors state or writings argument? (49-52)

If Elizabeth does not provide protection for this English, Protestant, and politicized poetry, then men might not 'confess' the 'Wit' and 'Art' of English poetic production. And further, they might not admit – as the English do 'Yet here' – that Elizabeth is 'so meet a Patrones.'

Mary Sidney has reconstructed a patronage role that stands outside of the distribution of material grace and will turn to images of, and the exchange of, metaphysical grace. She now directs the Queen toward the figure for the psalms, King David, establishing a relationship between monarchs as this 'King' is sent to 'a Queene.' The union that Mary Sidney will propose recalls the earlier invocations of Philip and his poetry; she has created a situation in which Elizabeth will accept and read these psalms, a process that is made equivalent to receiving a suitor or lover. Like Philip's opening gamut in *Astrophel and Stella*, 'Pleasure might cause her read, reading might make her know / Knowledge might pity win, and pity grace obtain' (3-4). The evocation of Philip's Petrarchan sonnet sequence appropriately fuses the language of spiritual and physical forms of love and the distribution of 'grace'; Elizabeth's acceptance of the psalms becomes the 'grace' that she will offer to King David, and that he will provide for her.

Sidney consequently converts the political situation into a private space for the Queen's engagement with the psalms, a private space for reading but also for the undercurrent of romance. Mary Sidney returns again and again to the appropriateness of this match between the King and the Queen to whom she sends him: 'A King should onely to a Queene be sent. / Gods loued choise unto his chosen love: / Deuotion to Deuotions President' (53-5). The balance achieved in these lines continues in the next stanza as the figure of David is transformed into a perfect mate:

> And who sees ought, but see how justly square
> his haughtie Ditties to thy glorious daies?
> How well beseeming thee his Triumphs are?
> his hope, his zeale, his praier, plaint, and praise,
> Needles thy person to their height to raise:
> Lesse need to bend them downe to thy degree. (57-62)

For a woman, a Queen, who had struggled over the issue of rank in considering a mate, Mary Sidney offers the ideal solution: King David. His traits match Elizabeth's; his poetry perfectly describes her. The ideal match, he is also a perfect Petrarchan courtier, mapping to the many forms of 'grace' that Elizabeth can provide and receive.

Throughout this sequence, Mary Sidney also provides to Elizabeth accounts of her unchallenged power which will be acknowledged by all: 'Kings on a Queene enforst their states to lay; / . . . / Men drawne by worth a woman to obey' (81, 83). Such descriptions of gender reversals accord with the courtly deference offered a lady in courtship but were also the political realities of Elizabeth's court. It was this power structure at court that Mary's brother found impossible to accept; the implicit challenges that Philip Sidney posed to Elizabeth's power are, ultimately, rejected in Mary Sidney's poem. She thus employs Philip as a strategy, invoking the competitive relationship between Queen and courtier, which she then replaces with images of union and descriptions of a reconstructed gender hierarchy pleasing to Elizabeth.

Mary Sidney complements this with another reconstruction of the relationship between Philip and the Queen. The language of love conventions, highlighted through resonance with *Astrophel and Stella*, also casts Mary Sidney as a matchmaker, even a panderess, as she arranges for 'A King [who] should onely to a Queene bee sent' (53). The procuring tone in this line invokes the different status of, and the different responsibilities of, the female courtier, a difference that glances back to Philip's interactions with the Queen but looks forward to a new relationship between Mary and Elizabeth. Mary Sidney returns to the very issue that had caused Philip to 'offend' the Queen. The French marriage controversy, in which Philip attempted to direct the Queen away from marriage, resulted in his devastating loss of court favor. Now, Mary invokes her brother's previous political error, but offers a new response: the spiritualized union with King David. The invocation of her brother's Petrarchan verses becomes the offer of the husband whom Elizabeth had been directed to reject by Mary's brother. This allows Mary Sidney to reconfigure the relationship of the Queen to the Sidney family, but it also allows her to establish a relationship between female courtier and Queen. In her brokering of a marriage deal, Mary Sidney appears to invoke the form of relationship that female courtiers did have with the female monarch: as a lady-in-waiting during her youth, Mary Sidney would have tended to the Queen's more personal needs and to the bed chamber. The interaction between Mary Sidney and Elizabeth is not about exchange of material favors, of land, of power. Such patronage would have been less useful for a female client. Mary Sidney establishes a different form of exchange between Queen and 'handmaid' (90): erotic and spiritual satisfaction for the Queen, poetic and religious protection for the Sidney alliance.

Mary Sidney's address to the Queen in 'Even now that Care' thus combines the concerns of a poet with the project of the Sidney-Dudley alliance. Employing the memory of her brother, both as the Protestant martyr and an English poet, Mary Sidney creates an audience for her psalms and her politics. As in 'To the Angell spirit,' the figure of Philip serves a strategic purpose: he recalls past engagements with Elizabeth as patron and as queen. While Mary Sidney may initially offer Philip as a figure embedded in a better patronage model, she employs these images in order to model for the queen the need to protect these poems and to promote Elizabeth's and the nation's spiritual happiness. Poetic production, personal desire, and politics are thus fused in Mary Sidney's bid for patronage.

It is in the dialogue among Mary Sidney's four poems that we can locate many of the difficulties that a woman writer faced, but more importantly discern what techniques she employed to validate her own acts of writing. Though also a translator of great skill, Mary Sidney's translations do not offer us the same view of creating an audience nor do they as fully expose the complex matrix of poetic strategies she uses to offset cultural resistance to women's compositions; neither the *Tragedy of Antonie* nor the *Discourse of Life and Death*, the two translations that Mary Sidney publishes, carry with them the intricate dedicatory apparatus that accompanied the Psalms. It is in the context of appealing for patronage, of making public her own acts of creation, that Mary Sidney most fully shows the inventive strategies which allowed her to combine issues of political action, personal remembrance, and poetic production within her writings.

Notes

[1] The 'Lay of Clorinda' is the other poem that could be considered an original work by Mary Sidney. The debate about its authorship is clearly and succinctly summarized by Margaret Hannay in *Philip's Phoenix* 64-67; she also makes a successful argument here for Sidney's authorship, one which is the basis of my decision to include the poem in this discussion of Sidney's works. The recent attribution of the poem to Edmund Spenser is one of the strongest reasons to question his authorship of the 'Lay.' As Hannay explains, it was 'generally accepted' to be by the Countess until 1912; that year, Ernest de Selincourt argued that Spenser wrote it in her name (65). Besides Selincourt's questionable attribution, in the face of the original publication of the poem as Mary Sidney's, the internal evidence of the poem argues for Mary Sidney's authorship. The poem repeats many of the motifs within Sidney's other two poems which preface the translated Psalms. The physicality of one

of the opening images in the poem, 'where shall I unfold my inward pain / That my *enriven* heart may find reliefe?' (3-4), is stylistically parallel to Mary Sidney's imagery of wounding in 'To the Angell spirit.' More unique is Sidney's use of economic language to describe her emotional loss in the 'Lay': 'to my selfe my plaints shall back retourne, / To pay their usury with doubled paines' (21-2). The language of debts which cannot be repaid runs through both of the dedicatory poems to the Psalms, and we see this same vocabulary of accounting used to describe her relationship to Philip: 'Oh! when to this Accompt, this cast upp Summe, / this Reckoning made, this Audit of my woe' (43-4). The tradition of attribution, combined with such stylistic connections, seems adequate reason to accept Mary Sidney's authorship.

2 Wendy Wall's 'Our Bodies/Our Texts?: Renaissance Women and the Trials of Authorship' does explore Mary Sidney's strategies. Yet the prominence that she gives to the memory of Philip in Sidney's elegy implies that Mary Sidney's abnegation of herself as a writer within the poem, her 'poignant self-erasure' (58), is a product more of emotion than of poetic strategy.

3 Locke's configuration of the family in his 'Treatises on Government' offers a counter-image to the homology of king rules over the state as father rules over the family that had been the basis of Renaissance political theory. See Leonard Tennenhouse and Nancy Armstrong's *Imaginary Puritan* for a discussion of this shift and its dependence on rationality (171-4). For the explicit use of 'public' versus 'private' and the development of the opposition of these terms after the Restoration, see J.G.A. Pocock.

4 A notable exception to this in work on Mary Sidney is Margaret Hannay's article, '"Doo What Men May Sing": Mary Sidney and the Tradition of Admonitory Dedication,' which outlines the many explicit political parallels and topical references in the dedicatory poem to the Queen, 'Even now may Care.'

5 The focus on biography in much of the criticism has become a standard complaint. Jonathan Goldberg is a major critic of this approach in his *Desiring Women Writing*; in praising Elaine Hobby's work, he remarks that 'unlike many other studies, its focus is not on individual authors, and it does not aim at biographical readings, in which women's texts are indices to their lives or the lives of women *tout court*, inevitably cast in privative terms' (13).

6 Elizabeth would visit Wilton at a later time, but Mary Sidney, busy attending to her sick husband, was unable to be there (*Philip's Phoenix*

240n3).

[7] Margaret Hannay suggests that Mary Sidney finished the psalms specifically for Elizabeth's planned visit (*Philip's Phoenix* 84).

[8] This collection of seven elegies, *Astrophel: A Pastorall Elegie upon the Death of the Most Noble and Valorous Knight, Sir Philip Sidney*, was published in 1595, though Sidney himself had died in 1586. The collection includes elegies by Edmund Spenser, Lodowick Bryskett, Matthew Roydon, Sir Walter Raleigh, and Edward Dyer. The gap in time between Philip Sidney's death and the publication of this collection of elegies points to the larger political purpose of the volume.

[9] According to the editors of the Oxford edition of Mary Sidney Herbert's poetry, 'the need to commemorate the dead could override gender restrictions, making the elegy one of the few forms of original writing open to women' (120). They list the numerous Renaissance women who authored elegies, including Anne, Margaret, and Jane Seymour, Lady Elizabeth Cooke Russell, and Anne Dacre Howard, Countess of Arundel.

[10] One's attribution of this poem – to Edmund Spenser or to Mary Sidney – obviously influences one's reading of it. Sacks, who attributes 'The Doleful Lay of Clorinda' to Edmund Spenser, reads the lament and the framing poetry as Spenser's; this produces a very different judgment of how, or how successfully, the elegy functions. He reads it as an extremely successful elegy, in his terms, because it does the 'work' of elegy by generating another figure onto whom the mourner can reattach: 'It is to this new-found or rather newly created object [the consolatory figure of the heavenly infant] that the mourner can now transfer her feelings and thereby complete the work of mourning' (60).

[11] One of the arguments used to negate Mary Sidney's authorship of the 'Lay' has been the poem's Spenserian echoes, an indisputable point. But the 'Dialogue' is filled with a similar number of Spenserian themes and motifs: the imagery of Astrea; Thenot's concern with raising his 'wits' (2); the concern with language's sufficiency. The Spenserian echoes within the 'Dialogue,' about which Mary Sidney's authorship has never been questioned, help support a claim for Sidney's authorship of the 'Dolefull Lay.'

[12] A footnote to the 'Dialogue' in the *Norton Anthology of English Literature*, Vol. 1, indicates that Thenot expresses Neo-Platonic values while Piers is a spokesperson for the Protestant plain style (1047n3).

[13] For discussion of the insufficiency of language in the 'Dolefull Lay,' see

Elaine Beilin, *Redeeming Eve* 141-2.

[14] Hannay makes this point in '"Doo What Men May Sing": Mary Sidney and the Tradition of Admonitory Dedication.' The opening stanzas 'serve primarily as a reminder that the fate of Europe rests in her hands . . . Like her family and like the Geneva Protestants, Mary Sidney apparently believed that Elizabeth herself was the key to the establishment of the Protestant faith, in Europe as well as England' (152).

[15] Critics such as Louis Montrose have documented the effect of Philip Sidney's often audacious literary directives to the Queen, but for an exploration of a more personally-interactive sequence between Philip and Elizabeth, see Maureen Quilligan's 'Sidney and his Queen.'

[16] The line also means that in the face of such political cares, her presentation of poems may be considered inappropriate because of 'that Care which in thy Crowne attends . . . my Muse offends' (1, 3).

[17] Mary Sidney's language here seems to invoke her brother's sonnet #18 in *Astrophel and Stella* which also draws upon the conceit of an 'audit' and a financial reckoning.

Works Cited

Armstrong, Nancy and Leonard Tennenhouse. *The Imaginary Puritan: Literature, Intellectual Labor, and the Origins of Personal Life*. Berkeley: U of California P, 1992.

Goldberg, Jonathan. *Desiring Women Writing: English Renaissance Examples*. Stanford: Stanford UP, 1997.

Hannay, Margaret P. "'Doo What Men May Sing' Mary Sidney and the Tradition of Admonitory Dedication.' *Silent But for the Word: Tudor Women as Patrons, Translators, and Writers of Religious Works*. ed. Margaret P. Hannay. Kent: Kent State UP, 1985. 149-65.

_____. *Philip's Phoenix: Mary Sidney, Countess of Pembroke*. New York: Oxford UP, 1990.

_____, Noel J. Kinnamon and Michael G. Brennan. 'Introduction.' *Collected Works of Mary Sidney Herbert*. Vol. 1. 1-77.

Lamb, Mary Ellen. *Gender and Authorship in the Sidney Circle*. Madison: U of Wisconsin P, 1990.

Lewalski, Barbara. *Protestant Poetics and the Seventeenth-Century Religious Lyric*. Princeton: Princeton UP, 1979.

Montrose, Louis. "The Elizabethan Subject and the Spenserian Text." *Literary Theory /Renaissance Texts*. eds. Patricia Parker and David Quint. Baltimore: Johns Hopkins UP, 1986. 303-40.

Norton Anthology of English Literature. eds. M. H. Abrams, et al. 6th Edition. Volume 1. New York: W.W. Norton & Company, 1993.

Pocock. J. G. A. *Virtue, Commerce, and History: Essays on Political Thought and History, Chiefly in the Eighteenth Century*. Cambridge: Cambridge UP, 1985.

Quilligan, Maureen. 'Sidney and His Queen.' *The Historical Renaissance: New Essays on Tudor and Stuart Literature and Culture*. eds. Heather Dubrow and Richard Strier. Chicago: U of Chicago P, 1988. 171-96.

Sacks, Peter. *The English Elegy: Studies in the Genre from Spenser to Yeats*. Baltimore: Johns Hopkins UP, 1985.

Sidney, Mary. *The Collected Works of Mary Sidney Herbert, Countess of Pembroke*. eds. Margaret P. Hannay, Noel J. Kinnamon and Michael G. Brennan. 2 vols. Oxford: Clarendon P, 1998.

Sidney, Philip. *Astrophil and Stella*. *Sir Philip Sidney*. ed. Katherine Duncan-Jones. Oxford: Oxford UP, 1989.

Spenser, Edmund. *The Faerie Queene*. Harmondsworth: Penguin Books, 1984.

Wall, Wendy. 'Our Bodies, Our Texts?: Renaissance Women and the Trials of Authorship.' *Anxious Power: Ambivalence in Narrative by Women*. eds. Carol J. Singley and Susan Elizabeth Sweeney. Albany: State U of New York P, 1993. 51-71.

9

'Subdu'd by You': States of Friendship and Friends of the State in Katherine Philips's Poetry

Andrew Shifflett

Katherine Philips was born in 1632, married in 1648, became a literary celebrity in 1663, and died in 1664. But 1651, the year of Worcester, Limerick, and *Leviathan*, should stand out in any study of her career as a poet. It marks her first publication of a poem ('To the Memory of the most Ingenious and Vertuous Gentleman Mr. WIL: CARTWRIGHT, my much valued Friend,' in an edition of William Cartwright's *Comedies*), her composition of most of the poems for which she is now famous, and finally her conception of a 'design . . . to unite all those of her acquaintance' – in the words of Sir Edward Dering, whom she called 'the worthy Silvander' – into one societie, and by the bands of *friendship* to make an alliance more firme then what nature, our countery or equall education can produce' (Thomas 11; my emphasis).

Dering was writing in 1665, a time when such a man might not be expected to be nostalgic for Philips's 'societie' or think that it 'would in time have spread very farr, & and have been improved with great and yet unimagind advantage to the world' (Thomas 11). Perhaps it will seem curious that a 'design' launched during the high-water mark of the Commonwealth was still of such interest to readers well after the Restoration.[1] Obviously there was something greatly attractive about friendship – nobody can doubt the esteem in which it was held by seventeenth-century intellectuals – but what makes Philips's approach so fascinating is her projection of enmity as natural and friendship as a 'sacred union' ('L'amitié' l. 21, Thomas 142) that, though it mimics a higher nature, is nevertheless competitive and even coercive in practice. That concord could not be separated from violence and the threat of violence was a lesson taught by the decade of Cromwell, Monck, and Hobbes, and while it may have been suppressed in 1660, it was never quite forgotten. Spokesmen for the new regime might pretend that its 'pleasures' were not also matters of force,[2] but better mottoes for the times were Orinda's effusion to Lucasia, 'We court our own captivity' ('Friendship's Mysterys' l. 16, Thomas 90), and Hobbes's statement in *Leviathan* that 'Feare and Liberty are consistent' (262). Indeed, Philips did for friendship in her way what Hobbes did for politics, and if clarifying the operations of friendly passions was more palatable to readers than demystifying the bases of government and religion, she made it difficult to continue thinking of friendship in traditional ways favored by traditional authorities: as a gift of nature and as the natural foundation, bond, and goal of the state.

'Our Gasping English Royalty'

Philips's interest in friendship has often been remarked, but some problems and prejudices have kept us, I think, from getting a true sense of its range and significance.[3] One problem arises from our reasonable belief that Philips's friendship poems were written to friends. Of course, many of them do appear to have been written to friends – often they include the name of an addressee in their titles – but surely the interest of these poems to Philips's general readership lay less in what they said about Philips or about Anne Owen, Mary Aubrey, or Regina Collier than in what they said about friendship itself. The tendency has been to read them rather too narrowly as records of her life and loves, much in the manner of popular television documentaries that use scenes from films to represent the private lives of film actors.[4] Another challenge is posed by the great number of poems in question: five have dates from 1651 in their titles, two are dated 1650, two are dated 1652, and at least twenty more poems on friendship, some of them quite long, appear to have been written in the early or middle 1650s. With so many poems to consider it has been tempting to critics to generalize about Philips's beliefs based on impressions from one or two poems, and thus make something simple out of something rather complicated. We shall see that her true achievement involved the creation of a body or world of poetry which presents friendship, not as a single experience or 'philosophy,' but as a relationship passing through several moods or phases.

And then there is the prejudice against the very idea of the English Commonwealth and Protectorate, a thing so ingrained in the critical tradition that it will be necessary to contend with it in one form or another throughout this essay.   Patrick Thomas, whose edition of Philips's poems makes it possible as never before to read them with an eye to the choices of image and argument that she made in changing circumstances, speaks for the critical tradition when he argues that Philips's 'philosophy of friendship' amounted to 'a plea for harmony and a protest against the perpetual discord and disturbance that characterized the years that followed the execution of Charles I.' With one king dead and another in exile, friendship could be cultivated only in 'private groups' that 'were manifestations, on a smaller scale, of the principles that underlie a cohesive social system' (Thomas 12).   Thomas is thinking here of the lengthy, 'philosophical' poems that Philips wrote in the mid-1650s, but much the same is said of the earlier, more personal poems addressed to friends such as 'L'amitié,' which 'contrasts the harmony of friendship with the disharmony of a society ruled by "Envy, pride and faction"' (356).   Deprived of a 'cohesive social system' based on Stuart kingship, the poet was forced – or so the argument goes – to create her own system in miniature.

Like most prejudices involving confidence in 'cohesive' social systems, this one begins to collapse as soon as things are studied and compared.   Typical is Thomas's assertion that 'Charles's defeat at the battle of Worcester' was 'lamented' by Philips in her poem 'On the 3d September 1651' (6).   But that poem is such a strange kind of lament – strange enough to make us doubt that Thomas has gotten it or the 'political element' (12) of Philips's many poems on friends and friendship quite right.   Indeed, '3d September 1651' deserves closer reading than it usually receives, and it happens that by reading it closely we can begin to see why Philips was so exciting to her early readers.   It begins with a carefully balanced simile relating the setting sun to the demise of the Stuarts, 'our Gasping English Royalty':

> As when the Glorious Magazine of Light
> Approaches to his Cannopy of night,
> He with new splendour cloth's his dying rays,
> And double brightness to his beams conveys;
> As if to brave and check his ending fate,
> Puts on his highest looks in's lowest State;
> Drest in such Terrour as to make us all

> Be Anti=persians, and adore his fall;
> Then quits the world, depriving it of day,
> While every herb and Plant does droop away:
> So when our Gasping English Royalty
> Perceiv'd her period now was drawing nigh,
> She summons her whole strength to give one blow,
> To raise her self, or pull down others too.
> Big with revenge and hope, she now spake more
> Of Terrour then in many months before;
> And musters her attendants, or to save
> Her from, or wait upon her to the Grave:
> Yet but enjoy'd the miserable fate
> Of setting Majesty, to dy in State.
>   (ll. 1-20, Thomas 82-83)

The simile is 'epic.' It tells a story and may be imagined to have a place, not only in '3d September 1651,' but in some much larger epic narrative. I am speculating, of course, but we may be able to get closer to the spirit of this short poem by recalling Hobbes's contention in his 'Answer' to Sir William Davenant's 'Preface' to *Gondibert* (1650) that 'Sonets, Epigrams, Eclogues, and the like pieces . . . are but Essayes, and parts of an entire Poem' (Davenant 22). The 'entire Poem' that concerns Hobbes in the 'Answer' is 'the Heroique Poem narrative,' and one supposes that for him, at least, '3d September 1651' would be 'but' an essay preparatory to some unwritten 'Epique Poem' on 'the manners of men' (Davenant 21-22).

The first verse paragraph of Philips's poem has the character of an epic fragment, *circa* 1651. Because the 'manners' which it treats are not so much 'feigned' as 'found in men' (Davenant 22), the poetic whole to which it aspires would seem to be not some Davenantian fantasy but a hybrid of epic and history such as Hobbes rejected in Lucan's *Pharsalia* and Abraham Cowley attempted in his fragmentary epic of the Stuart catastrophe, *The Civil War*. Cowley himself never carried his dismal story to 1651, having determined that it was 'so uncustomary, as to become almost *ridiculous*, to make *Lawrels* for the *Conquered*' (A4r). Cowley stopped at the first battle of Newbury, but Philips carries the theme through to the aftermath of Worcester:

> Unhappy Kings! who cannot keep a throne,
> Nor be so fortunate to fall alone!
> Their weight sinks others: Pompey could not fly,

But half the world must beare him company;
Thus Captive Sampson could not life conclude,
Unless attended with a multitude.
Who'd trust to Greatness now, whose food is ayre,
Whose ruine sudden, and whose end despaire?
Who would presume upon his Glorious Birth,
Or quarrell for a spacious share of earth,
That sees such diadems become thus cheap,
And Heroes tumble in the common heap?
O! give me vertue then, which summs up all,
And firmely stands when Crowns and Scepters fall.
                    (ll. 21-34, Thomas 83)

If the allusion to Samson and the Philistines seems bleak, the example of
Pompey is 'Unhappy' in the extreme. Pompey, as Lucan tells the story in
Pharsalia 8, flees to Egypt after his defeat by Julius Caesar and is killed by
men he thinks are his friends. If Caesar was Cromwell, Egypt was the
Continent. The poem 'reveals . . . sympathy for the defeated king' (Thomas
329), but that sympathy is balanced by sympathy for those left trailing in his
wake – 'half the world,' 'a multitude,' the 'others too' who are 'pull[ed]
down' and who 'sink' under the 'weight' of kings.[5] This is quite different
from the mood of the poem 'Upon the double murther of K. Charles' (Thomas
69-70), where Philips writes of 'Great Charles,' whose 'double misery was
this, / Unfaithfull friends, ignoble enemies' (ll. 15-16, Thomas 69). Certainly
there is a sense of loyalty in '3d September 1651,' but there is also a sense that
loyalties have been misplaced. There is even a hint of disgust in the grotesque
imagery. 'Gasping,' 'Big with revenge,' 'she now spake more / Of Terrour,'
and all the talk of death and the grave are in keeping with Cowley's *Civil War*
and especially with Lucan's *Pharsalia*, where monstrous death serves as the
great leveller of men.

  '3d September 1651' is a poem on a great public theme, and it implies
a narrative involving more than the story of the 'defeated king' or the poet's
feelings about that story. Philips's purpose is not so much to express
sympathy for an individual as to put forward a moral-political thesis on which
most if not all of her readers could agree. The personal voice is not heard
until the second verse paragraph, and when it declares itself openly in the final
couplet it is not idiosyncratic but communal, normal, choric. What begins as a
fragment of some unwritten 'Heroique Poem narrative' comes to suggest what

Hobbes called the 'Heroique Poem Dramatique, [which] is Tragedy' (Davenant 21). But this tragedy, crucially, is not the speaker's tragedy. The moral of '3d September 1651' unites the individual with a community of virtuous men and women, and it is because of that unity that the mood at the end of this otherwise somber poem is not at all somber. 'Only the wise man is a king,' says the contented Stoic; separating 'vertue' from 'Crowns and Scepters' was an early and rather easy step in the progress to Commonwealth *sapientia*. There is boldness, relief, and perhaps even some laughter in 'O! give me vertue then.' This is the cry of a survivor, of someone 'in the position of refusing, or at any rate resisting, the tragic movement toward catastrophe,' a 'chorus character [who] is, so to speak, the embryonic germ of comedy in tragedy' (Frye 218). Philips finds her voice when she realizes that she lives in the 'half the world' that has *not* been brought down by the Stuarts.

It is significant that Philips did not take up tragedy in the proper sense until after the Restoration in *Pompey* (1663), a work that is, as I have argued elsewhere, at once fascinated by and stridently critical of absolutist rhetoric.[6] In 1651, however, there was simply no need to 'trust to Greatness . . . whose food is ayre,' no need to follow Pompey to Egypt (or to France), no need to draw too near to the tragedies of kings and tyrants. The saving comedy of virtue was at hand, and the Matchless Orinda was free to make of it what she wished. To speak of 'felicity' being 'Crown'd' by friendship in July 1651, as Orinda does in 'To My excellent Lucasia' (l. 2, Thomas 121), was to pluck a crown from a king and place it on the head of happiness itself.

'Both Princes, and Both Subjects Too'

1651 was a year of conquests and consolidations. Whether or not to 'engage' with the new government was still a troubling question for some, but it must have seemed increasingly moot given the military successes of Cromwell in the north, Ireton in Ireland, and the inevitable submission of the American colonies. As the wife of a successful Cromwellian, the question of loyalty was unlikely to arise for Philips in any intelligible public way,[7] but at any rate we have no evidence that she found the political environment of the early 1650s constricting or – to recall Thomas's phrasing – perpetually discordant and disturbed. Instead, we find evidence of a great deal of creative activity by a maturing poet who must have felt free, as never before, to do as she pleased.

And if in fact Philips did become, as Thomas insists, 'increasingly inclined towards orthodox Anglicanism and the royalist cause' (5), then that, too, shows how fluid the ideological situation was during the period, and how many avenues of political and religious association were open to a person of her talents in her position. It is fitting that she liked to call her husband 'Antenor' in her poems – probably a reference to the Trojan peacemaker of the *Iliad* and *Aeneid* – for she, too, was more a peacemaker than a partisan in her poems on friends and friendship.

All of these poems are – *pace* Thomas – politically neutral in their condemnation of the world's vices.[8] Their criticisms are no more nor less applicable to the 1650s than they are to the 1640s and 1660s, although one assumes that Philips preferred the peace that England enjoyed after September 1651 to the frequent bloody battles of her adolescence. If Orinda and a friend 'pitty Kings, and Conquerours despise,' their contempt for Cromwell is countered by nothing more than crocodile tears for Charles I and Charles II: 'we that sacred union have engrost, / Which they and all the sullen world have lost' ('L'amitié' ll. 20-22, Thomas 142). In 'A retir'd friendship, to Ardelia,' Orinda condemns less the 'scorching Age' than those who would betray 'their own peace':

> In such a scorching Age as this,
>   Whoever would not seek a shade
> Deserve their happiness to misse,
>   As having their own peace betray'd.
>   (ll. 29-32, Thomas 98)

'Come,' she calls to Ardelia at the beginning of this poem, 'Let's innocently spend an houre, / And at all serious follys smile' (ll. 1, 3-4; Thomas 97). While those 'that place content / In Liberty from Government' become slaves when they are 'deprave[d]' by their passions, it is also true that contentedness 'ne're dwelt about a Throne' ('Content, to my dearest Lucasia' ll. 8, 25-27; Thomas 91-92). The world is a 'dull brutish world' to Orinda ('Friendship' l. 1, Thomas 150), but there is seldom any suggestion in the poems that it is any duller or more brutish when governed by commoners than when ruled by kings.

Even poems that use partisan terms seem to do so in order to invalidate partisanship. In 'For Regina,' for instance, Regina is immediately denounced as a 'Triumphant Queen of scorne' – Philips is playing on the woman's name, of course – who is 'Unjust and cruell,' and who, 'by a tiranny that's strange and new, / . . . murther[s] him because he worships you' (ll. 1, 3, 7-8; Thomas 125). This is hardly the support for 'the royalist cause' that a strong royalist would expect in a poem called 'For Regina' (Regina is denounced also in 'To the Queen of inconstancie, Regina, in Antwerp' [Thomas 120-21]). In the final lines, Orinda confuses matters further by asking Regina to 'Redeem the poison'd age' by 'let[ting] it be seen / There's no such freedome as to serve a Queen' – a surprisingly positive judgement given the cruelty mentioned earlier – but then concluding that this particular 'Queen' is actually a 'Roundhead' after all: 'But you I see are lately Roundhead growne, / And whom you vanquish you insult upon' (ll. 17-20, Thomas 125).

When a friend can be a 'Queen' and a 'Roundhead' in the same poem, we may conclude that neither 'party' is being elevated over the other but that they are being equated. They are being equated, it should be stressed, in ways consistent with classical ideas of friendship and the relationship between friendship and political concord. One thinks immediately of Aristotle's *Nicomachean Ethics*, although there is no need to trace the classical heritage here in any detail.[9] Friendship 'appears to be the bond of the state' to Aristotle because the 'chief aim' of lawgivers is 'to promote concord, which seems akin to friendship,' while 'faction, which is enmity, is what they are most anxious to banish' (453). By the mid-1650s Philips could find Aristotle's views on friendship in the pages of Thomas Stanley's *History of Philosophy* (1655-62), but there were other authorities in Cicero, Montaigne, and her friend Francis Finch, the 'Palaemon' whose 'incomparable discourse of Friendship' she praises at length in a poem (Thomas 83-84). Cicero, whom Philips probably knew better than the Stagirite, stressed the naturalness of friendly impulses in *De Amicitia*; just like the beasts, humans 'search for a partner whose personality they can unite so utterly with their own that the two are almost transformed into one' (217). And, like Aristotle, Cicero likens friends' 'complete identity of feeling about all things' (187) to political concord: 'Take away the bond of kindly feeling from the world, and no house or city can stand' (189). Implicit in this tradition is the idea that 'letters' – posted or published, in prose or verse – can play a crucial role in friendship's progress. '*Friendship is the great Chain of human Society*,' writes James Howell in his *Epistolae Ho-Elianae* (1645-55), '*and Intercourse of Letters is one of the chiefest Links of that Chain*' (qtd. in Miner 263).

In early-modern texts, however, the functional relationship between friendship and the good and peaceful state often collapses into a vision of friendship as being itself a good and peaceful state. Friendship is a sovereign state composed, somehow, of two independent sovereigns. 'This mirroring form of sameness,' writes Laurie Shannon in an essay on 'sovereign friendship' in Renaissance drama, 'signifies a radical (or at least exotic) political equality in an otherwise fully hierarchized world . . . Somewhere between one and two, friends share a full slate of rights and powers' (92). Philips was alive to the 'radical' or 'exotic' possibilities of what might, in a lesser poet, have registered as mere convention. There were still mysteries to explore in her poem on 'Friendship's Mysterys':

> Divided Joys are tedious found,
> And griefs united easyer grow:
> We are our selves but by rebound,
>   And all our titles shuffled so,
>   Both Princes, and both subjects too.
>   (ll. 21-25, Thomas 91)

The 'shuffl[ing]' of 'titles' and 'selves' occurs in many of the most difficult poems, generating throughout a sense of sublimity. 'Soule of my soule! my Joy, my crown, my friend!' Orinda exclaims at the beginning of 'L'amitié' (l. 1, Thomas 142). 'They are, and yet they are not, two,' we are told of friends in 'Friendship in Emblem' (l. 24, Thomas 107). Not only is there the strongest of bonds between friends: they are themselves extremely powerful and derive their great power, as we say today, from their marginality. 'United thus, what horrour can appeare / Worthy our sorrow, anger, or our feare?' she asks in 'L'amitié' (ll. 13-14, Thomas 142). More positively, friends have the power together 'To teach the world heroique things' and prescribe 'Law to all the rest' ('Friendship in Emblem' ll. 40, 44; Thomas 108).

Sometimes, however, the powers of friends are used against each other – used, as Philips so often points out, against Orinda herself. It seems odd to me that this has suggested to some critics unique emotional failings on Philips's part. For while classical friendship 'tends toward equality' (Hutter 10), and while the 'polity' of friendship was 'governed by extraordinary principles that were not to be found anywhere else in Renaissance culture' (Shannon 92), rarely did it seem to constitute a union of self-effacing, power-sharing democrats. Indeed, friends were often said to be equals in the same way that equally powerful monarchs were equals. Orinda is in step with this

Renaissance tradition when she praises 'excellent Lucasia' to the skies after having 'Crown'd' her *own* 'felicity' ('To My excellent Lucasia' l. 1, Thomas 121), when she makes Aubrey a 'crown' that is also 'my crown' in 'L'amitié,' and when in 'Friendship's Mysterys' she claims that she and Lucasia are 'Both Princes.' We should not expect such ententes to be long-lasting.

The analogy of sovereignty could become a problem when monarchs made friends with those of lower station or when a poet of Philips's class tried to convert 'vertical' relationships into 'horizontal' ones.[10] 'Ador'd Valeria,' she asks in 'To my lady Ann Boyle's saying I look'd angrily upon her,'

> can you conclude
> Orinda lost in such Ingratitude?
> And so mispell the language of my Face,
> When in my heart you have so great a place?
> (ll. 1-4, Thomas 201)

Lady Anne could 'conclude' anything she wished. Although Orinda can bestow her own kind of titles on the Boyles – 'Valeria' on Anne, 'Celimena' on Elizabeth – there is no avoiding the class dilemma:

> But say, bold trifler, what dost thou pretend?
> Wouldst thou depose thy Saint into thy Friend?
> Equality in friendship is requir'd,
> Which here were criminal to be desir'd.
> ('To Celimena' ll. 5-8, Thomas 227)

But social hierarchy, confronted in these courtly poems of the early 1660s, was less problematic and a good deal less interesting to Philips than sovereign equality itself. For although friends might seem like equal sovereigns in books, experience showed that actual sovereigns were seldom good friends. Indeed, they were the most immediate examples one could find, as Hobbes pointed out in the thirteenth chapter of *Leviathan*, of the 'NATURALL' and wholly miserable 'CONDITION of *Mankind*':

> But though there had never been any time, wherein particular men
> were in a condition of warre one against another; yet in all times,
> Kings, and Persons of Soveraigne authority, because of their
> Independency, are in continuall jealousies, and in the state and
> posture of Gladiators; having their weapons pointing, and their

eyes fixed on one another; that is, their Forts, Garrisons, and Guns
upon the Frontiers of their Kingdomes; and continuall Spyes upon
their neighbours; which is a posture of War. (187-88)

When Philips represents friendship in its most unpleasant phases she uses
images of what Hobbes would call 'Persons of Soveraigne authority' and
'Independency.' One could almost say of Philips in this regard what C. B.
Macpherson says of Hobbes – that he wrote 'as a scientist, not as a partisan'
(Hobbes 14). Thus 'For Regina' explores misunderstandings characteristic of
friendship by taking the form of a mock communiqué between rival camps.
Regina, the 'Queen of scorne,' refuses to do what is right, and even risks
becoming the 'wretched Captive' of another if she does not change her course
(ll. 1, 16; Thomas 125). 'To the Queen of inconstancie, Regina, in Antwerp,'
although not nearly as coherent a poem as 'For Regina,' also presents itself as
a diplomatic ultimatum filled with references to something 'decreed,' to an
'exchange,' to 'revenge,' 'treacheries,' 'faiths . . . betraid,' a 'desperate game,'
'private ruines,' and, last but not least, 'French men' (ll. 1, 5-8, 17-18, 21;
Thomas 120-21). One gathers from such poems that friendships between
equals can be both sublime and nasty – 'nasty, brutish, and short' (Hobbes
186). The nature of friendship in Philips ranges from the friendly nature
praised by Cicero to something resembling Hobbes's 'meer Nature.' If
friendship was like a relationship between equal monarchs, it was also like
war – a 'warre of every man against every man' (Hobbes 188).

There is, then, a sense in which the characteristic, wholly traditional
'shuffl[ing]' of 'titles' and 'selves' allowed by the equality and unity of
friends in Renaissance tradition tends in Philips's poems to become an 'ill
shuffled game':

> Why are the bonds of friendship tyed
> With so remisse a knot,
> That by the most it is defyed,
> And by the rest forgot?
>
> ....
>
> If friendship sympathy impart,
> Why this ill shuffled game,
> That heart can never meet with heart,
> Or flame encounter flame?
> What doth this crueltie create?
> Is it th'intrigue of love or fate?

('The Enquiry' ll. 31-34, 37-42; Thomas 152-53)

Certainly, we do not always see sparks flying in the 'shade' of friendship ('A retir'd friendship, to Ardelia' l. 30, Thomas 98). But just as Hobbes knew that 'the nature of Foule weather, lyeth not in a showre or two of rain; but in an inclination thereto of many dayes together,' and that 'the nature of War, consisteth not in actuall fighting; but in the known disposition thereto' (186), so there always seems to be the *potential* for recrimination and competition within Philips's friendly polity. 'We both diffuse, and both engrosse,' says Orinda in 'Friendship's Mysterys' (l. 13, Thomas 90) – a 'Platonick' image of mutual exploitation reminiscent of John Donne's erotic micro-commonwealths.[11] And, as in Donne, the impulse to 'engrosse' readily moves beyond the 'shade.' The 'design' of friendship may be 'innocent' in 'To My excellent Lucasia,' but Orinda is pleased to have gained 'all the world' by gaining Lucasia (ll. 20, 23; Thomas 122). As allies in 'To the excellent M[rs.] A. O.,' the glorious and greedy friends are able to wrest 'all worth, all happiness' from the 'dull World' (ll. 3-4, Thomas 101-02).

Such boasts are usually taken, I suppose, as compensatory philosophical platitudes, but they are made so often and pointedly that they become 'real,' or at any rate unavoidable, features of the world created by the poems. In 'Injuria amici,' a fascinating poem that is no less about friendship for dealing with the 'injury' of friendship, Orinda assigns to her 'Lovely apostate' a Neronian 'desire / . . . to survey the Rome you set on fire' (ll. 1, 10; Thomas 123). The 'complete identity of feeling about all things' that Cicero praises in *De Amicitia* – the happy feeling that friends are, as Orinda says, 'of one another's mind / Assur'd' ('A retir'd friendship' ll. 33-34, Thomas 98) – leads in 'Injuria amici' to a special kind of hell:

> While wounded for and by your power, I
> At once your martyr and your prospect dy.
> This is my doome, and such a riddling fate
> As all impossibles doth complicate:
> For obligation here is injury,
> Constancy crime, friendship a haeresy;
> And you appeare so much on ruine bent,
> Your own destruction gives you now content:
> For our twin-spirits did so long agree,
> You must undoe your self to ruine me.

And, like some frantique Goddess, you'r inclin'd
To raze the Temple where you were enshrin'd;
And (what's the miracle of cruelty!)
Kill that which gave you imortallity.
(ll. 11-24, Thomas 123-24)

If friendship is now a 'haeresy' to this friend, it is because friendship with Orinda made such heresies and enmities possible to begin with. Friends are always potential fiends.

'We Court Our Own Captivity'

Within the full sweep of Philips's friendship poetry, the naturalness of friendship leads inevitably to the naturalness of enmity, and indeed to the perception that friendship is not so much the opposite of enmity as its co-conspirator. One might tease out hints of this tendency in the tradition – in, for example, Cicero's vexed recognition in *De Amicitia* that while friendship is the basis of political concord it is also the vehicle of political faction (198-99). But the best analogue, and the most contemporary analogue to these poems of 1651, is the 'stylized background' which Hobbes created for his great 'epic' of political philosophy (Wolin 24). 'The notions of Right and Wrong, Justice and Injustice have there no place,' says Hobbes of our 'NATURALL CONDITION,' and it 'is consequent also to the same condition, that there be no Propriety, no Dominion, no *Mine* and *Thine* distinct; but onely that to be every mans that he can get; and for so long, as he can keep it' (188). When the sun is shining on Orinda and her friends – or rather when they are in their 'shade' – their equality is a joy. But when the weather turns foul, the equality of friends can become a nightmare.

For Hobbes, the only way out of the misery of our natural equality – other than death – is the conferral of all our 'power and strength upon one Man, or upon one Assembly of men, that may reduce all [our] Wills . . . unto one Will' (227). Whether this happens through 'mutuall transferring of Right . . . which men call CONTRACT' (192) or comes about violently by 'conquest' is a matter of indifference to Hobbes (252-53), there being 'scarce a Common-wealth in the world, whose beginnings can in conscience be justified' (722). And while Hobbes himself thought friendship a matter of

'GIFT, FREE-GIFT, GRACE' (193), it seemed reasonable to others to place
it, too, within a contractual setting. 'Nature hath made friendships' so that we
might 'relate to all the world,' wrote Jeremy Taylor in his learned 'letter' to
Philips, *A Discourse of the Nature and Offices of Friendship* (1657),

> but when men contract friendships, they close the commons; and
> what nature intended should be every man's, we make proper to two
> or three. Friendship is like rivers, and the strand of seas, and the air,
> common to all the world; but tyrants, and evil customs, wars, and
> want of love, have made them proper and peculiar. (1:72)

Of course, what is natural for Hobbes is only customary for Taylor, an
Anglican divine who must have hated Hobbes's doctrine. But Taylor is too
severe and too intelligent to think that custom can simply be done away with.
Our constriction of natural friendship, however lamentable it may be, must be
accepted as a fact of our *fallen* nature: 'universal friendship . . . must be
limited, because we are so' (1:74). Real human friendship, fine as it surely is,
is a 'contract' – a drawing together of interested parties – necessitated by
politics, enmity, and violence.

   Having encountered the dangers of friendly equality in Philips's
poems, one may turn in two directions, as it were, for safety: toward poems
like 'Friendship' (Thomas 150-51), 'A Friend' (Thomas 165-68), and
'L'accord du bien' (Thomas 169-73) that stress the 'Unity' and natural
'Harmony' of friendship and the universe, or toward those poems that find
some measure of emotional security and peace in less 'natural' solutions.
When we take the first route we are taught to forget that friendship 'must be
limited, because we are so.' The second route leads back to Taylor, Hobbes,
and the realities of 1651, and forward to the panegyrics written by Cowley and
other 'friends' of Philips in the 1660s. Here the pleasures attained through
'conquests' seem no different from those attained through consent, and
friendship is a happy consequence of Taylor's reign of 'tyrants':

> Madam,
>   As in a triumph conquerours admit
> Their meanest captives to attend on it,
> Who, though unworthy, have the power confest,
> And Justify'd the yielding of the rest:
> So when the busy world (in hope t'excuse
> Their own surprize) your conquests doe peruse,

And find my name, they will be apt to say
Your charmes were blinded, or else thrown away.
> ('To the truly noble, and obleiging Mrs: Anne Owen' ll. 1-8,
> Thomas 102-03)

The tone may suggest Donne, and the imagery ancient Rome, but the rhetoric of 'confes[sion],' 'Justif[ication],' and 'yielding' places these lines squarely in the 1650s. The power of friendship is 'Justify'd,' not by recourse to the justice or naturalness of its origins, but simply by our 'yielding' to it. There is no way, as Orinda says in a similar mood in the poem on 'Lucasia,' 'to obleige Lucasia by my voice'; nor is there anything to be done to 'Justify my choice' beyond submitting to that choice (ll. 1-2, Thomas 103). It is as if Orinda has thought of the question posed in another, more contractualist poem, 'Nay, to what end did we first barter minds, / Onely to know and to neglect the claime?' and chosen to embrace the answer she there dismisses:

If this be all our friendship does design,
    We covet not enjoyment then, but power:
To our Opinion we our bliss confine,
    And love to have, but not to smell, the flower.
> ('To my Lucasia in defence of declared friendship' ll. 13-14,
> 17-20; Thomas 154)

Friendly conquest is so one-sided in 'To . . . Anne Owen' that it is beside the point whether our 'conquerors' are really friends to us at all. 'Submission . . . implyeth . . . all' for Hobbes (720) and, in this mood at least, 'Power' *is* 'enjoyment' and 'bliss' *is* 'Opinion' for Orinda.

What is a mystery in 'Friendship's Mysterys' – that 'We court our own captivity' (l. 16, Thomas 90) – becomes in 'To . . . Anne Owen' the enabling condition of happiness and the best chance for happy survival. Orinda is certain that she will benefit from her defeat:

But this will cleare you, that 'tis generall
The worst applaud what is admir'd by all.
But I have plots in't: for the way to be
Secure of fame to all posterity,
Is to obtain the honour I pursue,
To tell the world I was subdu'd by you.
> (ll. 11-16, Thomas 103)

Such friendship, much like Hobbes's peace and human industry, is achieved through a violence that must be accepted so that some greater violence or privation can be avoided.

Since the poet, too, has 'plots in't,' it may seem best to relegate these poems to anthologies of tempests and teapots. And yet we have seen that the fiction or, as Taylor puts it, the 'fine romance' (1:81) of friendship is not reducible to platitudes or limited by a rhetoric of mock hyperbole. Orinda's world is much larger than that. Beyond the romance of friendly conquest lies the tragic expanse of 'Dangerous Friendship,' a theme that made Philips famous in her day. Indeed, the greatest advocate of friendship in *Pompey*, Julius Caesar, is also the greatest conqueror. His real 'end' in warring with Pompey and the republicans, he claims in act 3, scene 2,

> Was of a Foe subdu'd, to make a Friend;
> ....
> And my Ambition only this Design'd,
> To Kill their Hate, and force them to be kind;
> How blest a Period of the War't had been,
> If the glad World had in one Charriot seen
> *Pompey* and *Caesar* at once to have sate
> Triumphant over all their former Hate!   (Philips 30)

But Pompey has already been killed by treacherous Egyptians. The tragedy is not that Caesar was wrong to force his enemy to be a friend but rather that he was too late in doing it.

Caesar's friendly defeat of Pompey is a hypothesis within a play, Lucasia's conquest of Orinda is 'fine romance,' and the 'great LEVIATHAN' who enforces peace and security in Hobbes's philosophical epic is '*One Person, of whose Acts a great Multitude, by mutuall Covenants one with another, have made themselves every one the Author*' (227-28). All these things are fictions that seek to redeem violence for a violent world – a 'dull brutish world' – and all stand as striking examples of seventeenth-century social dreaming on the theme of peace. Cowley caught the spirit in 'Upon Mrs. *K. Philips* her Poems':

> Ah cruel Sex! will you depose us too in Wit?
> ....
> Verse was love's fire-arms heretofore:

In Beauties Camp it was not known,
Too many arms beside that Conquerour bore.
'Twas the great Cannon we brought down,
T'assault a stubborn Town.
Orinda first did a bold sally make,
Our strongest quarter take,
And so successful prov'd, that she
Turn'd upon *Love* himself his own Artillery.
                    (ll. 3, 9-17; Philips B2v)

Notes

[1] Here I shall avoid any attempt to 'account' for Philips's popularity in the seventeenth century. The traditional explanation for her popularity after 1660 – that she had preserved 'the old court tradition' from the 1630s (Souers 277) – simply does not bear a reading of the poems themselves or reflect what readers said about them at the time. An intriguing alternative – that the poems were enjoyed because of their heart-felt expressions of 'intense same-sex love between women' (Andreadis 37) – begs more questions than it answers, both about Philips and about the sexual mores of seventeenth-century readers. By far the best study of Philips's reception in the seventeenth and eighteenth centuries has been provided by Loscocco, who argues that 'mid-century readers did not limit themselves to issues connected with her gender,' that they 'repeatedly and pointedly broadened their discussions to include other aspects of her poetry' (260), that she was praised in the 1660s as much for her 'masculine strength' as for her 'feminine sweetness,' and that gendered terms of praise, 'though deriving from and specific to the poems' female subject, also participate in general poetic discourse in ways separate from the sex of the poet' (262).

[2] On the 'politics of pleasure' during the Restoration, see Zwicker 90-129.

[3] See Andreadis, Hiscock, Hobby 134-42, Libertin, Limbert 32-36, Miner 300-02, and Souers 39-78.

[4] Thomas, for instance, writes that Philips 'vented her spleen' to Regina, that her 'deluded belief in unanimity between friends was experienced by those close to her as tyranny,' that she was 'baffled and deceived' by those she sought to influence (12), and that she 'cried herself nearly blind' when informed of Lucasia's marriage ceremony (16).

[5] See Evans for a reading of '3d September 1651' that stresses its 'deliberate, richly crafted balance, an equilibrium characteristic not only of Philips's poetic

skill but also of her nuanced political insight' (184-85). Even Souers, who felt that Philips 'was probably ready to welcome the Restoration several years before that event took place' (83), noticed that the poem 'shows a point of view on politics curiously detached for one at that time' (80).

[6] See Shifflett 75-106.

[7] The affair alluded to in 'To (the truly competent Judge of Honour) Lucasia, upon a scandalous libell made by J. Jones' (Thomas 114-16) and 'To Antenor, on a paper of mine wch J. Jones threatens to publish to his prejudice' (Thomas 116-17) must not have been as damaging as it sounds. After all, the obscure 'J. Jones' did not actually 'publish' anything against the Philipses, and neither 'To Lucasia' nor 'To Antenor' were published until 1664. See Thomas 346-48.

[8] See Hobby, who observes that 'the extant poems that she addresses to friends make few overt comments on state politics' (134); Miner, who allows that she 'expresses no fervent Royalism in her poems' (301); and Souers, who admits that 'her poetry maintains an almost guarded silence concerning the political troubles and religious difficulties of the time' (80).

[9] The intersection of friendship and politics in antiquity has been treated at length by Hutter, who claims that 'Western political speculation finds its origin in a system of thought in which the idea of friendship is the major principle in terms of which political theory and practice are described, explained, and analyzed' (2).

[10] 'The rules of *amicitia* run afoul of the monarch's proverbial singularity, his public function of representing polity in generic terms, and his duty to sublimate his affective life to the good of the realm. A monarch so engaged to a particular friend is, from the constitutional perspective of the realm's priority, a captured sovereign – a sovereign subject to an interest at odds with his political purpose' (Shannon 93).

[11] On Donne as a model for Philips see Andreadis 39-43.

Works Cited

Andreadis, Harriette. 'The Sapphic-Platonics of Katherine Philips, 1632-1664.' *Signs* 15 (1989): 34-60.

Aristotle. *The Nicomachean Ethics.* Trans. H. Rackham. Cambridge: Harvard UP, 1962.

Cicero. *On the Good Life.* Trans. Michael Grant. Harmondsworth: Penguin Books, 1971.

Cowley, Abraham. *Poems.* London, 1656.

Davenant, Sir William. *The Works of Sir William Davenant.* London, 1673.

Evans, Robert C. 'Paradox in Poetry and Politics: Katherine Philips in the Interregnum.' *The English Civil Wars in the Literary Imagination.* eds. Claude J. Summers and Ted-Larry Pebworth. Columbia: U of Missouri P, 1999. 174-85.

Frye, Northrop. *The Anatomy of Criticism: Four Essays.* Princeton: Princeton UP, 1957.

Hiscock, W. S. 'Friendship: Francis Finch's Discourse and the Circle of the Matchless Orinda.' *Review of English Studies* 15 (1939): 466-68.

Hobbes, Thomas. *Leviathan.* ed. C. B. Macpherson. Harmondsworth: Penguin Books, 1968.

Hobby, Elaine. *Virtue of Necessity: English Women's Writing 1649-88.* Ann Arbor: U of Michigan P, 1989.

Hutter, Horst. *Politics as Friendship: The Origins of Classical Notions of Politics in the Theory and Practice of Friendship.* Waterloo: Wilfrid Laurier UP, 1978.

Libertin, Mary. 'Female Friendship in Women's Verse: Toward a New Theory of Female Poetics.' *Women's Studies* 19 (1982): 291-308.

Limbert, Claudia A. 'Katherine Philips: Controlling a Life and Reputation.' *South Atlantic Review* 56 (1991): 27-42.

Loscocco, Paula. '"Manly Sweetness": Katherine Philips among the Neoclassicals.' *Huntington Library Quarterly* 56 (1993): 259-79.

Miner, Earl. *The Cavalier Mode from Jonson to Cotton.* Princeton: Princeton UP, 1971.

Philips, Katherine. *Poems by the Most Deservedly Admired Mrs. Katherine Philips the Matchless Orinda.* London, 1667.

Shannon, Laurie. 'Monarchs, Minions, and "Soveraigne" Friendship.' *South Atlantic Quarterly* 97 (1998): 91-112.

Shifflett, Andrew. *Stoicism, Politics, and Literature in the Age of Milton: War and Peace Reconciled.* Cambridge: Cambridge UP, 1998.

Souers, Philip Webster. *The Matchless Orinda.* Cambridge: Harvard UP, 1931.

Taylor, Jeremy. *The Whole Works.* ed. Reginald Heber. Rev. Charles Page Eden. 10 vols. London: Longmans, 1854.

Thomas, Patrick, ed. *The Poems. The Collected Works of Katherine Philips, The Matchless Orinda.* Vol. 1. Stump Cross: Stump Cross Books, 1990.

Wolin, Sheldon S. *Hobbes and the Epic Tradition of Political Theory.* Los Angeles: Clark Memorial Library, 1970.

Zwicker, Steven. *Lines of Authority: Politics and English Literary Culture, 1649-1689.* Ithaca: Cornell UP, 1993.

PART IV

Writing the Female Poet

10

'First Fruits of a Woman's Wit': Authorial Self-Construction of English Renaissance Women Poets

Helen Wilcox

When we try to reconstruct an image of the Renaissance Englishwoman, what archetypes spring to mind? Most of us will probably visualize one of the many portraits of Elizabeth I, the virgin queen and icon of late sixteenth-century England, emblem of what John Knox in 1558 called 'the monstrous regiment of women' (Knox A1r). Others might think of a less public and more familial 'regiment,' with the Renaissance mother heading ranks of children in descending order of height; we will recall many a family portrait or memorial sculpture in which the woman features in this role, often as one of several wives (chronologically speaking) to a long-lived patriarch.[1] We might, on the other hand, call to mind the visual image of the woman in peaceful domestic activity, most commonly sewing or perhaps – if books are to enter the picture – reading the bible or an appropriately devotional text (see Figure 1). The Renaissance woman is constructed for us by history and the evidence of the visual arts as either exceptional – the virgin queen with the heart and stomach of a king – or as domestic, bearing and bringing up children and upholding their (and her own) spiritual standards. How, in the spectrum of these existing stereotypes, do we begin to visualize the Renaissance woman as *writer*? What are the available icons here?

Apart from a few late Renaissance paintings by artists such as Johannes Vermeer and Gerard ter Borch, in which women are seen writing letters (see Figure 2), it is very difficult to discover any visual depictions of the early modern woman as writer. The nearest we come to such an image is perhaps Simon van der Passe's well-known 1618 engraving of Mary Sidney, Countess of Pembroke, in which she is shown holding a copy of the Psalms.

At first glance this would seem to confirm the traditional association of women with (passive) holiness, except that Mary Sidney herself had completed a translation of the Psalms into English lyric verse. The choice of the book in her hands is, therefore, significant, but nevertheless still in keeping with female modesty; the work may be in some sense hers, but she would not claim 'authorship' of the Psalms in English verse (since that still belongs to God). Despite the presence of a poet's laurel wreath at the top of the frame with which van der Passe enclosed Mary Sidney's portrait, she is not shown writing verse but holding the open book, as though ready to make practical use of the completed work in private or communal devotion. Already, in contemplating this one engraving, we begin to see something of the complex and paradoxical nature of the female authorial image in Renaissance England.

Images of writers, of course, are as likely to be verbal as visual. We can learn a great deal about the ways in which Renaissance English women poets were viewed, both by themselves and others, through studying the written self-portraits to be found in the prefatory material preceding or framing their works. The preface is always a significant opportunity for authorial self-fashioning, but it is particularly so in the early modern period when the relationship of a text to a chosen literary genre, and of the writer to a chosen patron, needs to be established by means of the preface. At the very entrance to the work – Jonathan Swift called the preface a 'porch'(1) – the prefatory material takes the reader across the border from the private world of the writer to the public world of literature. It gives the writer a chance to shape the readers' expectations before they enter the work itself; furthermore, it offers the woman writer a vital opportunity to justify what she is doing in writing at all, and thereby to establish her own presence as author.[2] Paradoxically, all of this must be achieved through a rhetoric of modesty and self-denial; the authorial image in the Renaissance preface, male or female, is conventionally that of the reluctant and apologetic public speaker. My concern in this essay is to highlight the tropes and strategies of self-construction used by women poets in particular, and then to consider how we can relate these authorial images to the wider issue of the emergence of the woman writer in the early modern period.

I

Of the huge range of prefatory material by English women poets from the late sixteenth to the mid-seventeenth centuries, I have selected a small number of examples from prefaces in prose and verse which highlight different aspects of female authorial self-fashioning. The chosen prefaces provide appropriate and revealing variety in terms of the chronological moment from which the particular preface comes, the poetic vocation of its author, the mode of publication of her poetry and its subsequent reception. We will thus encounter texts from throughout the period from 1590 to 1680, by widely-known as well as less familiar authors, prefacing poetry on devotional as well as secular subjects and from printed as well as manuscript sources. By taking a representative sample of self-constructing prefaces, the essay aims to raise important questions concerning the women writers' entry into authorship.

My first example is from the work of Mary Sidney, whose translation of the Psalms – as depicted in the engraving described above – was in fact the completion of a task begun by her brother, Sir Philip Sidney. After Philip's death at the Battle of Zutphen in 1586, Mary revised the Psalms which he had versified, and turned the remaining 107 into lyric stanzas of her own. The collection which resulted – presented to Queen Elizabeth in 1599 – was to have a profound influence on English devotional and lyrical writing in the seventeenth century. Bearing in mind the origins of the text, it is not surprising that Mary Sidney prefaced the translation with a poem dedicating the work to her late brother, 'To the Angell spirit of the most excellent Sir Phillip Sidney':

> To thee pure sprite, to thee alone's addres't
>   this coupled worke, by double int'rest thine:
>   First rais'de by thy blest hand, and what is mine
> inspird by thee, thy secrett power imprest.
>   So dar'd my Muse with thine it selfe combine,
>   as mortall stuffe with that which is divine,
> Thy lightning beames give lustre to the rest. (Sidney xxxv)

Her brother's spirit is addressed in terms which other writers might have used for the Holy Ghost or the inspiring muse which gives 'secrett power' to the poet. Viewed from this perspective, the work of translation was not Mary Sidney's at all but 'doubly' Philip's, as he was, according to Mary's opening stanza, both its originator and its continuing inspiration. An explicit binary distinction is made between the earthly poet and her brother – between 'mortall' and 'divine,' impure and 'pure' – and this opposition runs parallel with the female/male binary which also divides them. She only 'dar'd' to write because her mortal (female) inadequacy could be 'combined' with his perfection. Though the gendering of these contrasts remains implicit here, it is fundamental to Renaissance modes of thought and recurs in explicit form in a number of the prefaces which follow.

Meanwhile, three stanzas later in this prefatory poem, Mary Sidney repeats the idea that her writing was daring and presumptuous, and goes on to justify it to the spirit of her brother, not in any literary terms, but as a work of love:

> Yet here behold, (oh wert thou to behold!)
>   this finish't now, thy matchlesse Muse begunne,
>   the rest but peec't, as left by thee undone.
> Pardon (oh blest soule) presumption too too bold:
>   if love and zeale such error ill-become
>   'tis zealous love, Love which hath never done,
> Nor can enough in world of words unfold. (Sidney xxxvi)

Mary Sidney's completion of the translation begun by her brother, and the subsequent circulation of what she had written so that others might read it, is depicted in her own words here as an 'error,' a 'presumption' which will require 'pardon' and can be justified only on the grounds of 'love and zeale,' as she expresses it in the shared vocabulary of familial and spiritual devotion. Although the task of translating Scripture was always considered a very high vocation, the focus of Mary Sidney's prefatory verse is, significantly, not on that aspect of her work but specifically on her relationship *as a writer* to her late brother. In her construction, the woman writer is a devoted follower, not an initiator; she has, she claims, simply 'peec't' together what her brother had begun, itself derived from the biblical text assumed to have been sung originally by David.[3] In fact, as we now know, Mary Sidney did the major part of the work herself, and reworked her brother's early translations to a considerable extent; but in the prefatory poem she casts herself in the role of the subservient partner whose actions are the result of devoted love. I do not suggest that there is anything insincere in this self-image; what is fascinating is how closely it anticipates the practice of many other women writers who, without Mary Sidney's circumstantial justification, represent themselves in a language of relative passivity and emotional dependency rather than of skill or artistic initiative in the 'world of words.'

The importance of prefatory gestures to the Renaissance English woman writer is vividly exemplified by the case of Aemilia Lanyer, more than a third of whose 1611 publication *Salve Deus Rex Judaeorum* consists of dedications and prefaces (fifty out of the 128 pages in the modern edition). All of Lanyer's dedicatees are women – suggesting a very self-consciously female fashioning of her literary product – and prominent among the named female readers is none other than Mary Sidney, who as a patron and a writer is of double significance to Lanyer:

> For to this Lady now I will repaire,
> Presenting her the fruits of idle houres;
> Thogh many Books she writes that are more rare,
> Yet there is hony in the meanest flowres:
>
> Which is both wholesome, and delights the taste:
> Though sugar be more finer, higher priz'd,
> Yet is the painefull Bee no whit disgrac'd,
> Nor her faire wax, or hony more despiz'd.   (Lanyer 30)

Once again, the woman poet constructs herself by negation; where Philip Sidney was the 'matchless' model under whose shadow his sister Mary wrote, here Mary Sidney herself is, in turn, held up as the author of 'rare' and highly 'priz'd' works which can never be matched by the writing of Lanyer. However, the uncertainty of Lanyer's position is suggested in the contradictions between her metaphors. On the one hand, she offers her poetry as the 'fruits of idle houres,' continuing the idea of the woman writer's harmless passivity; yet, on the other hand, she urges sympathy for the bee who takes careful 'pains' over what she does as she busily makes her honey and wax, even if these products are not as refined as pure sugar. Is the woman writer, then, casual or earnest? The inevitable tensions between humility and commitment – the opposition of feminine ideology and female vocation – show very clearly in Lanyer's language here.

Lanyer resolves (at least temporarily) the clash between self-deprecation and self-justification in this dedicatory poem by turning the spotlight back onto her dedicatee, the 'learned damsell' Mary Sidney:

> So craving pardon for this bold attempt,
> I here present my mirrour to her view,
> Whose noble virtues cannot be exempt,
> My Glasse beeing steele, declares them to be true. (Lanyer 31)

The way for Lanyer to justify her work, she implies, is to make it an image of female virtues as exemplified in Mary Sidney. The writer's boldness here is intertwined with, and supported by, the reader's qualities; if the text is a 'mirror,' then its worth is defined as much by those who look into it as by the woman who created it. The mirror is a traditional image for the didactic function of literature, but it carries a special resonance with reference to women;[4] here Lanyer combines these associations and puts them to positive use in implying the vital relationship of woman reader to woman writer. As she confirmed in her prose preface 'To the Vertuous Reader,' 'I have written this small volume, or little booke, for the general use of all virtuous Ladies and Gentlewomen of this kingdome; and in commendation of some particular persons of our owne sexe' (Lanyer 48). By writing a work which is self-consciously both *for* and *about* virtuous women, Lanyer finds a niche for herself as the author of a useful work which is given an assured status through the readers to whom it is contracted.

II

Mary Sidney found authorial daring through the inspiring spirit of her brother; Aemilia Lanyer entered the literary market place with, at least in anticipation, a powerful group of female sponsors. Both women, in presenting themselves as poets, crucially disarmed their critics by simply admitting that their vocation as authors was 'bold' or even 'erroneous.' If a woman writer's place is always in the wrong, then some strength can be gained by claiming that position, however undesirable it may be. As Elizabeth Cary wrote in the brief prefatory epistle to her dramatic *History of the Life, Reign and Death of Edward II* (1627),

> I strive to please the Truth, not Time; nor fear I Censure, since at the worst, 'twas but one Month mis—spended; which cannot promise ought in right Perfection. If so you hap to view it, tax not my Errours; I my self confess them. (Cary 216)

There is a striking absence of apology or self-justification in Cary's account of her writing – emboldened, perhaps, by the knowledge that her work was in manuscript with a limited circulation. Her preface asserts a defiant disregard for contemporary opinion, and she forestalls criticism by confessing her faults while seeming casually unconcerned about them: ''twas but one Month.' A similar trope, though in a rather more gracious tone, is employed by Rachel Speght in the prefatory verse to her poem *Mortalities Memorandum*, published in 1621:

> But, courteous Reader, who ever thou art,
> Which these my endeavours do'st take in good part,
> Correcting with judgement the faults thou do'st finde,
> With favour approving what pleaseth thy minde,
> To thee for thy use, and behoofe, I extend
> This poore *Memorandum* of our latter end. (Speght 142)

The anticipated collusion of a 'courteous Reader' who will correct the writer's 'faults' and at the same time 'approve' and 'use' the ensuing poem is a hope commonly expressed in prefatory writing. Among women writers, however, this sense of partnership with the reader is often most confidently asserted when the expected readership is of the same sex. Diana Primrose, publishing her poetic *Chain of Pearl* in 1630 in honour of the memory of Elizabeth I, dedicated her work to 'All Noble Ladies and Gentlewomen' (a phrase strikingly reminiscent of that used by Lanyer twenty years earlier):

> To you, the honour of our noble sex,
> I send this chain with all my best respects,
> Which if you choose to wear for her sweet sake,
> For whom I did this slender poem make,
> You shall erect a trophy to her name,
> And crown yourselves with never-fading fame. (Primrose 229)

As Lanyer justified her own position as a writer by invoking the respected poet Mary Sidney (as well as many other named noble women), so Primrose launches her own 'slender poem' through its devotion to Elizabeth ('for her sweet sake'). Both poets addressed a specifically female readership, here termed by Primrose 'the honour of our noble sex.' In fact, so concerned is she with her readers that Primrose hardly mentions herself or her work, other than to belittle it (as 'slender') and to describe it metaphorically as a 'chain' which she hopes her readers will 'wear.' By doing so, she suggests, they will give glory to Elizabeth and earn themselves 'never-ending fame.' Any possible fame for the writer – as the maker of a decorative chain, perhaps – is the reflected glory of her subject and her readers. The confidence of Primrose's tone, however, and the conscious femininity of poem, metaphor and readership, are most revealing.

In the 1650s, the tone of the epistle 'To the Reader' prefacing an anonymous collection of poems called *Eliza's Babes* was again determined by the fact that the writer anticipated a female readership: she dedicates her verse to her 'Sisters.' In this case, the authorial self-presentation is also guided by the explicitly devotional nature of the work:

> When first the motion came into my minde, that these Babes of mine, should be sent into the world; I would faine have supprest that motion, for divers reasons which may be imagined, by them, that shall read them: But especially by those, that knew my disposition. But rising one day, from my Devotions, it was suggested to my consideration, that those desires were not given me, to be kept in private, to my self, but for the good of others.
>   And if any unlike a Christian shall say; I wrote them, for mine owne glory, I like a Christian, will tell them; I therefore sent them abroad; for such a strict union is there betwixt my deare God and mee, that his glory is mine, and mine is his; and I will tell them too, I am not asham'd of their birth; for before I knew it, the Prince of eternall glory had affianced mee to himselfe; and that is my glory.
> (Eliza A2r)

The author of this work – whom we only know as 'Eliza' from the title of her collection of devotional verses – begins here by adopting the passive role of the instrument of God. In the context of her 'Devotions,' she claims, it was 'suggested' to her that her poetry should be 'sent into the world' to work for 'the good of others.' This conventional scenario of the religious poet as medium for the divine is given a gendered nuance by Eliza's choice of metaphors: her poems are her 'Babes' and are the result of a 'strict union' between the female poet and her affianced Lord, the 'Prince of eternall glory.' In a reversal of the conventional relationship between the male poet and his female muse, here the female poet is inspired by a divine partner whose textual (and spiritual) offspring she subsequently bears. Against all the odds, the female poet achieves a (second) virgin birth; the title-page announces the poems as *Eliza's Babes: or the Virgin's-Offering*.   As Martha Moulsworth cryptically claimed in her poetic *Memorandum* (1632), 'The muses females are / And therefore of us females take some care.' [5]

Despite the rhetoric of modesty concerning the decision to publish her poems, Eliza achieves an almost triumphant tone in her account of her 'owne glory' to her women readers.   The trick of self-construction here centers on the way in which she responds to the unchristian assumption that she might be publishing her poems for her own benefit.   In a witty twist of the expected retort, she says instead that she is indeed writing for her own glory, because she is so bound up with God that his glory is hers.   The final effect of this apparent self-denial (all that she has is God's and therefore her own self is nothing) is ultimately a self-assertion (all the glory that goes to God also goes to Eliza).   In this representation of herself and her writings as God's, Eliza paradoxically goes against the religious and gendered assumptions which underpin her justification.   She anticipates the attitudes of those who criticize her for speaking out:

> And if any shall say, others may be as thankefull as shee, though they talk not so much of it; Let them know that if they did rightly apprehend the infinite mercies of God to them, they could not be silent. (Eliza A3r)

The female author thus claims an obligation to write or speak out; she cannot remain silent once she has perceived the 'infinite mercies of God.' In this claim she is going directly against the advice given by St Paul concerning women in the church, frequently cited during the seventeenth century: 'let the woman learn in silence with all subjection' (2 Timothy 2:11). In solidarity with her female readers, and in community with many other medieval and early modern women writers who responded to a higher vocation to break silence in order to praise God, Eliza wittily negotiates space for herself (and others still who may follow) as a woman writer of devotional poetry.

The delicacy of Eliza's task, manoeuvering between literary and devotional expectations, is highlighted by her insertion of a second discussion of her position, further on in *Eliza's Babes*. It is as though she feels the need (Tristram Shandy-like) to write a preface when she is in the midst of the work. Once again, her self-construction as writer is dependent upon the subtly interwoven elements of gender and religion, though on this occasion she is addressing God rather than her human readers:

> And now I dare not say, I am an ignorant woman and unfit to write,
> for if thou wilt declare thy goodness, and thy mercy by weak and
> contemptible means, who can resist thy will. My gracious God, I
> will be now so farre from being unwilling to doe it, that I will not
> rest until I have done it, for in all ages thou wilt not leave thy selfe
> without a witnesse of thy mercy and goodnesse to thy children, and
> therefore I will send out my words to speak thy praise. (Eliza 75)

Unlike Elizabeth Cary or Rachel Speght, who took the blame for any
shortcomings squarely upon their own shoulders, Eliza here transfers all the
responsibility – and the initiative – to God. It is his 'will' that so 'weak and
contemptible' a woman should have been chosen to write, as a sign of his
infinite compassion. Once again, a traditional rhetorical stance is intensified
through gendering; many writers will consider themselves (or present
themselves as) inadequate, but Eliza is specifically that socially condemned
figure, an 'ignorant woman' who ought to know that she is deemed 'unfit to
write.' However, the implication of Eliza's self-justification is that God has
overcome even those boundaries in fathering her poetic 'Babes.'

III

The argument of privacy is a very important one in the construction of early
women's authorship. Like all writers of the Renaissance period, women poets
were working at that moment of transition from the limited circulation of
manuscript culture to the unknown public encountered through publishing in
print. For women to emerge into the public arena, however, even if only
through their writings, was potentially a far more scandalous undertaking than
for their male equivalents. As we have already seen in Eliza's preface, the
reluctant mother-poet claimed that she did not want her poems to leave home
(as it were) and be 'sent into the world.' Eliza's contemporary and fellow
devotional lyricist, An Collins, wrote in a similar vein that

> Unto the publick view of every one
> I did not purpose these my lines to send,
> Which for my private use were made alone. (Collins 3)

If her *Divine Songs and Meditacions* are to be given to 'the publick view' – as indeed they were in 1653 – then Collins goes on to say that the reader she has in mind is a 'pious friend' who will judge her writing as an expression of grace rather than a demonstration of 'Art.' Here we are encountering another well-known trope, a fundamental assumption concerning devotional style: plainness is next to godliness, since high art is a sign of unholy pride. Collins's rejection of 'Art,' however, is given added significance in the context of women's devotional writing, which must very specifically dissociate itself from the cosmetic or deceptive arts conventionally associated with femininity. In this gendered setting, artlessness is not weakness but a form of honesty, which in turn implies purity.[6]

As her prefatory poem proceeds, An Collins introduces the idea that, perhaps in place of artistry, her poetry might create an impression of the writer's self:

> And lastly in regard of any one,
> Who may by accident hereafter find,
> This, though to them the Author bee unknown,
> Yet seeing here, the image of her mind;
> They may conjecture how she was inclin'd:
> And furthermore, that God doth Grace bestow,
> Upon his servants, though hee keeps them low. (Collins 4)

This is one of the most interesting authorial self-constructions I have so far discovered in Renaissance English writing, for two main reasons. Firstly, instead of spending the preface sketching an image of herself, as so many of her contemporaries did, Collins uses this preliminary moment to point to her presence in the subsequent main body of the text. Her writing itself is, as she terms it, 'the image of her mind'; the whole of her work bears the stamp, not of a Christian spirit or a human personality in general, but very specifically of her own individuality. A similar expression had been used by Elizabeth Grymeston in 1604 when she offered her *Miscelanea* to her son as a 'true portrature of thy mothers minde' (Grymeston A3v). But while Grymeston was passing on a miscellany of aphorisms, advice, verse and meditation for the benefit of her last remaining child, Collins was presenting herself consciously as the 'Author,' whose mind and personality were encapsulated within her collection of devotional poems. Secondly, Collins's use of the title 'author' for herself is intriguing. Although a number of Renaissance women

writers use the term to refer to themselves in abstract terms (as in Aemilia
Lanyer's 'Authors Dreame'), Collins is among the first to flesh it out with
distinctly female details. This 'Author,' though 'unknown' and 'low' (as both
woman and individual), is, according to Collins, to be found revealed in her
text; readers may see in the words of her songs 'the image of *her* mind' and
begin to conjecture 'how *she* was inclin'd' (my italics). The choice of the
word 'author,' used with these unashamedly female pronouns, implies certain
radical connections: it links her with God, the 'Author' and creator of life
itself, and thus with the supreme patriarchal source of 'authority.' Though
modest and 'low,' Collins is blazing a trail toward a more fundamentally
emancipated idea of authorship.

IV

Literary prefaces, while being a means of entrance to a work, are also always
a moment of letting go; they are a greeting to the reader but at the same time
constitute the author's farewell to the text. In many cases, Renaissance
women writers' prefaces were actual farewells, since the women were often
moved, like Elizabeth Grymeston, to release their work when facing death or
approaching the mortal dangers of childbirth. For a healthy and childless
woman writer such as Margaret Cavendish, however, the process of
publication still involved a sense of parting. In her *Poems, and Fancies* of
1653, Cavendish explains how protective she feels towards her book as it
begins to face the rigors of critical reception:

> Condemne me not for making such a coyle
> About my Book, alas it is my Childe.
> Just like a Bird, when her Young are in Nest,
> Goes in, and out, and hops, and takes no Rest;
> But when their Young are fledg'd, their heads out peep,
> Lord what a chirping doe the Old one keep.
> So I, for fear my Strengthlesse Childe should fall
> Against a doore, or stoole, aloud I call,
> Bid have a care of such a dangerous place:
> Thus write I much, to hinder all disgrace. (Cavendish A8v)

The dominant metaphor, as in *Eliza's Babes*, is that of writing as motherhood;

however, here the emphasis falls more heavily on the dangers to the child, which needs a wrapping or 'coyle' around it for protection. The writer is likened to a motherbird who at first is restlessly concerned for her young (making a 'coyle' about her offspring, in the other meaning of coil, a fuss). With ironic self-reflection, Cavendish describes the writer-mother noisily warning against impending danger: 'Lord what a chirping doe the Old one keep.' Though the poem tends towards self-mockery of the poet as this 'Old one,' the last line is poignantly revealing. Writing itself becomes a protective mechanism against 'disgrace,' the anticipated reception of poetry by a woman writer. For, as Anne Bradstreet commented in her 'Prologue' (1650) on the fate of the work of the 'Female wits' such as herself, 'If what I doe prove well, it wo'nt advance, / They'l say it's stolne, or else, it was by chance' (Bradstreet 7). In the prefatory poems of both authors, humor is a means of protection against the continuing vulnerability of the woman writer's position.

The representations of herself and her work given by Bradstreet in her later poem, 'The Author to her Book,' stem, like Cavendish's, from the basic metaphor of the writer as mother. However, Bradstreet describes a harsher scene in which the mother feels her poverty and inadequacy, and the poetic offspring is seen to be 'ill-form'd.' Out of maternal compassion the poet tries to 'amend' the 'blemishes' of the child she has produced:

> I wash'd thy face, but more defects I saw,
> And rubbing off a spot, still made a flaw.
> I strecht thy joynts to make thee even feet,
> Yet still thou run'st more hobling then is meet;
> In better dress to trim thee was my mind,
> But nought save home-spun Cloth, i'th'house I find.
> In this array, 'mongst Vulgars mayst thou roam,
> In Criticks hands, beware thou dost not come;
> And take thy way where yet thou art not known,
> If for thy Father askt, say, thou hadst none:
> And for thy Mother, she alas is poor,
> Which caus'd her thus to send thee out of door. (Bradstreet 178)

The allegory is clear and telling: when the woman poet alone produces an offspring, it has no 'Father' and is therefore illegitimate, a bastard product.[7] When the woman poet seeks to present her child in the 'better dress' of rhetoric or learning, all she can find in her experience is 'home-spun Cloth,' which proves inadequate once the poem meets the critics. Even in the 1670s

it was still dangerous for a 'Mother' to send her poetry 'out of door.'
Bradstreet, however – unlike Cavendish, whose mothering is represented as
careful, even as fussy – seems to confront this danger with an audacious
carelessness. Here, indeed, is a woman prepared to advertise not only her
writing, but also her ineffectual attempts at (metaphorical) mothering. This is
not so much a painstaking justification of her 'home-spun' art as a daring
challenge to her critical readers.

V

We have considered a sequence of prefatory and dedicatory texts by
Renaissance Englishwomen in roughly chronological order. But it would be
wrong to conclude that the survey has suggested a positive pattern of
development in the way women writers introduced themselves to their readers
during the period. Indeed, the last two writers, different though they are in
their use of the trope of motherhood, remain among the most negative in their
outlook, stressing the dangers and disgraces awaiting the work of the woman
writer as it enters the fierce public world opened up by print culture. This
sense of unease is confirmed in the preface to Katherine Philips's poems,
published in 1667:

> I am so far from expecting applause for anything I scribble, that I
> can hardly expect pardon; and sometimes I think that employment so
> far above my reach, and unfit for my sex, that I am going to resolve
> against it for ever. (Philips n.p.)

The sense of writing as unsuitable for her sex leads here, as in other examples
we have seen, to a conscious down-grading of the woman writer's skills and
achievements. Philips, an accomplished poet known in her lifetime as the
'Matchless Orinda,' describes her own work as 'scribble.'[8] This is the very
same term as was used by Margaret Cavendish in her autobiographical
memoir, *A True Relation of my Birth, Breeding and Life* (1656), in which she
commented that, whereas her husband wrote what his 'wit' dictated, she
passed her time 'rather with *scribbling* than writing, with words than wit'
(Graham et al. 93; my italics). The self-deprecating mode of description and
the tendency towards binary contrasts on the literary as well as social and

spiritual levels, in which the woman writer is always the lower, persist far beyond the Renaissance.

It is clear from this sample of prefaces that the emergence of the woman poet, as perceived in the self-images used by such women, was not a straightforward process of evolution. The language of the later prefaces is, if anything, more troubled and bitter than that of the earlier examples. Across this range of texts, however, a number of clear issues arise. First, it is striking that gender is not merely a modern critical category but was a feature of the women's own thinking and self-construction as writers. My title quotation, 'First fruits of a woman's wit,' taken from another of Aemilia Lanyer's many dedicatory poems to her 1611 volume (in this case to Princess Elizabeth), encapsulates Lanyer's sense of her own poetry as the 'fruit' of a specifically female poetic capacity(11).[9] This consciousness of womanhood may also be seen in the extracts from Primrose, Eliza, Moulsworth, Collins, Grymeston, Cavendish, Bradstreet and Philips. Though it is often a negative feature, characterizing womanhood as a handicap for a writer, femininity can sometimes be teasingly turned to the writer's advantage, as in the case of Eliza's prefaces.[10]

The metaphors for their work that these writers chose are strongly gendered, too; the poets are often depicted in a maternal relation to their texts, whether as human mothers or fussing mother-birds learning to let their babes flee the nest. The hostile world of readers, explicitly expecting the worst from women writers, lurks at the fringes of these prefatory pleas, making their defensiveness understandable as well as consciously gendered. This anticipated rejection renders the impact of the maternal metaphor significantly different from that of contemporary male authors who consciously depicted their texts as offspring.[11] The fathers of the women's texts are often implied in the prefaces; poetic partners range from Christ, the Word himself to whom Eliza is 'affianced,' to – at the other extreme – the unnamed father who has caused Anne Bradstreet's poems to enter the world as bastard offspring. In all of these ways the rhetoric of self-presentation takes on a broader aspect than the conventional language of authorial modesty. The topos of humility, when conventionally used by highly educated male authors, is not intended to highlight the author's weaknesses. The woman writer who asks for 'pardon' for her 'error' in writing, on the other hand, is drawing attention to her transgression against social and religious ideology as well as literary convention. However, the familiar trope of the reluctant author can play a vital role for the woman whose writing, if construed as deliberate, might be seen as a flouting of a woman's proper passivity (for which read also chastity and holiness). Thus the stress on the justification of women's writing on emotional grounds, such as Mary Sidney's 'love and zeale' or An Collins's 'true intent,' is a further gendered feature of their self-construction, linked with the need for women to root their activities in devotion to a superior cause.

The women writers whom we have observed justified their work by reference to a number of higher authorities, including God the Father, Christ the divine fiance, a brother and the muses. Where there is no reference to an external figure of this kind, the women tend to explain their writerly activity in relation to a particular readership, whether it comprises individual patrons or a general class of readers.[12] The conscious contract between some early modern women poets and a specifically female readership – as, for example, in the cases of Aemilia Lanyer, Diana Primrose and Eliza – adds a unique dimension to the confidence of the women authors themselves. Lanyer's poetry is presented as a 'Glasse' of 'steel' – true and unwavering – while Primrose's verse will give her readers 'never-fading fame' and Eliza is defiantly 'not asham'd' of her poems' 'birth.' Equally noteworthy is the poise with which An Collins writes of her presence as 'Author,' by which the reader will be able to discern 'the image of her mind' throughout her text. Perhaps it is in that moment – the rendering feminine by both Collins and Bradstreet of the hitherto patriarchal term 'author' – that the rise of the English woman poet as a distinct entity really begins. It is also no coincidence that this gendering of authorship emerges in the same period as the identification of the author as an individual (rather than as a member of a coterie) and potentially as a professional rather than as a leisured amateur.[13] As soon as writing becomes a matter of public competition, financial remuneration and social status, then gender difference among authors becomes a more conscious factor, and anticipation of criticism (as in the case of Margaret Cavendish's poem) becomes more likely.

These conclusions must, of course, remain speculative since there is so much still to be discovered and understood in the area of early modern women poets and their self-construction as writers.[14] We need to continue to raise the questions addressed in this essay, starting with the exploration of images, visual as well as verbal, associated with women and poetry in the Renaissance, and proceeding through issues of authority and gender (conscious and unconscious) to the formulation of women's creativity as writers and as readers. The pursuit of these matters will be of significance not only to the study of Renaissance women poets, but also to our knowledge of changing patterns of gender roles and rhetorical assumptions in the early modern period, and to the history of writing in connection with emerging concepts of individuality. This discussion is thus (I hope) set to continue.

Figure 1: 'Old Woman Reading,' sometimes also known as 'Rembrandt's Mother,' by Gerard Dou, c. 1630-35, reproduced by kind permission of the Rijksmuseum, Amsterdam

Figure 2: 'Woman writing a Letter' by Gerard ter Borch, c. 1655, reproduced by kind permission of the Friends of the Mauritshuis, The Hague

Acknowledgements

With thanks to colleagues in Groningen, York, Lancaster, Bloomington and Stony Brook for stimulating discussions during the evolution of this chapter, and to the Rijksmuseum, Amsterdam, and the Mauritshuis, The Hague, for permission to reproduce the illustrations.

Notes

[1]   See, for instance, the (anonymous) portrait of Baron Cobham and his family, in the collection of the Marquiss of Bath at Longleat House in Wiltshire, Great Britain, in which the Baron is shown, anachronistically, in the presence of his two wives and their many offspring.

[2]   For a useful general discussion of the early modern literary preface, but with an almost exclusively male focus, see Kevin Dunn, *Pretexts of Authority*. For an extensive discussion of early modern authorship, see Wendy Wall, *The Imprint of Gender*.

[3]   On the issue of women as translators in the early modern period, see Suzanne Trill, 'Sixteenth-Century Women's Writing' and Tina Krontiris, *Oppositional Voices*. For further discussion of Mary Sidney as author and translator, see the chapters by Shannon Miller and Margaret Hannay elsewhere in this volume.

[4]   The most famous early modern example of literature as looking-glass is the 1559 collection of tragedies entitled *A Mirror for Magistrates*. For women writers, the metaphor is complicated by the association of femininity itself with contemplation and self-reflection – and thus, by implication, with vanity as well as beauty. For further discussion of the multiple meanings in Lanyer's mirror references, see Jacqueline Pearson, 'Women Writers and Women Readers.'

[5]   'The gendering of inspiration is a complex issue and is addressed in its seventeenth-century context, particularly in the work of devotional writers, by several contributors to Danielle Clarke and Elizabeth Clarke's *The Double Voice*. The gender stereotypes of authorship and the muse in this period are vividly summed up in the opening lines of Dryden's prologue to his play *An Evening's Love* (performed in 1668):

When first our poet set himself to write,
Like a young bridegroom on his wedding night,
He laid about him, and so did bestir him,
His muse could never lie in quiet for him:
But now his honeymoon is gone and past,
Yet the ungrateful drudgery must last (1-6)

[6] See, for example, Ben Jonson's lyric 'Still to be neat' for an exploration of the links between his dislike of women's artificiality in dress, make-up and manner, and his fondness for the literary art of plainness (291-292). Significantly, this poem is from *Epicoene*.

[7] For a fuller consideration of this metaphor of bastardy, see Alison Findlay, *Illegitimate Power*.

[8] For further discussion of Philips's self-definition as a writer, see Dorothy Mermin, 'Women Becoming Poets.'

[9] 'First fruits' is a biblical term for the part of the harvest given as an offering to God (Leviticus 23:10).

[10] For further discussion of the intermingling of victimization and enablement in women's writing, see Wall 279-340.

[11] For more detailed discussions of the concept of the writer as parent in early modern texts, see Susan Stanford Friedman, 'Creativity and the Childbirth Metaphor' and Margaret Dupuis, 'Birthing the Text.'

[12] It is interesting to note the relative absence of the familiar trope of the 'friend' who encourages the author to publish. This is fairly common among male writers of the period, but, as far as I can discover, is less frequently invoked by women, who tend either to sidestep secular authorization and claim their justification directly from God, or to anticipate the support of their (often female) readers.

[13] The rise of the self-conscious author in England is generally linked to Ben Jonson's first folio of his *Works* (1616), and subsequently to the position of Dryden and his contemporaries in the later seventeenth century. For another perspective on this phenomenon, see Kevin Pask, *The Emergence of the English Author*. The relationship between the individualizing of authorship and the emergence of women writers has yet to be fully explored.

[14] As part of the evolving discussion, see Margaret W. Ferguson 'Renaissance Concepts of the "Woman Writer".'

Works Cited

Bradstreet, Anne. *The Complete Works of Anne Bradstreet*. eds. Joseph R. McElrath Jr and Allan P. Robb. Boston: Twayne, 1981.

Cary, Elizabeth. *The History of the Life, Reign and Death of Edward II*. London, 1680. *Paradise of Women*. ed. Betty Travitsky. 216-18.

Cavendish, Margaret, Duchess of Newcastle. *Poems, and Fancies*. London: 1653.

Clarke, Danielle, and Elizabeth Clarke, eds. *The Double Voice: Gendered Writing inEarly Modern England*. London: Macmillan, 2000.

Collins, An. *Divine Songs and Meditacions*. London, 1653.

Dryden, John. *An Evening's Love*. London, 1671.

Dupuis, Margaret. 'Birthing the Text: Authorship and Childbirth in Early Modern England.' Diss. U of Oregon, 1998.

Dunn, Kevin. *Pretexts of Authority: The Rhetoric of Authorship in the Renaissance Preface*. Cambridge: Cambridge UP, 1994.

Eliza. *Eliza's Babes: or the Virgin's-Offering. Being Divine Poems, Meditations. Written by a Lady, who onely desires to advance the glory of God, and not her own*. London, 1652.

Ferguson, Margaret W. 'Renaissance Concepts of the "Woman Writer".' *Women and Literature in Britain 1500-1700*. ed. Helen Wilcox. Cambridge: Cambridge UP, 1996. 143-68.

Findlay, Alison. *Illegitimate Power: Bastards in Renaissance Drama*. Manchester: Manchester UP, 1994.

Friedman, Susan Stanford. 'Creativity and the Childbirth Metaphor: Gender Difference in Literary Discourse.' *Feminist Studies* 13 (1987): 49-82.

Graham, Elspeth, Hilary Hinds, Elaine Hobby, and Helen Wilcox, eds. *Her Own Life:Autobiographical Writings by Seventeenth-Century Englishwomen*. London: Routledge, 1989.

Grymeston, Elizabeth. *Miscelanea, Meditations, Memoratives*. London, 1604.

Jonson, Ben. *The Complete Poems*. ed. George Parfitt. Harmondsworth: Penguin, 1975. Rpt. and rev. 1996.

Knox, John. *The First Blast of the Trumpet against the monstrous regiment of women*. Geneva, 1558.

Krontiris, Tina. *Oppositional Voices: Women as Writers and Translators of Literature in the English Renaissance*. London: Routledge, 1992.

Lanyer, Aemilia. *The Poems of Aemilia Lanyer*. ed. Susanne Woods. Oxford: Oxford UP, 1993.

Mermin, Dorothy. 'Women Becoming Poets.' *ELH* 57 (1990): 335-55.

Moulsworth, Martha. *'The Birthday of My Self': Martha Moulsworth, Renaissance Poet*. eds. Ann Depas-Orange and Robert C. Evans. Princeton: Critical Matrix, 1996.

Pask, Kevin. *The Emergence of the English Author: Scripting the Life of the Poet in Early Modern England*. Cambridge: Cambridge UP, 1996.

Pearson, Jacqueline. 'Women Writers and Women Readers: The Case of Aemilia Lanyer.' *Voicing Women: Gender and Sexuality in Early Modern Writing*. eds. Kate Chedgzoy, Melanie Hansen and Suzanne Trill. Keele: Keele UP, 1996. 45-54.

Philips, Katherine. *Poems by Mrs. Katherine Philips, the Matchless Orinda*. London 1667.

Primrose, Diane. *A Chain of Pearl*. London, 1630. *Women Poets of the Renaissance*. ed. Marion Wynne-Davies. 229-38.

Sidney, Mary. *The Psalms of Sir Philip Sidney and the Countess of Pembroke*. ed. J. C. A. Rathmell. New York: New York UP, 1963.

Speght, Rachel. *Mortalities Memorandum*. London, 1621. *Paradise of Women*. ed. Betty Travitsky. 141-42.

Swift, Jonathan. *A Tale of a Tub*. London, 1704.

Travitsky, Betty, ed. *The Paradise of Women: Writings by Englishwomen of the Renaissance*. Westport: Greenwood P, 1981.

Trill, Suzanne. 'Sixteenth-Century Women's Writing: Mary Sidney's *Psalmes* and the Femininity of Translation.' *Writing and the English Renaissance*. eds. William Zunder and Suzanne Trill. London: Longman, 1996. 140-58.

Wall, Wendy. *The Imprint of Gender: Authorship and Publication in the English Renaissance*. Ithaca: Cornell UP, 1993.

Wynne-Davies, Marion, ed. *Women Poets of the Renaissance*. London: J. M. Dent, 1998.

11

A Rhetoric of Innocence: The Poetry of Katherine Philips, 'The Matchless Orinda'

Bronwen Price

The Preface to the posthumous 1667 edition of Philips's work pinpoints the slippery relationship between the symbolic and material, text and body, that features in much writing by seventeenth-century women. Presented as a private letter from 'Orinda' (Philips's pseudonym) to 'Poliarchus' (Charles Cotterell), it specifically responds to the apparently unauthorized, adulterated appearance of Philips's poetry in 1664, shortly after which she contracted smallpox and died.[1]

In her letter the figure of Orinda is concerned to establish the 'innocence' of her textual activity and 'ignorance' of the processes by which her corpus was published (Philips 'The Preface').[2] She refers to her indebtedness to Cotterell in aiding its withdrawal from the public domain, asserting that she 'never writ any line in my life with an intention to have it printed,' her compositions being undertaken 'only for my own amusement in a retir'd life' ('The Preface'). She alludes to her work as 'scribble' and 'careless blotted writing' composed upon 'rags of Paper,' conceding that poetic creation is 'far above my reach, and unfit for my Sex' ('The Preface'). The integrity of her feminine virtue is asserted through the fragmentary condition of her corpus. Moreover, publication is associated with bodily disease and mutilation: the 'injury' and 'unworthy usage' resulting from having her 'private . . . imaginations rifled and exposed' cost her 'a sharp fit of sickness,' while the anticipation of future publication is envisaged 'with the same reluctancy as I would cut off a Limb to save my Life' ('The Preface'). Literary production is apparently physically corrupting.

Poliarchus's printed response to Orinda's letter takes up these metaphors. The injury her work suffers at the hands of the stationer, which 'seized unexpectedly upon her, the true Original' and 'violently tore her out' of the world

('The Preface'). Poliarchus's edition of her poems attempts to repair the damage by restoring 'their native Shape and Beauty' which had been 'deformed' 'when they appeared in that strange disguise' ('The Preface'). The reformation of Philips's verse in print will, in turn, resurrect her from the ravages of smallpox and death by recovering her reputation and granting her eternal life as 'the matchless Orinda.'

Such corporeal images draw attention to the dominant cultural construction of women during the period in which feminine identity was linked to the female body and its status and, by association, female speech, especially in the public domain, was equated with sexual promiscuity.[3] Throughout the letters, though, Orinda and Poliarchus play with these standard sets of tropes, Orinda's mortal sin in taking up the pen being punctuated by an insistence on her modesty and chastity. An excessive innocence underscores her textual excess. However, as Elaine Hobby argues, we should not take Orinda's protestations too literally (129-30, 132). The content and mode of circulation of Philips's work clearly signal her political allegiances and poetic practices. Her first poem appeared, albeit anonymously, as early as 1651 prefixed to a royalist volume of William Cartwright's work (Thomas, 'Introduction' 6-7). While it is true that in the 1650s the distribution of her verse was largely confined to her 'Society of Friendship,' a select circle of friends residing in West Wales and London with whom she corresponded and to whom she wrote poetry, coterie circulation had particular political significance during the Interregnum. It symbolized political loyalty and community, offering a means through which royalist values could implicitly be protected (Thomas, 'Introduction' 7-8, 12). Moreover, Philips wrote numerous occasional verse addressed to members of the royal family during the Restoration, including 'On the faire weather at the Coronacon' and 'To the Queene on her arrivall at Portsmouth. May 1662' (73, 74-5). This suggests a call for public recognition, especially as she now began to send her work directly to the Court. By the time of Charles II's accession, it is evident that Philips's work was well-known and had begun to be given serious consideration. Indeed, her translation of Pierre Corneille's *Pompée*, performed in 1663, won royal acclaim.

It is the appearance of her work in print from which Orinda is most anxious to distance herself in the letter, for print was particularly associated with social and feminine impropriety, while coterie circulation was aligned to social privilege (Wall 281; Barash 81). She goes so far as to point out that it was Cotterell, and not her, who first discovered that her poems had gone 'abroad so impudently . . . for I had not seen the Book, nor can imagine what's in't' ('The Preface'). Wendy Wall draws attention to the way in which 'abroad' was 'a word that was commonly used to describe publication, travel, and harlotry' in the seventeenth century (299). While Orinda's letter calls forth these resonances, the printed text seems to be given an independence and agency quite separate from herself. She, by contrast, is identified in reference to her physical confinement, passivity and debilitation. Although she has been corporeally damaged by her text, its harmful activities are set against her harmlessness: 'those fugitive Papers' 'escap'd my hands' so as to produce 'this most afflictive accident' ('The Preface'). It is the text which commits the illicit act over which she has no control. Indeed, the movement of her poems from private thought to public exposure is the result of her subjection and sacrifice to the desires of her friends, as 'others [sic] commands' 'seduc'd me to write' ('The Preface'). From the outset Orinda is presented as being the object of exploitation and persuasion, responsibility for any appearances of her work being placed firmly outside her command. Ironically, it is apparently her initial innocence that allowed such excesses to occur.

A close examination of the letter clearly reveals, as Hobby convincingly shows, that it 'was not the "private" communication it is presented as, but was designed for a public audience' (132). It is intricately and knowingly argued at every turn, the carefully formulated figure of Orinda providing a strategic mode of self-presentation whereby Philips's act of writing is made to appear more acceptable both in terms of her gender and social position (130).[4] Moreover, apologies such as Philips's letter conventionally preface women's printed poetry during this period, registering, as Susan Wiseman suggests, 'a particular self-consciousness . . . about their status as gendered texts' (12), thus highlighting women writers' need to negotiate prevailing concepts of feminine decorum. This process of negotiation is premised on a rhetoric of innocence in Philips's letter.

There are, however, other meanings at play in the text. Orinda's allusions to physical adulteration not only concern the appearance of her poems in print, but are also connected with an anxiety about her own loss of control over her work and its meanings.[5] It is the invasion of what implicitly was once her chaste, unsullied corpus by the tamperings of others when it 'escap'd my hands' ('The Preface') that especially troubles her. On learning that her poems are 'abominably transcribed,' she fears that they 'must be more abus'd than I think possible' ('The Preface'). In this sense, the insistent rhetoric of innocence is not only employed as a means of legitimizing Philips's writing, but also implies other things: it is a code for signalling a desire for authorial autonomy and self-definition. If this double-edged deployment of 'innocence' is apparent in the letter, it is even more intricately and subtly woven into the poetry itself. The reiterated trope of 'innocence' throughout Philips's verse releases still more complex meanings than in the letter.

I Political Innocence

On the surface Philips's work brings few surprises, operating within familiar poetic discourses and conventional forms for the period. The majority of her poems comprise occasional verse and lyrics, often addressed to specific people, who are frequently assigned pastoral names: 'To Mr Henry Vaughan, Silurist, on his Poems,' 'To my Lucasia,' 'A Farewell to Rosania.' Standard pastoral themes and motifs, together with allusions to Virgil's eclogues, pervade Philips's verse. In particular, Philips's remodelling of Platonic tropes and courtly codes as a means of elevating female friendship is initially most striking in her work and marks her out as a new voice of the period.[6] This combination of conservative forms and themes with innovative practice signals her poetry's ambivalent relationship to prevailing contemporary ideas about femininity.

   The poems are nonetheless littered with references to the innocent, chaste and spiritual concerns of their subject matter. Female friendship is continually extolled because it is founded on 'an incomparable mixture' of souls ('L'amitié: To Mrs M. Awbrey' 142, l. 4) and is therefore 'next to Angells Love, if not the same' ('A Friend' 166, l. 9). Indeed, the figures to whom Orinda's 'spotless passion' ('To my Lucasia, in defence of declared friendship' 154, l. 27) is directed frequently epitomize feminine 'virtue': Lucasia, for example, embraces an 'excess' of 'humility alone' so as to make her worthy of being 'cannoniz'd' ('Lucasia' 104-5, ll. 58, 40): 'Nay innocence it self less cleare must be, / If innocence be any thing but she' (ll. 41-2).

   It is also worth noting that the first person subject is often far less central than we might usually expect in the lyric form. In Philips's poetry the concept of friendship in the abstract frequently collapses into 'we' and continually takes precedence over 'I.' In spite of its personal address, 'Friendship in Emblem, or the Seale' begins with a general analysis of the refined and refining union that friendship comprises. The third person is employed throughout and it is not until the final line that these qualities are emblazoned on 'Lucasia's and Orinda's name' (108, l. 64).

When the first person subject does appear it often mutates into 'we' or 'thee.' It manifests itself in order to mask itself. The speaker of 'To my excellent Lucasia, on our friendship' identifies 'I' only to signify its hollowness until it emerges as 'Thee' through the 'inocent' 'design' of 'our Soule' (121-2, ll. 4, 23-4). In a number of poems the speaker is subsumed under the beloved's identity. In 'Rosania shaddow'd whilest Mrs M. Awbrey' the first person subject is overshadowed by the idolized figure of Rosania, whom, 'Such innocence within her Brest doth dwell, / Angells themselves doe onely parallell' (118, ll. 41-2). Although the speaker appears at the beginning and end (and at line 25), she remains veiled for the central part of the poem, incorporated into the general abstract body of people on whom Rosania produces her miraculous effects and enters primarily to indicate the inadequacy of her ability to contain Rosania in language (120, ll. 85-90). While such self-debasement is a commonplace of courtly love poetry, this feature takes on another dimension when the speaker is identified as being female. Rather than highlighting the speaker's abject state of anguish and despair, as might be expected in Petrarchan love poetry, her self-deprecation seems to be aligned to an anxiety about taking up an appropriate speaking position. Speech melts into silence and self-effacement.

Yet on closer inspection these features of innocence, chastity and privacy come to signify something more ambivalent than might initially be apparent. As Barash has recently argued, Philips's allusions to feminine honor and virtue are underscored by a complex network of political referencing.[7] Concepts of friendship and private community became of course important tropes in cavalier writing during the Civil War and Interregnum periods, forming part of a discourse signifying allegiance and loyalty to royalism. A number of Philips's occasional verse from the 1660s connect the loss of the Crown with the demise of the values of friendship. In 'Arion on a Dolphin to his Majestie' Charles II's exile is linked with his being 'by friends betraid' (71, l. 22). It is 'heaven, his secret potent friend' that 'kept him upright / Midst flattering hope and bloudy fright' (ll. 24-5). Friendship is identified with divine order. This, in turn, is associated with a private, coded mode of communication resonant with what Lois Potter has termed 'a philosophy of secrecy' through which the royalist community established 'its sense of itself as elite' during the 1640s and 50s (113). 'To the noble Palaemon on his incomparable discourse of Friendship' (83-4), a poem probably written as a response to Francis Finch's treatise *Friendship* (1653/4) which was dedicated to 'Noble *Lucasia-Orinda*' (Thomas,

'Introduction' 330), provides a more elaborate, ritualized figuration of friendship. Palaemon's deliverance of friendship from its recent misappropriation when it 'had a scorn or mask been made' (l. 9), is conceived in terms of a chivalric romance. Friendship is feminized, 'discover'd,' 'rescu'd,' protected and saved by the 'conqu'ring truths' of Palaemon (ll. 16, 28, 22), whose heroic deeds are not only equated with 'honour' and loyalty to the king (ll. 27, 20), but are also specifically linked with an image of restoration when he 'Unvayled her face, and then restor'd her Crown' (l. 18). As Barash points out, here Orinda's and Lucasia's friendship is represented as an emblem of monarchy (77). In revealing the true values of friendship Palaemon also unveils and exposes the political encoding of Philips's poem.

In addition, sequestered havens, rural retreats and enclosed, private domains, topographies that are central to Philips's friendship verse, feature regularly in cavalier poetry during the Interregnum. Potter shows how these settings are often endowed 'with a transcendental meaning,' operating as sites in which 'rituals of loyalty' may be protected and sustained (138). The Platonic cast of the ideals set out in such contexts in Philips's verse could be regarded as functioning in this way to some degree. The idealization of Platonic codes and rituals was introduced by Henrietta Maria from the French cult of *préciosité* and was cultivated in Caroline court culture during the 1630s (Parry 29-31; Thomas, 'Introduction' 7).[8] In the 1640s and 50s allusion to these practices became, as Thomas indicates, 'one way of demonstrating loyalty' and was 'an important cohesive influence among defeated Cavaliers' ('Introduction' 8, 10). Richard Lovelace, for example, draws on these ideas in a number of his poems. Indeed, it is worth noting some significant connections in the images presented in his and Philips's verse.[9] The loyalty of the royalist speaker in Lovelace's 'To Althea from Prison' is defined in reference to his Platonic love for 'my divine Althea' and is associated with 'Minds innocent and quiet' (78-9, ll. 3, 27). More specifically, the female figure in 'The Lady *A.L. My* Asylum *in a great extremity*' performs a function similar to the feminized figure of friendship in 'To Palaemon.' In the latter poem she is the location of 'Men's (and Angells) bliss' (83, l. 8) and the means through which values that have been corrupted or lost may be restored when Palaemon reveals her 'vertue' and transforms her into 'a glorious monument' (ll. 28, 34). In Lovelace's poem the woman is the source of spiritual ecstasy and is also linked with images of monarchy and restoration when the speaker enacts a similar coronation ritual to Palaemon in crowning her with the 'Bayes' and 'Lawrels' of his poetry (Lovelace 62-5, ll. 20-21, 73-6).[10]

Where, however, Palaemon rescues friendship with his 'conqu'ring truths' (l.22), in Lovelace's poem it is the woman who rescues the speaker through her 'Conquering Goodness' (64, l. 75) and it is not until later in the poem that she becomes the object of his discursive authority.

In these various ways Philips's poetry forms a link with a broader set of aesthetics associated with royalist allegiances which provide an implicit set of political signals in her work. In this respect the private and public arenas are not as clearly demarcated as they might seem to be on the surface, but rather intersect in ways which complicate such boundaries.

II Innocent Speech

Philips's rhetoric of innocence, however, has a more far-reaching significance than the specific party political undercurrents that I have outlined here. Her poems' allusion to cavalier poetics does not simply indicate social and political allegiance, it also frequently has the effect of complicating and redefining those aesthetics. While it is important to acknowledge the ostensible conservatism of many of her poems' depictions of gender difference, this often masks a more complex set of references in her verse. The political encoding of her poems signals other more problematic codes operating beneath the surface of her work.

'To the truly noble, and obleiging Mrs: Anne Owen (on my first approaches)' (102-3) is one of a number of poems which draws on Petrarchan conventions, a discourse traditionally reserved for the masculine courtship of women. Initially the poem seems to comprise stock Petrarchan features. The speaker addresses the revered woman from a position of abjection and humility – she is her 'meanest captive[s],' 'unworthy,' 'The worst' (ll. 2, 3, 12), while Anne Owen stands as a remote, elevated and exalted figure, 'admir'd by all' and possessing 'all wonders' (ll. 12, 17). The relationship between them is presented in standard terms of conquest, in which the speaker is a 'yielding' captive, a votary willingly 'subdu'd' and gratified by her subjection to Owen's superior powers (ll. 4, 18, 16).

The Petrarchan motif, however, is placed in reference to a set of values which highlight the strains and tensions produced by the poem's mimicry of that discourse. The speaker's justification of her relationship with Owen and swift anticipation of 'the busy world''s condemnation of it (l. 5) ironically draws attention to its possible threat to social propriety. The question of the (in)appropriateness of their relationship indeed lies at the foreground of the poem. This, in turn, polarizes the significance of their female exchange, even though specific reference to this remains unmentioned. Rather the poem's considerations of gender are subsumed under those concerning social value.

In particular the poem focuses on the economy underlying the social parameters of the speaker's relationship with Owen. In the Petrarchan model the power that the woman appears to possess on the surface ultimately belongs to the male speaker. Irigaray's discussion about sexual economy is illuminating when applied to this discourse, for the Petrarchan woman is *'a product of man's "labor"'* through which she is disinvested of qualities of her own and merely supplied with a 'value-bearing form,' thus becoming *'a mirror of value of and for man'* (Irigaray 175, 180, 177).[11] Philips's poem, however, complicates this set of relations, because the speaker is implicitly a woman. Both women are sited as being objects of a speculative public gaze where propriety is understood as being a matter of property. Owen is the property of another – she is married – but she also possesses a treasury of conquests which add to her value. The speaker, by contrast, commodifies herself in terms of lack. She is scrap merchandise, a poor investment, possessing nothing of her own. Most seriously, rather than conferring value on Owen, she has the potential to cause her property damage and loss:

> So when the busy world (in hope t'excuse
> Their own surprize) your conquests doe peruse,
> And find my name, they will be apt to say
> Your charmes were blinded, or else thrown away. (ll. 5-10)

At one level, then, the speaker identifies herself in appropriately feminized terms. At another, however, she signals the tenuousness of her position and relation to Owen. The allusion to 'honour' at line nine underlines this, for not only does it refer to social worth in general terms, but specifically to chastity when applied to a woman. Ironically, the possible threat the speaker poses to Owen reminds the reader of the implicitly illicit and erotic overtones of Petrarchan love, despite the poem's apparent exclusion of them. The complications underpinning the poem's use of this discourse are thus kept at the forefront.

The speaker, however, redefines the terms of her relationship with Owen in a way which will make it appear innocent and socially viable. Unlike the conventional Petrarchan woman, Owen endows her conquests with capital and thus increases her own worth. In her 'all wonders common are' enabling her to enrich and transform what is commonplace (ll. 17-18). In acknowledging that she was 'subdu'd' by Owen, the speaker gains market value. Not only does she thereby have a 'share' in Owen's 'vertues' but is also metamorphosed by them through Owen's creation within her of 'a noble soule' (ll. 18, 24). The corporeal pleasure and pain of the Petrarchan lover are replaced by spiritual gain. The speaker is thus enabled to 'obtain' 'honour' which, in turn, reflects and enriches the honor that Owen already possesses (ll. 15, 23-4).

This renegotiation of the Petrarchan sexual economy with an innocent, feminized one hinges on the speaker's admission that she has 'plots' in this exchange (l. 13). On the surface these plots refer to the profits the speaker acquires through her association with Owen: Owen invests in Orinda, yet Orinda has a stake in that investment. They also indicate, however, the literary capital Orinda procures from Owen in providing her with a position from which to produce a narrative. On the one hand, her licence to assume authorship is released through her denial of autonomy; on the other, this denial seems to lie outside patriarchal parameters, for it is Owen who is the generative source of the speaker's plots, through whom the terms 'name' and 'fame' are redefined from being signs of indecorum to ones of chaste surrender. Yet if the speaker articulates herself through Owen, Owen is also articulated through the speaker as she is the agent of Owen's creative power. Such plots suggest the way in which innocent propriety slides into feminine excess.[12]

'To my Lucasia, in defence of declared friendship' (153-6) also reinscribes the terms of a masculine economy, but in a way which is more explicitly and elaborately linked to feminine speech. Here, too, feminine propriety is recast:

> O! my Lucasia, let us speak our Love,
>   And think not that impertinent can be,
> Which to us both does such assurance prove,
>   And whence we find how Justly we agree. (ll. 1-4)

Speaking involves a process of rethinking, for it demands that the women friends set their own terms for self-representation – ones that reconceive feminine speech from an act of indecorum to one of innocent exchange. To articulate their love is a way of continually investing the 'treasures' they 'gain'd' when 'did we first barter minds' (ll. 5, 9, 13). Such revenue will lose its value without 'use' and

'Circulation' (ll. 24, 40). To 'convey transactions' is to 'repeat' and so 'increase' their bond (ll. 32, 25, 28). '[O]ur free and deare converse' is a form of 'commerce' that 'we ow our' love, for being silent would be like 'misers' who 'bury thus their gold' (ll. 74, 76, 21).

The masculine economy that Irigaray describes in which women are the objects of exchange, reduced to 'the visible, material correlative' of man's labor (183), is thus reformulated by the textual economy transacted by the women friends. Irigaray's analysis explains '*women's role as fetish-objects*' as being 'the manifestation and the circulation of a power of the Phallus.' In performing this function women 'no longer relate to each other except in terms of what they represent in men's desire, and according to the "forms" that this imposes upon them,' so that woman herself may 'never have access to desire' (183, 188). The poem, however, argues for the women friends to become subjects of discourse and thereby to express and affirm desires of their own, through which the sign of the Phallus is implicitly rendered invalid. The circulation of feminine desire through speech enables an 'increase' of pleasure rather than signalling the claims of property and power, for 'to tell' their 'passions' is to 'obleige and please' (ll. 28, 33-34). Such an exchange provides mutual gratification, as value is both conferred and received: to 'take' is also to 'give' 'satisfaction,' their hearts both 'obtein' and 'produce' enjoyment (ll. 55, 51-2). The 'use' of their verbal 'stock' results not in expenditure through arrival at one, fixed destination of 'bliss.' Instead, it reaps continual returns, for they do not 'spend' but 'by motion multiply' their 'Joys' (ll. 24, 35):

> And as a River, when it once has pay'd
>   The tribute which it to the Ocean ow's,
> Stops not, but turns, and having curl'd and play'd
>   On its own waves, the shore it overflows:
>
> So the Soul's motion does not end in bliss,
>   But on her self she scatters and dilates,
> And on the Object doubles, till by this
>   She finds new Joys, which that reflux creates. (ll. 41-48)

The women's transactions are not fixed within a stable rate of interest, but are fluid, forever recreating and reshaping themselves so as to supply an endlessly remunerative circulation of pleasure.

Throughout the poem, then, the speaker plays with and recasts a web of references which, as we have seen from Orinda's and Poliarchus's letters, are conventionally connected during the period. The standard link between feminine textual and sexual utterance is invested with new meaning. The reconception of this commonplace alignment is highlighted by the poem's allusion to Donne's 'The Ecstasy.'[13] Philips's poem follows closely Donne's description of the fusion of the lovers' souls, which are doubled and transformed by becoming one (Donne 54, ll. 33-40). Donne's poem presents the body as a 'book' on which 'Love's mysteries' are inscribed and without whose use 'a great prince in prison lies' (55, ll. 71-2, 68). In Philips's poem, by contrast, the body does not illuminate or reveal, but operates as a prison for the soul, from which speaking allows release (ll. 29-32), speech that enables a redefinition of the feminine from its traditional position of object-body. Whereas sexual coition indicates a descent into the worldly domain in Donne's poem by signifying 'That subtle knot, which makes us man' (55, l.64), verbal exchange guarantees the continuance and regeneration of spiritual ecstasy in Philips's poem. The textual form in which Lucasia's 'look' is clothed when it 'is dress'd in words' figures nothing visible, but rather 'The mystique power of musick's Unison' through which speculation gives way to the reverberation of Lucasia and the speaker's voices (ll. 69-72). The opening of the women's lips articulates a 'spotless passion' (l. 27) where their textual intercourse is innocently productive.[14]

III Innocent Alternatives

In the above poems the conception of a feminine voice and exchange as 'innocent' seems also to be a means of redefining the feminine and its location within the Symbolic Order. Elsewhere Philips's verse provides a more explicit critique of patriarchal parameters, identifying friendship as a preferable alternative to matrimony.[15] 'A Friend' (165-8), for example, presents friendship as 'Nobler then kindred or then mariage band, / Because more free,' ''Tis love refin'd and purg'd from all its drosse' (ll. 13-14, 8). It is innocent of the material claims – both bodily and property – that marriage demands. In this poem, as elsewhere in Philips's corpus, innocence seems to signify a refusal to be penetrated by implicitly masculine terms.

Indeed, friendship itself is continually feminized, often conceived as an interiorized, autonomous space, unbreached by the world outside. In 'To My excellent Lucasia, on our friendship' (121-2) Orinda and Lucasia's union is controlled by 'no bold feare,' but has an 'inocent' 'design' that exceeds 'Bridegroomes' and 'crown'd conqu'rour's mirth' (ll. 22-3, 17). It is not based on property and possession – 'pieces of this Earth' (l. 18) – but a fusion of identities where 'I am not Thine, but Thee' (1.4), the permeation of Orinda's empty corporeal frame by Lucasia's soul producing a 'world' of its own (l. 20).

'A retir'd friendship, to Ardelia' (97-8) also attempts to map out an exclusive, private sanctuary, whose 'innocence' is defined by its rejection of 'the boistrous world' (ll. 24, 34). Instead, 'In one another's hearts we live' through 'kindly mingling Souls' (ll. 16, 2). Framed by personal pronouns, friendship's 'bowre' is 'unconfin'd' as is it not subject to 'any Slavery of State' (ll. 1, 35, 8), but sets out its own terms of validity.

'L'amitié: To Mrs M. Awbrey' (142) presents friendship as being constructed within a similarly internalized domain, protected from invasion by 'the dull world,' thus enabling the friends 'To pitty Kings, and Conquerours despise' (ll. 15, 20):

> I have no thought but what's to thee reveal'd,
> Nor thou desire that is from me conceal'd.
> Thy heart locks up my secrets richly set,
> And my brest is thy private cabinet. (ll. 7-10)

Operating through a private, hidden network of codes and rituals, their 'sacred union' (l. 21) provides a secret language, available to them alone. It is only to each other that their 'inocent' 'flame' is revealed (l. 17).

IV Innocent Erotics

The presentation of friendship as an unseen, 'unterritorialized space' (Irigaray 141) providing its own self-contained grammar of desire and pleasure is a major feature of many of Philips's friendship poems. Like the previous poems, 'Friendship's Mysterys, to my dearest Lucasia' (90-1) identifies female friendship in terms of an enclosed domain that transcends worldly concerns. Here, however, we are given a fuller account of how this utopian realm operates:

> 1
> Come, my Lucasia, since we see
> That miracles men's faith do move

By wonder and by Prodigy,
  To the dull, angry world let's prove
There's a religion in our Love.
                2
For though we were design'd t'agree,
  That fate no liberty destroys,
But our election is as free
  As Angells, who with greedy choice
  Are yet determin'd to their Joys...
                6
Our hearts are mutuall victims lay'd,
  While they (such power in friendship ly's)
Are Altars, Priests, and offerings made,
  And each heart which thus kindly dy's,
  Grows deathless by the sacrifice. (ll. 1-10, 26-30)

Typically, Philips draws on Christian Platonism and conceives of friendship in terms of a divine mystery. The speaker/Lucasia look back at 'the dull, angry world' (l. 4), though, and observe that men need proof in order to have faith. They must see in order to believe. The friends thus invite themselves to become objects of the world's gaze.

There is no body in view, however. The divine revelation that the speaker/Lucasia present is unsightable, for their religion transports them from the terms in which women are conventionally sited. Rather, it provides an ex-stase: it is outside place and so cannot be placed, comprising an invisible, indivisible touching of female hearts and minds. Their union elicits a series of divine paradoxes: it combines free will and predestination as 'liberty' and 'election' become the same (ll. 7-8). But this unorthodox religion of female friendship both incorporates and blurs the boundaries between different denominations, combining the Calvinist principle of divine election and high Anglican ritual (l. 28). The distinct symbolic forms of the church, are dissolved, however, for the women are at the same time the places, agents and objects of worship (ll. 27-30).

As we have seen already, Philips's imagery seems to draw on Donne's love poetry, where we would also expect to find such ingenious exploitation of religious concepts. In Donne's verse, though, the speaker almost invariably takes center-stage with the woman positioned as the passive, silent recipient of his rhetorical performance. In Donne's 'Air and Angels,' for example, the ambiguous 'lovely glorious nothing' which the speaker 'see[s]' (Donne 41, l. 6) in the opening of the poem becomes the sexual vehicle through which he expresses his more refined love by the end. Whereas men, it is argued, are capable of possessing the pure love of angels, women are the impure 'sphere,' the air, which angels inhabit (41, ll. 23-8). 'The Sun Rising' similarly affirms the power lines that underlie gender relations in charting its exclusive world of love when the speaker declares, 'She'is all states, and all princes, I, / Nothing else is' (80, ll. 21-2).[16] By contrast, Philips's ecstatic union of female friendship enables the polarities of subject and object, presence and absence to melt. Difference is undone, giving way to an intersubjective, reciprocal mode of exchange, where 'you' and 'I' become interchangable, for 'We are our selves but by rebound' and 'Never, yet ever are alone' (ll. 23, 15). The self becomes not 'I.' To be is not to be. They are plural and one, for, as in 'Friendship in Emblem or the Seale' 'They are, and yet they are not, two' (107, l. 24).

In addition, by recalling and reworking the intense, sexually charged language of Donne's love poetry, Philips's verse produces a different type of erotics, while apparently maintaining its 'innocence.' The rapturous state of spiritual coition presented at the end of 'Friendship's Mysterys' centers around the paradox and ambivalence of 'death,' a term which could signify orgasm in the seventeenth century. While the friends' hearts ultimately become 'deathless,' it is the preliminary 'death' of each as they are ecstatically consumed by one another that breeds eternal life (ll. 29-30).

However, the poem's configuration of friendship's ecstasy not only troubles the sexual and power relationships found in much heterosexual love poetry of the period, it also unsettles the conditions by which 'the dull, angry world' functions in broader terms. The speaker and Lucasia are both and neither male and female in being like 'Angells' (l. 9); they are 'Princes' and 'subjects,' victors and victims (ll. 25-7). Classifications of space and matter are confounded, for to 'diffuse' is to 'engrosse,' to be captive is to be liberated, to lose is to gain, to possess is to be dispossessed (ll. 13, 16-20, 26-30). Hierarchical and oppositional modes of identification are thus 'shuffled' (l. 24) so as to create a newly defined feminine space.

The formulation of the feminine in terms that rework divine imagery and problematize implicitly masculine modes of understanding is apparent in a range of Philips's poems. In 'To my Lucasia' (128-9) exploration into 'nature's womb' for the purpose of discovering and explaining the 'causes' of her 'secret Unions' (ll. 2-3, 5) is regarded as being 'low experiments' conducted by 'dull Philosophers' (ll. 7, 1). Such observations fail to 'view' 'nature's harmony entire' which 'will admit / No rude spectatour to contemplate it' (ll. 8-9, 13-14).

Rather the feminine 'body' (l. 4) is recast in terms of innocent, eroticized, de-anatomized 'agreeing soules' whose 'soft touches' 'greet and kiss, / And in each other can compleat their bliss' (ll. 9, 11-12). Here the boundaries between the spiritual and sensual collapse and merge to create an impenetrable, unseeable site of 'wonder' through a 'mixture' 'sweet,' 'full' and 'true' (ll. 13, 10). The plenitude of divine ecstasy figured in the form of Platonic friendship is set against the reductive knowledge of natural philosophy.

In the last part of the poem, though, the speaker reflects on her own position in relation to the 'morallity' (l. 20) set out in the opening as she considers her relationship with Lucasia. Acknowledging the imperfect state of her 'unimproved Soule,' she seeks 'vertue' to make her 'fit to be Lucasia's friend' (ll. 21, 27-8). Her atonement will take the form of death, but a death in which self-sacrifice will guarantee salvation and resurrection when she submits to the Christ-like Lucasia: the speaker will 'forsake' herself so as to 'seek a new / Self' in Lucasia's breast; 'Then glorious in its funerall' it will obtain 'Eternity' (ll. 29-30, 35-6). As in 'Friendship's Mysterys' consummation means recreation. The speaker rises from the ashes to become clothed in a new form, her own disembodiment enabling her to be embodied within Lucasia. Virtue embraces rapturous communion to produce a religion of a different kind.

In these poems images of death and self-sacrifice are figured in terms of erotic exchange. While Philips's verse continually seems to deny or exclude the body, it is through the motifs of disembodiment, absence and death that the body surfaces and the overt demarcations between the corporeal and spiritual are destabilized. As Wall argues in reference to Mary Wroth's *Pamphilia to Amphilanthus*, absence and negation are significant themes in women's writing of the period, often calling attention to omissions and silences in the text and pointing to what cannot or will not be spoken (335).[17] Just as Philips's poetry reconceptualizes feminine 'innocence,' so references to absence and negation suggest not merely omissions, but also imply redefinitions of those concepts.

In 'To Mrs. Mary Awbrey at parting' (145-7) physical separation indicates not an empty space or lack, but is a sign of the melting of physical identities, space and boundaries:

> Our chang'd and mingled soules are growne
>   To such acquaintance now,
> That if each would assume their owne,
>   Alas! we know not how.

> We have each other so ingrost,
> That each is in the union lost.
> And thus we can no absence know,
>   Nor shall we be confin'd;
> Our active soules will dayly go
>   To learne each other's mind.
> Nay, should we never meet to sence,
> Our soules would hold intelligence. (ll. 13-24)

In these lines parting suggests a refusal to conceive the body as a sign of enclosed, autonomous identity and distinction between selves. The desires it elicits are formulated outside the terms of anatomy. Instead, parting signals an intersubjective space of free movement and exchange, where selves meet, merge and blend, producing the possibility for transformation and mutation. Here identities are given no origin or essence, for one may become the other, each part dissolving into the whole.

The body, however, has not entirely disappeared. While the clandestine meetings in which the speaker and Lucasia share their intimacies are cloaked in innocent terms of spiritual intercourse, as in the previous two poems, their disembodied exchange is presented through images of corporeal activity and sensual pleasure (ll. 43-8). The borderlines between body and soul are thus complicated, where parting points to a gap that represents not absence, but eroticized possibility through which Orinda and Lucasia may 'teach the World new love' (l. 50).

V Excess Innocence

Here absence and negation suggest a space that is in excess of 'innocence.' However, it is also in the parting poems and, in particular what Barash terms 'elegies for friendship' (99), where the concept of innocence often breaks down and becomes troubled by the idea of excess.

In 'To Rosania (now Mrs Montague) being with her' (127-8) it is through the process of parting company with her beloved after she marries that the speaker identifies the extreme effects Rosania's 'presence' has upon her. These are represented through the sexually resonant metaphors of liquid and aridity applied to the earth:

> So when the Earth long gasps for raine,
> If she at last some few drops gaine,
> She is more parched then at first;
> That small recruit increast the Thirst. (ll. 37-40)

The speaker's fulfillment by her beloved is now experienced by Orinda in fragmentary form, the 'snatches' of 'blisse' (l. 36) she currently receives making her forthcoming separation from Rosania even more painful to contemplate. It is in the interstice between presence and absence and through the anticipation of loss and denial that the speaker's sense of excess is articulated.

This sense of excess, signalling both Orinda's movement beyond accepted boundaries and her sense of identity as being reduced to residual, waste matter, is apparent in a number of poems. In 'Orinda to Lucasia parting' (211-12) it is again the impact of Lucasia's loss on Orinda's identity that expresses Orinda's 'Love's excess' (l. 1). Having imparted her 'whole self once to thee,' to whom she still directs her 'same fervent and unchanged heart' (ll. 3-4), Orinda now experiences herself in a defamiliarized form. Lacking any coherent sense of identity, she is

> so entangl'd and so lost a thing . . .
> That would'st thou for thy old *Orinda* call,
> Thou hardly could'st unravel her at all. (ll. 13, 14-15)

To lose Lucasia results in a state of dispossession and alienation, in which Orinda's deranged condition is a sign both of the effects of feminine propriety in renouncing her relationship and of having overstepped its limits.

It is in 'To Mrs M. A. upon absence' (141-2) that the self-estranged identity Orinda inhabits as a result of separation from her beloved is most in the foreground:

> 'Tis now since I began to dy
>   Foure moneths and more, yet gasping live;
> Wrapp'd up in sorrows doe I ly,
>   Hoping, yet doubting a reprieve.
> Adam from Paradise expell'd
> Just such a wretched being held. (ll. 1-6)

Here absence does not open up an ecstatic mingling of souls. Rather it indicates deficiency. While parting does not destabilize love, 'That will in spight of absence hold' (ll. 7-8), absence reduces its value by enriching 'nothing but conceipt' (l. 12). Love requires commerce, thought material exchange, without which love will lose its 'benefit and use' becoming like 'imprison'd Gold' (ll. 9-10).[18] Moreover, in yielding 'conceipt' alone, such a deficit in love seems to be reenacted in poetic production. In this sense, the poem appears to perform the very absence and lack it bemoans: it is about nothing, consisting merely of words without substance. Lacking the free-flowing circulation of capital generated by 'To my Lucasia''s oral/aural textual economy, parting with M. A. produces sterility in both love and poetry.

Yet, as in the other poems, absence and death open up a space of unspeakable trouble. Articulating itself through mere conceit – thought and metaphor – love without physical presence creates 'but conceipt' (l. 12) – 'A (morbid) seizure of the body or mind' (*OED*) in the speaker. The poem's status as residual, waste matter inscribes Orinda's wasted condition. It is Orinda's half-dead state as she diminishes into waste and excess, however, which becomes a metaphor for the excesses of her love, revealing that 'my love all Love excells' (l. 17). Her corpse-like bearing, which is 'Wrapp'd up in sorrows' that know no bounds (ll. 3, 18), signals the unfixing and exceeding of boundaries.

Here the alternative religion set out in 'Friendship's Mysterys' and 'To my Lucasia' is revised. In particular, the analogy between the speaker's 'wretched being' and the fallen Adam (ll. 5-6) indicates not only the loss of an Edenic state, but also a prior act of transgression. Like Adam's expulsion from Paradise, Orinda's separation from M. A. results in mortality, a division between body and soul. But this, in turn, suggests disobedience to the Law of the Father through participation in forbidden activities, where the speaker's decaying body becomes the implicit sign of her sin. Her marginal position between presence and absence infers a loss of innocence, pointing to the borderline between censorship and desire, the licit and illicit operating within the utopian realm of female friendship.

In addition, the mingling, melting and mutation of identities that underscore feminine exchange in other poems is replaced by an insistently isolated, self-enclosed first person subject here. Removed from the site of desire, however, the assertion of 'I' contains only a sense of its fissured, spent, self-alienated condition. The speaker is both beside and inescapably engulfed inside herself, as she becomes the object of her own gaze, 'Coppys of my wild 'state' unremittingly reflecting back on 'I,' who 'am their epitomy' (ll. 21-2). Orinda's 'I' perceives a continuous repetition of self-mirroring images which affirm only her emptiness and loss of self-presence as she dissolves into nothing. The misplacement of the speaker's love figured by her dislocated state is ultimately allowed no space, however. The excesses suggested by absence, displacement and death give way to denial, which seems to be a condition of their acknowledgement. Her 'wild 'state' is harnessed by images of lifelessness in the final stanza, for 'Sapless and dead as winter here / I now remaine' (ll. 19-20). Transgression reverts to innocence, dispossession to renunciation when Orinda finally asks her beloved to 'Love me no more! for I am grown / Too dead and dull for thee to own' (ll. 23-4).

VI

Philips's rhetoric of innocence indicates the subversive complexity that seeps through the texture of her verse. Beneath the surface of her work's seeming conservatism lies an intricate network of codes and references which belie the poems' 'innocence' and which often operate in complicated, contradictory ways. The insistent reiteration of 'innocence' throughout her verse is frequently put to non-innocent uses to produce meanings in excess of those which appear at first glance. Most obviously her poems' seeming preoccupation with virtue and withdrawal is underwritten by their entry into public debates, where these very motifs are employed as political signals. The political encoding of Philips's verse, however, points to other more troublesome enciphering which, in turn, redefines the limits of royalist aesthetics. In particular, Philips's poetry produces a set of codes in which the conventional alignments between feminine identity and the body, and feminine speech and promiscuity are challenged. Instead, innocence is reconceived, becoming the means through which the masculine world and its values are critiqued, as well as inscribing a self-defining, separate feminine space in which an alternative discourse of desire and pleasure is mapped out.

As we have seen, though, Philips's rhetoric of innocence is often underscored by a sense of anxiety and ambivalence. Like much women's writing of the period, Philips's verse problematizes any neat demarcations between conservatism and subversion. Rather, it signals a precarious negotiation between silence and speech, denial and excess, innocence and transgression. Nonetheless, Philips's poetry reconfigures the terms by which feminine identity was conventionally understood and extends the aesthetic ideas and forms with which it engages. By the end of the century Philips acquired a number of imitators, establishing a new, feminized poetics devoted to romantic female friendship, feminine withdrawal and a sexually politically encoded 'innocence.'

Notes

Parts of this essay first appeared as '"Spotless Passion": Public Face and Private Space in the Poetry of Katherine Philips, the "Matchless Orinda".'

[1] In his edition of Philips's poetry, Patrick Thomas notes that there are in fact very few discrepancies between the 1664 version and the Folio edition of 1667 (Introduction 19). All references to Philips's poems come from Thomas's edition.

[2] All references to Philips's letter to Poliarchus come from 'The Preface' to the 1667 edition of Philips's poems, no page numbers.

[3] Barash discusses the link between the metaphor of rape and the publication of Philips's allegedly stolen manuscript (55, 81-3), while Mermin suggests that Orinda's anxiety about being suspected of 'a secret consent' (Philips 'The Preface') is 'like a woman complaining of rape' (Mermin 338). Numerous critics have observed the standard association between woman's body and textual production. See, e.g., Gallagher 1-48; Jardine 103-40; Wall 279-340.

[4] More recently Barash has explored how the figure of Orinda is complexly shaped in reference to Philips's political allegiances (55-100).

[5] Hageman also notes this feature of Philips's letter (578-9).

[6] Hageman notes how 'atypical' Philips's 'idea of female friendship was' by setting it in reference to male friendship poetry and Jeremy Taylor's *A Discourse of the Nature and Offices of Friendship*, which was addressed to Philips (573-5).

[7] Barash identifies Philips's deployment of the *femme forte* tradition, adopted from the French salons, as being especially significant to her poems' political resonances (see 56-9, 62-8).

[8] Andreadis rightly points out, however, that Philips's poetry only uses the rhetoric of *préciosité* superficially and that to treat her work as exemplifying these conventions is reductive (37-8). See also Swaim 77-108 and Barash 66, 70 on Philips's use of *préciosité*.

[9] Barash suggests that Philips's name for Anne Owen, Lucasia, derives from Lovelace's Lucasta (71). It is worth noting that Lovelace implicitly alludes to

Philips in his satire 'On Sanazar's being honoured with six hundred Duckets by the Clarissimi of Venice.' The poem draws on the standard equation between women's writing and prostitution (200, ll. 242-8) which signals in explicitly sexualized terms the displacement of masculine power by feminine unruliness: 'He to her fury the soft plume doth bow, / O Pen, nere truely justly slit till now!' (200, ll. 240-1). Philips, however, is set apart from such irregular activities in being held up as the 'one *Sapho* left' who 'may save' all other women writers (200, l. 249).

[10] For a more detailed analysis of this poem see my discussion in '"Th'inwards of th'Abysse"' 118-23.

[11] See also Vickers' important discussion about the complex sexual and textual power lines underscoring Petrarch (95-109).

[12] Celia Easton highlights the association of 'plots' with scheming and planning in her analysis of this poem (94-5). This implies both Orinda's agency and creativity, enabling her not only to challenge 'the conventional male/female structure of a conquest poem,' but also to create 'a woman's voice that can be simultaneously submissive and aggressive' so as to dismantle 'the power relations of erotic expression' (94).

The erotic resonance of Philips's poems has been well documented. See, for example, Andreadis 34-60, Hobby 128-40 and Stiebel 223-36. However, there is little detailed analysis of the particular forms this eroticism takes. Andreadis's essay rightly identifies Philips's 'manipulations of the conventions of [heterosexual] male poetic discourse' (60). Stiebel criticizes Andreadis, however, for 'writing sensuality out of' Philips's work through her suggestion that it is 'eroticized' and yet 'desexualized' (225). But while Stiebel persuasively argues that the poems 'may enact their sexuality on quite different terms from their male counterparts' (230), she has a tendency to reduce her readings to a process of 'outing' Philips and her beloved. Mermin, however, goes too far in the opposite direction when she suggests that Philips's poems are 'asexual, respectable,' reflecting a 'general blindness to the possibility of female homosexuality' (343), though she later refers to 'Orinda's erotics of female friendship' (347).

[13] Philips's reworking of Donne's poetry has been noted by numerous critics. See, for example, Hageman 572-3, Hobby 137-8, and, in particular, Andreadis 39-43.

[14] In her reading of this poem, Easton focuses on the 'contradiction of senses (Eye/Ear) and contradiction of behaviors (expected/resisted).' These, in turn,

point to the contradictions between Philips's repressed and Orinda's expressed desires (98).

[15] The few poems which celebrate marriage are occasional verse. See Hageman on Philips's reworking of epithalamion conventions (568-9).

[16] Hageman draws attention to Philips's specific reference to Donne's 'The Sun Rising' in this poem (572-3).

[17] Wall's observations about the 'thematization of absence' in Wroth's verse are pertinent to Philips's poetry. Wall argues that 'As readers, we are directed not only to discover and give voice to silences within the work, but also to understand how silence, absence and vacancy themselves define both text and speaking subject' (335).

[18] Philips's image of 'imprison'd Gold' to signify the effects of physical separation parallels Donne's metaphor for the body's disuse in 'The Ecstasy,' when he states 'Else a great prince in prison lies' (55, l. 68).

Works Cited

Andreadis, Harriette. 'The Sapphic-Platonics of Katherine Philips, 1632-1664.' *Signs* 15 (1989): 34-60.

Barash, Carol. *English Women's Poetry, 1649-1714: Politics, Community and Linguistic Authority.* Oxford: Clarendon P, 1996.

Donne, John. *The Complete English Poems.* ed. A. J. Smith. Harmondsworth: Penguin, 1971.

Easton, Celia A. 'Excusing the Breach of Nature's Laws: The Discourse of Denial and Disguise in Katherine Philips' Friendship Poetry.' *Restoration* 14 (1990): 1-14; rpt. in *Early Women Writers: 1600-1720.* ed. Anita Pacheco. London: Longman, 1998. 89-107.

Gallagher, Catherine. *Nobody's Story: The Vanishing Acts of Women Writers in the Marketplace, 1670-1820.* Berkeley: U of California P, 1994.

Hageman, Elizabeth H. 'The Matchless Orinda, Katherine Philips.' *Women Writers of the Renaissance and Reformation.* ed. Katharina M. Wilson. Athens: U of Georgia P, 1987. 566-82.

Hobby, Elaine. *Virtue of Necessity: English Women's Writing 1649-88.* London: Virago, 1988.

Irigaray, Luce. *This Sex Which Is Not One.* Trans. Catherine Porter. Ithaca: Cornell UP, 1985.

Jardine Lisa. *Still Harping on Daughters: Women and Drama in the Age of Shakespeare.* New York: Harvester Wheatsheaf, 1983.

Lovelace, Richard. *The Poems.* ed. C. H. Wilkinson. Oxford: Clarendon P, 1930.

Mermin, Dorothy. 'Women Becoming Poets: Katherine Philips, Aphra Behn, Anne Finch.' *ELH* 57 (1990): 335-55.

Parry, Graham. *The Seventeenth Century: The Intellectual and Cultural Context of English Literature, 1603-1700.* London: Longman, 1989.

Philips, Katherine. *Poems by the most deservedly Admired Mrs Katherine Philips: The Matchless Orinda.* London: H. Herringman, 1667.

———. *The Collected Works of Katherine Philips, the Matchless Orinda, Vol. I: The Poems.* ed. Patrick Thomas. 3 vols. Stump Cross: Stump Cross P, 1990.

Potter, Lois. *Secret Rites and Secret Writing: Royalist Literature 1641-1660.* Cambridge: Cambridge UP, 1989.

Price, Bronwen. '"Th'inwards of th'Abysse": Questions of the Subject in Lovelace's Poetry.' *English* 43 (1994): 117-37.

———. '"Spotless Passion": Public Face and Private Space in the Poetry of Katherine Philips, the "Matchless Orinda".' *Poetry Wales* 33 (1997): 44-9.

Stiebel, Arlene. 'Subversive Sexuality: Masking the Erotic in Poems by Katherine Philips and Aphra Behn.' *Renaissance Discourses of Desire.* eds. C.J. Summers and Ted-Larry Pebworth. Columbia: U of Missouri P, 1993. 223-36.

Swaim, Kathleen M. 'Matching the "Matchless Orinda" to her Times.' *1650-1850 Ideas, Aesthetics, and Inquiries in the Early Modern Era.* Vol. 3. ed. Kevin L. Cope. 5 vols. New York: AMS P, 1997. 77-108.

Vickers, Nancy. 'Diana Described: Scattered Woman and Scattered Rhyme.' *Critical Inquiry* 8 (1981): 265-79; rpt. in *Writing and Sexual Difference.* ed. Elizabeth Abel. Brighton: Harvester, 1982. 95-109.

Wall, Wendy. *The Imprint of Gender: Authorship and Publication in the English Renaissance.* Ithaca: Cornell UP, 1993.

Wiseman, Susan. 'Britain 1500-1800.' *Bloomsbury Guide to Women's Literature.* ed. Clare Buck. London: Bloomsbury, 1992. 11-22.

12

'Very Like a Fiction': Some Early Biographies of Aphra Behn

Jeslyn Medoff

[I]n reviving the dead, the prevalence of
the imagination is less dangerous than
its absence. (Stauffer, *Art* 131)

In 1863 a skeptical *Notes and Queries* reader wanted to know more about the purportedly female author of a biography that had been prefixed to Aphra Behn's collected novels generations earlier. Not only was the biographer's identity unknown, but the biography itself, including letters that were attributed to Behn, seemed questionable:

Is anything known of this fair writer? And is the Life to be at all depended upon? It reads very like a fiction; and the letters introduced are the most unlike real letters I have ever seen. (368)

The Victorian inquirer's questions remain unanswered to this day. We still do not know with any real certainty the gender or the identity of the biographer, nor can we claim unequivocally that the letters are genuine. We can safely say, however, that this early biography, the first version of which was published in 1696, seven years after Behn's death, has remained a remarkably influential text in the long history of the biographical pursuit of Aphra Behn.

It is not insignificant that Behn died just at the time when authorship was beginning to be viewed as a profession, and therefore at a time when literary biographies as a genre were starting to come into their own. In a sense, she could not have chosen a better time to die. Behn's earliest biographies demonstrate the nascence of both their subject's posthumous reputation and their own form. The amorphousness that one associates with Behn; the multiple personae she employed; the biographical, factual 'self' that remains elusive to some degree even to recent biographers; the phosphorescence that tempts all of us critics, then and now, to fall into the biographical bog of literal interpretation – all these ironically also provide us with a touchstone, by which we can test developments in that relatively new genre, literary biography. The manner in which Behn was 'written' at *any* given point in time after her death was determined perhaps as much by the perceived purposes of biographical writing and its role in the literary marketplace as it was by partisan or sexual politics, or by the vicissitudes of literary taste. Hopefully, the present undertaking will both highlight the necessity for detailed examination of the ways in which Aphra Behn has been 'written' and re-written through three centuries of biographical and critical treatments and contribute to the study of the development of literary biography as a genre.[1]

In the late seventeenth century the boundaries between fiction and biography, particularly literary biography, were not yet distinctly drawn, as literary historians have long acknowledged.[2] The term 'history' was indiscriminately employed to denote both fiction and biography, as it is in the editions of Behn's fiction referred to here. The 1696 biography (and its many subsequent versions) shows evidence of this genre-blurring by presenting for the first time a 'rumor' that Behn had had a real-life love affair with the married protagonist of her novel, *Oroonoko* (1688), the African 'royal slave' (though the rumor is refuted by the ostensible female author). Contributing significantly to the already-current view of Behn as sexual adventurer while appearing to exonerate Behn, the late-seventeenth-century biographer simultaneously planted seeds of doubt regarding the author–subject's character and fashioned her into a romantic heroine, part of an interracial triangle that does indeed sound 'very like a fiction.'[3]

Initially entitled 'Memoirs on the Life of Mrs. Behn, Written by a Gentlewoman of her Acquaintance,' the eighteen-page biography was prefixed to the first edition of Behn's collected fiction, *Histories and Novels*, published by Samuel Briscoe in 1696. Two years later, in 1698, the 'Memoirs' was substantially expanded to sixty pages and revised for a new edition of the *Histories and Novels* also brought out by Briscoe. The revised biography now incorporated eight 'Love Letters to a Gentleman' attributed to Behn which had appeared among Behn's fiction, separate from the prefatory biography, in the 1696 *Histories and Novels*.[4] The prefatory essay was further padded with more amatory letters, previously unpublished, and ostensibly written by 'Astrea' (Behn's *nom de plume*) about her amorous conquests in the Low Countries. This extended biographical piece was renamed 'The History of the Life and Memoirs of Mrs. Behn' and attributed simply to 'One of the Fair Sex,' who has been assumed by many literary historians to be Charles Gildon, author of the dedication of the 1698 edition, all-around hack, and possibly a personal acquaintance of Behn, but his authorship has never been fully substantiated.[5] The likelihood of Gildon taking on the role of textual transvestite is strengthened by a remark in his brief biographical preface to Behn's posthumously-published play, *The Younger Brother* (1696), that 'to draw her to the Life, one must write like her, that is with the softness of her Sex, and all the fire of ours' (A4r). In 1705 the 'History' was slightly corrected, and it was in this form available to readers for decades into the eighteenth century, through the many subsequent editions of the *Histories and Novels*.[6] The biographical 'History,' then, had no little influence on eighteenth-century readers' ideas of Behn's life and writings, and it remains, to the present day, an important source for most, if not all, biographical treatments of Behn.[7]

Composed in an age when literary biography as we understand it was just beginning to take shape,[8] the biographical 'history' by 'One of the Fair Sex' demonstrates in provocative ways the protean nature of the embryo genre: the possible cross-dressing of its author; the obvious efforts to underscore both the veracity of the purported female biographer and the verisimilitude of the fiction to follow (which is reminiscent of the prefaces of Defoe and others); and the propagation of Behn (or 'Astrea') as a creature much like some of her own heroines. Indeed, the author of the expanded version of the prefatory biography includes material and occasionally employs a tone better suited for comic fiction or satire. The post-1696 versions of the biography are distinguished by epistolary narratives that can only be read as fiction, or as highly fictionalized autobiography, in which Behn ostensibly features herself as the heroine of comic romantic intrigues. In one case, she is addressed by a Dutchman who likens her to a ship in over-the-top, parodic language:

> thy Nose like her Rudder, that steers my Desires, thy Mouth the well-wrought Mortar, whence the Granado's of thy Tongue are shot into the Gun-room of my Heart, and shatter it to pieces; thy Teeth are the grappling Irons that fasten me to my Ruin, and of which I wou'd get clear in vain . . . ('History' 16).

Picking up this light tone, the biographer interprets the amorous attentions of yet another Dutchman as proof that '[t]hey are mistaken who imagine that a *Dutch*-man can't love; it sometimes happens that Love does penetrate their Lump' ('History' 5).[9] In this early biography, then, we find Behn not only re-inscribed in her own fiction by way of the Oroonoko rumor, but also inscribed in epistolary fictions that may have been the creation of nearly anyone: Behn, 'One of the Fair Sex,' or someone who might have assisted 'her' efforts by contributing what Montague Summers described as 'imaginative and invented flotsam [that] accumulated and were heaped about the memory of Aphra Behn' (1:xv-xvi). Just as Behn fictionalized elements of the 'true history' of Oroonoko's 'life,' so did the author of Behn's 'History' contribute to the fictionalizing of her 'life.'[10]

   Conversely, Behn scholars have also culled her fiction for biographical information. The premise that *Oroonoko* is not entirely fictional and that there are indeed some important autobiographical elements in the text is as meaningful for biographers today as it was for the author of the 'History,' but the *manner* in which the 'History' makes an absolute equation between Behn the author and the narrator of *Oroonoko* mark it as very much a product of its time, the post-Behn 1690s. To set the stage, the 'fair' biographer first employs a then-current literary convention, claiming that Behn 'lisped in numbers' like Pope: 'ev'n in the first Bud of Infancy at the first Use almost of Reason in Discourse, she wou'd write the prettiest, soft engaging Verses in the World' (2). However, the member of the 'fair sex' stretches this convention in a manner that marks the piece as being particularly of its time, by suggesting that her subject was precocious in other, more gendered and sexualized ways.

   Behn is described as leaving England for Surinam, the setting of *Oroonoko*, at a tender but provocative age. (According to the work of recent biographers, Behn would have been in her early twenties at the time *Oroonoko* takes place.) As this biographer would have it, when 'our Future Heroine, and Admir'd *Astrea*,' her father's 'promising Darling,' departs for Surinam, she

> leav[es] behind her the Sighs and Tears of all her Friends, and breaking Hearts of her Lovers, that sigh'd to possess, what was scarce yet arriv'd to a Capacity of easing their Pain, if she had been willing. But as she was Mistress of uncommon Charms of Body, as well as Mind, she gave infinite and raging Desires,

before she cou'd know the least her self. (2)

After introducing a gender-defined, sexualized variation on the theme of a
young poet's 'promise,' the author of the 'History' praises Behn for removing
Oroonoko from obscurity by granting him 'immortality' through her eye-
witness account, and then carries on to present 'her' ostensible 'vindication'
of Behn against accusations of sexual misconduct. Just as Behn has assured
Oroonoko's fame by publicly recording his 'vertues and constancy,' so her
biographer attempts to rescue Behn's character and restore her good name:

> The Misfortunes of that Prince had been unknown to us, if the
> Divine *Astrea* had not been there, and his Sufferings had wanted
> that Satisfaction which her Pen has given 'em in the Immortality of
> his Vertues, and Constancy; the very Memory of which, move a
> generous Pity in all, and a Contempt of the brutal Actors in that
> unfortunate Tragedy. Here I can add nothing to what she has given
> the World already, but a Vindication of her from some unjust
> Aspersions I find, are insinuated about this Town in Relation to
> that Prince. I knew her intimately well; and I believe she wou'd
> not have conceal'd any Love-Affair from me, being one of her own
> Sex, whose Friendship and Secrecy she had experienc'd; which
> makes me assure the World, there was no Affair between that
> Prince and *Astrea*, but what the whole Plantation were Witness of:
> A generous Value for his uncommon Vertues, which every one
> that but hears 'em, finds in himself; and his Presence gave her no
> more. Besides, his Heart was too violently set on the everlasting
> Charms of his *Imoinda*, to be shook with those more faint (in his
> Eye) of a white Beauty . . . (2-3)

Having reminded the reader of cultural differences in perceptions of female
beauty, as further refutation (and to underscore her subject's tender age), the
female friend offers the assurance that the young Aphra Behn's 'Relations,
there present, had too watchful an Eye over her to permit the Frailty of her
Youth, if that had been powerful enough' (3). With a few strokes of the pen,
the author of the 'History' manages in this passage to re-enforce 'her' identity
as female and as a particular friend of Behn, just as 'she' did at the opening of
the 'History':

> My intimate Acquaintance with the Admirable *Astrea*, gave me,
> naturally, a very great Esteem for her; for it both freed me from that

Folly of my Sex, of envying or slighting Excellencies I cou'd not
obtain; and inspir'd me with a noble Fire to celebrate that Woman,
who was an Honour and Glory to our Sex . . . (1).

In the course of recounting and refuting the Oroonoko rumor, the biographer
bolsters the verisimilitude of (and the 'History's' connections to) one of
Behn's own histories that will follow this prefatory essay. Just as Behn surely
knew Oroonoko and knew him well (but not *too* well), we are assured that the
biographer knew Behn 'intimately well.' Noting that *Othello*, the most
popular Shakesperian drama of the Restoration, had rendered exotic interracial
relationships 'glamourous' by this point (despite connotations of
'whorishness' found in lampoons), Janet Todd declares, 'The "Memoirs" was
aimed at a sophisticated readership' and suggests that the biography's
Oroonoko rumor served to 'spice' the novel's plot (*Secret Life* 37).

This anonymous text demonstrates that the fictionalizing of Behn and
the role of the literary biographer as understood in 1696 are intricate,
intertwined topics. Gildon's idea that Behn's biographer must be able to
'write like her,' i.e., as a kind of textual hermaphrodite whose style is both
masculine and feminine, with both 'softness' and 'fire,' implies that if the
biographer can replicate her style of writing he can then capture the author
herself, create a word portrait, 'draw her to the life.' In this prescription, the
female author's style and her identity are conflated, as are the tasks of the
biographer and the fiction writer. It is at least as likely, then, that a savvy and
enterprising hack along the lines of Charles Gildon may have constructed such
an Aphra Behn, as it is that a woman once close to the author strove publicly
to restore her dead friend's good character. In this light, it makes perfect
sense to include this 'anonymous life' of Behn in a list of mostly fictional
'defenses of dubious virtue' that encompasses the work of Madame d'Aulnoy,
Eliza Heywood, and Delariviere Manley (Stauffer, *Art* 72).

Regardless of her creator's identity, this pubescent Behn who is
capable of eliciting 'raging Desires' before she is old enough to experience
them herself is a Behn for the nineties, the 1690s. The precocious heart-
breaker, 'Mistress of uncommon Charms of Body as well as Mind,' who, we
are asked to believe, was really too young to have had a 'Love-Affair' with
Oroonoko, is disturbingly reminiscent of the very young actresses who recited
sexually tantalizing prologues and epilogues, reciting a kind of 'kiddie porn,'
in the plays of Behn herself and others in the 1670s (Greer et al. 405). After a

lull in the 1680s, the practice was revived, beginning in 1696 (the same year as the first appearance of the 'History' – then called 'Memoirs'), in the work of playwrights like Mary Pix, George Powell, and Delariviere Manley. For example, in Manley's *The Royal Mischief* (1696), a very young Mistress Bradshaw entices the audience with these lines:

> Nor think those Youthful Joys I have in store,
> Far distant Promises, unripen'd Oar,
> Meer Fairy-Treasure, which you can't Explore:
> The Play-House is a Hot-Bed to young Plants,
> Early supplies your Longings and your Wants. (Greer et al. 404)

This Lolita-like Behn is a function of what has been called the 'merchandizing' of the author we know as Aphra Behn (Greer, 'How to Invent a Poet', 7). An enticing image of the female author, whether as provocative ingenue or as passionate mature woman of letters, was part of the pitch, an element of the hype that began in Behn's own lifetime, encouraged by Behn herself, and carried on into the decade after her death and beyond (Gallagher). Paula McDowell has recently made the important suggestion that the late-seventeenth-century emergence of literary biography 'should be seen as a function of a burgeoning publishing industry' and that 'early literary lives were an entrepreneurial technique – designed primarily to encourage interest in, and boost sales of, an author's *works*,' citing the 1696 Behn 'Memoirs' as an example (222).[11]

We can see that whether male or female, hack or woman friend, the author of the 'History' was clearly engaged in the task of marketing Behn. As a Behn merchandizer, the 'fair sex' biographer seems to be of the same school as the biography's first publisher, Samuel Briscoe, as well as John Dunton, both notorious 'literary pimps' who, beginning in the 1690s, were quick to capitalize on the titillating possibilities presented by young women like Catherine Trotter and Elizabeth Singer who 'exposed' themselves publicly in print, writing quite personally (presumably) on the subject of love, in letters and in verse (Greer, 'Honest Sam. Briscoe' 34-35 and Medoff). In the last decade of the seventeenth century, when Behn's precedent for the next generation of women writers was well in place, the pioneering author and her successors were together the subjects of marketing strategies that conflated the availability of the author's text with the potential 'availability' of the author herself.

The ways in which the 'fair' biographer played on 'her' subject's sexuality and reputation were complex, and that complexity is sustained throughout the 'History.' The biography concludes very much as it began: citing the enviousness traditionally ascribed to women; reiterating a 'malicious' rumor in order to refute it; praising Behn's finer qualities; defending her against imputations of 'unbecoming' behavior; and finally, underscoring the intimacy between biographer and subject. 'One of the Fair Sex' attributes to 'the Envious of our Sex, and the Malicious of the other' the rumor that 'a very ingenious Gentleman' (whom scholars identify as either Behn's one-time lover, John Hoyle, probably Lycidas of the 'Love Letters to a Gentleman', or Edward Ravenscroft) was the real author of Behn's work.[12] Employing what Todd has called a 'gendered notion of art' (*Critical Fortunes* 27), 'she' protests that the works were Behn's 'own Product' because of their naturalness (50). Having detailed some of Behn's qualities, 'a generous and open Temper' as well as 'Wit, Honour, Good-humour, and Judgment,' and having described Behn as a 'Woman of Sense, and by consequence a Lover of Pleasure,'[13] the biographer closes with a spirited and colorful defense of Behn's 'modesty,' reminding readers of 'her' reliability as a direct source but tantalizingly pulling the 'veil' around her own identity:

> For my part, I knew her intimately, and never saw ought unbecoming the just Modesty of our Sex, tho more gay and free than the Folly of the Precise will allow. She was, I'm satisfy'd, a greater Honour to our Sex than all the canting Tribe of Dissemblers, that die with the false Reputation of Saints. This I may venture to say, because I'm unknown, and the revengeful Censures of my Sex will not reach me, since they will never be able to draw the Veil, and discover the Speaker of these bold Truths. (51)[14]

Nearly forty years after Behn was first 'promoted' as a nubile narrator, 'vindicated' in a manner that erased boundaries between English author and African subjects, and set up as an 'honour' to her sex, the Oroonoko 'triangle' was resurrected and Behn re-romanticized in *The General Dictionary* (1734-1741). The first serious critical biography of Behn, hitherto rarely examined, appears in the form of a long entry in this popular ten-volume work.[15] Though this biography shares with the 'History' a question of uncertain authorship as well as an exploitive view of Behn as female author, there are differences in generic formulations and, of course, the moments in literary history at which each appeared.[16] The *General Dictionary* biographer affords 'the tender History of Oroonoko' only a brief mention in the body of the entry, but his footnote on the few lines in the text, on the other hand, runs over two pages, (140-41). The form and structure of the entire entry on Behn betray this self-conscious scholarship, overtaken as it is by the apparatus; copious glosses, footnotes, marginal citations alongside the footnotes, critical commentary everywhere, much like other entries in the *Dictionary*. In his efforts to write a critical biography the author drew on or quoted from (and this is merely a partial list): 'The History;' Charles Gildon's lesser-known biography of Behn prefixed to the posthumous edition of her play, *The Younger Brother* (1696); Behn's novels themselves; a 1702 edition of her plays; various late-seventeenth and early eighteenth-century miscellanies containing Behn's poetry (including miscellanies edited by Behn herself); Thomas Southerne's dramatic adaptations of Behn's novels, and biographical and dramatic compendia assembled by Edward Philips, Gerard Langbaine, Charles Gildon and Giles Jacob.

However, the biographer was not without his own tendencies to imaginative writing and ruminations. Within the long commentary on *Oroonoko* he provides a synopsis of the plot, dutifully paraphrases the rumor and its refutation from the 'History,' which he acknowledges having read in the 1722 edition of Behn's *Histories and Novels*, and then counters that refutation, attempting to re-instate the possibility of an interracial relationship between Behn and Oroonoko with a Eurocentric view of female beauty:

> Oroonoko appears to have had an uncommon fondness for Imoinda; and if it was so great as Mrs. Behn has related, there is no probability that he could have had a passion for her; unless we suppose, that possibly the sight of so beautiful a white woman, might efface the idea of the charms he till then had found in his Imoinda, and substituted that of our Poetess in its stead. This to some, considering the violence of Oroonko's love for Imoinda, and the contrast of their complexions, might appear next to a miracle: but might not this contrast excite a certain curiosity, and are not miracles daily wrought by love? (Birch 3:141)[17]

Unlike the 'History,' this 'life' gives Behn pre-eminence over her own character, Imoinda, in the amatory competition between female observer/

recorder of a slave narrative and the female slave herself, the young Englishwoman and the pregnant African princess, the presumed family friend and the much-beloved wife, creator and created, the colonial and the kidnapped.

In this case, the emphasis is as much on Behn's whiteness as it is on her femaleness, while the age issue all but disappears. Indeed, race and gender in this hypothetical scenario are inseparable: European woman and African man meet in the New World, and the 'contrast of their complexions' leads to a 'certain curiosity,' i.e., sexual attraction, which is a 'miracle wrought by love.'[18] In the long *Oroonoko* commentary, which quotes extensively from the 'History,' the biographer initiates a 'dialogue' with an unknown predecessor of an earlier generation, going beyond mere compilation and summary to engage in his own speculations, on both the ostensible subject at hand (Behn) and on the powers of cultural and sexual difference. In fact, the biographer reaches even further back than the 'History,' all the way to the text of *Oroonoko* itself; his 'dialogue' is also with Behn. The biographer not only re-inscribes Behn in an old rumor, but rewrites his subject's fiction, undercutting the narrator's attestations of Oroonoko's 'uncommon' love for Imoinda and therefore undermining his subject's own authority as author. Although he first admits, 'If [Oroonoko's fondness] was so great as Mrs. Behn has related' it would have been impossible for Oroonoko to 'have had a passion for Behn,' he then posits the possibility that Oroonoko's loyalty to his wife may not have been quite as Behn described, thus giving primacy to Behn-as-lover over Behn-as-narrator or Behn-as-author. Though writing in a later age that had a developing sense of literary biography as a discipline, in some respects the *General Dictionary* biographer made use of his subject in a manner not unlike his predecessor's. Forty years on, Behn was still putty in her biographer's hands.[19]

Pronouncing *Oroonoko* as 'the best of Mrs. Behn's pieces,' he defends the plausibility of a 'savage African express[ing] himself in so tender and witty a manner,' with characteristic Eurocentricity as he reminds the reader that Oroonoko had been educated by a Frenchman, and then attempts to bridge the gap between cultures and races, albeit still in xenophobic and racist terms:

A difference of colour does not make any difference in the soul; and tho' some nations of Blacks appear incorrigible brutes, there

yet are others who discover a natural fund of wit and genius; and
we had but a few years since a Black, who made great
improvements in Languages, the polite Arts, and Mathematics . . .
(Birch 3:141)[20]

The biographer also accounts for Oroonoko's eloquence and Behn's ability to
draw 'the passion of love with great delicacy and softness' by suggesting that
Behn was 'herself so susceptible of the fond passion of love' and therefore 'no
doubt she heightened the expressions of her Hero, on this and other
occasions.' The 'heightened' representations of Oroonoko's speech are
attributed not to the author's artistry then, but to her own passionate nature.

If the Oroonoko rumor reinforced the image of Behn as passionate
female from 1696 through 1735 (and beyond), then certainly autobiographical
interpretations of her other works, especially the love poetry, played at least
an equal part. Just as he attributed Oroonoko's moving amatory expressions
to Behn's own disposition, so too did the *General Dictionary* biographer
attribute Behn's skill in love lyrics to her personality and private experience,
rather than to her art. The precedent had been set not long after Behn's death,
when it became common for editors and critics to ignore entirely the concept
of a persona, or any number of other literary conventions, as they commented
on Behn's amatory verse, conflating the love-struck speaker and the poet
without acknowledging mediating factors like artistic control or prosodic
mastery. In May, 1707, the short-lived *Muses Mercury* (1707-8) reprinted a
substantially revised version of Behn's 'The Dream. A Song,' first published
in *Poems on Several Occasions* (1684), a collection edited by Behn. Here
entitled 'Cupid in Chains,' the poem depicts a dream in which the female
persona converses with Cupid, who weeps because Amyntas has stolen his
bow and pinioned his wings. Asking only that Cupid wound Amyntas, she
sets him free and awakens to finds herself the wounded one. ('Amyntas' is
generally understood to designate Hoyle.) The editor finds Behn-as-poet and
Behn-as-lover inseparable:

> The Poem we now print under her name has something in it so
> soft, so amorous, so pretty, and so perfect, that it shews the Author
> to have been both a Poet and a Lover; both which Mrs. Behn was
> in a high Degree: few of her Sex having distinguish'd themselves
> more by their Wit and Amours than she has done. (111; rpt.
> O'Donnell 275)

In a later issue, the *Muses Mercury* editor ran another 'amorous' poem, 'made upon her Self and her very good Friend Mr. Hoyle,' that apparently needed to be revised in order to come 'within the Rules of Decency' (Dec. 1707, 273; rpt. O'Donnell 276).[21] Here, too, autobiographical readings during the fifty years after Behn's death tended to eschew serious considerations of Behn's artistry in favor of intensifying her erotic profile.

Like biographers and critics today, the *General Dictionary* biographer culls autobiographical elements from Behn's poetry (probably for the first time), but at the same time he reveals a particularly eighteenth-century sensibility by looking for evidence of Behn's presumed ruling passion, love, through literal readings of Behn's personae in passages that are not necessarily autobiographical revelations. To reinforce the veracity of the claim made in one of the Astrea-Lycidas letters, 'My soul is formed of no other material than love,' and to support his autobiographical reading of the letters, he cites Behn's paraphrase of the Lord's prayer, in which the speaker blames all her 'crimes' on 'soft bewitching love,' and reads *that* as pure autobiography as well (comparing this voice to that of Pope's Eloisa) (Birch 3:142). To substantiate his perception that 'this passion [love] entered into most of her compositions, or rather was the foundation of them all, and she was a perfect mistress of it,' he calls up Behn's commendatory poem prefixed to Thomas Creech's translation of Lucretius, in which she employs the standard device of deprecating her own skills:

> But I of feebler seeds design'd,
>   While the slow-moving atoms strove
> With careless heed to form my mind,
>   Compos'd it all of softer love. (Birch 3:146)

The biographer here commits a particularly egregious error by remaining blind to Behn's gendered play on the topos of the apologetic commender. Behn goes on to contrast her 'gentle Numbers' and 'Womanish Tenderness' with the 'Strong Manly Verse' such an undertaking requires; his reading of this section of the poem as the expression of an unmediated autobiographical voice is indicative of the skewed view of Behn early eighteenth-century critics were wont to adopt. They couldn't, or wouldn't, get the joke, but they did accept, wholesale, a public persona that Behn herself helped to create.[22]

The *General Dictionary* biographer's position on Behn's sexual reputation is problematic, entangled as it is with his era's general distaste for the license of an earlier age and an overall condescension toward women writers. The distinctions between the *General Dictionary* biographer's era and that of the 'History's' author, as well as the distinctions between the biographers themselves, are particularly obvious in the entry's comments on Gildon's dedication of the *Histories and Novels* (which first appeared in the 1698 edition) and on his life of Behn prefixed to *The Younger Brother* (1696). Taking at face value Gildon's claim to have been 'familiarly acquainted' with Behn, the biographer notes that Gildon 'speaks of her with enthusiasm' and quotes his lines about 'drawing her to the life' with the 'softness' of the female sex and the 'fire' of the male. Then he issues his caveat: 'But great deductions ought often to be made from the applauses of a Writer of our sex, when bestowed on a beautiful woman of genius, with whom he is intimate. Besides, Mr. Gildon's judgment will hardly pass for current with persons of good taste' (Birch 3:143). Despite his probably accurate warning regarding Gildon, the biographer betrays his own predilections in these remarks, apparently seduced himself by the image of Behn as a 'beautiful woman of genius' and preoccupied with other men's purported 'intimacies' with her.

The *General Dictionary* biographer's efforts to sort out Behn's 'virtue' continue. In the body of the entry he declares, 'Whether or no she was a woman of strict virtue, I shall not take upon me to determine,' but he considers her comedies to be wanting in 'moral instruction' and cites the Lycidas letters as evidence that she 'was of a very tender and amorous cast' (Birch 3:145). He then pronounces on what he imagines to have been Lycidas's awkward position:

> to be adored by a Poetess, and at the same time not value her, must subject the lover to no little perplexity; such languishing Ladies never cease to teize them (and no dunner can teize more) with billet-doux and messages, as long as they are able to set pen to paper. Love is ever predominant in their minds . . . (Birch 3:145)

In his lengthy gloss on these observations, he prissily cautions that he would 'by no means be understood, as though Lycidas had rifled the honey-comb of [her] sweets,' here apparently lapsing into a brief defense of Behn's honor, and describes Behn/Astrea as 'beautiful, witty, tender; in short, possessed of all the charms that could endear a woman to her lover.' He concludes by deeming another Astrea–Lycidas letter 'blasphemous rant' by 'a doating, distracted forsaken woman,' finding Lycidas 'a very Aeneas, and our Astrea a perfect Dido' (Birch 3:146).

In that instance, Behn/Astrea is romanticized and characterized as the epitome of the Ovidian heroine.[23] In a subsequent footnote, he seems to undercut his own assessment as well as his resolve not to pronounce on her honor by quoting a jibe from Steele's periodical, *The Lover*: '[Behn] understood the practic part of love better than the speculative' (Birch 3:146).[24] Elsewhere, he introduces the image of yet another Ovidian heroine, Sappho, and again appears to question Behn's honor when he repeats a slur from Delariviere Manley's *Memoirs of Europe* (1710) in which Behn, as 'Sappho the younger,' is described: 'owner of a soul as amorous as the elder, yet wanted much of that delicacy, and all that nice, yet darting spirit (of which hers is but a faint imitation) so applauded in Phaon's mistress.' Though admitting that, in the main, Manley's characterizations were 'not very famous for adhering to truth,' he suggests that in Behn's case, Manley gave a 'pretty just' character, but then qualifies that opinion by attributing Manley's malice to possible 'envy,' since 'Ladies can as ill bear a rival in the graces of the mind, as in those of the body, and for the very same reason' (Birch 3:143-4). In his efforts to assemble an Aphra (or 'Aphara') Behn, the biographer demonstrated a good deal of ambivalence – toward Behn, women writers, and women in general – not untypical of the time in which he wrote.[25] Not surprisingly, the abandoned women of antiquity seem to have taken possession of his biographical imagination.[26]

Regardless of his limitations, we must recognize that as a scholar of a later era, the *General Dictionary* biographer was helping to develop the relatively new genre of literary biography with a kind of self-consciousness about his task that the author of the 'History,' who ever he or she was, could not have shared. By 1735, non-prefatory literary biographies were beginning to proliferate, and compilations like the *General Dictionary* were 'the chief repositories of biographical knowledge concerning virtually all English authors who lived before 1700' (Altick 19). Unwilling simply to rehash what everyone who had read Behn's *Histories and Novels* – and with them the prefatory 'History' – already knew, the *General Dictionary* biographer rejected the paradoxical role of titillating vindicator adopted by the biographer of the 'History' and made an effort to put his own stamp on Behn's life. That 'stamp' included a view of poets' 'real' lives as being potentially as fascinating as fiction. In an attempt to make sense of the same fictional qualities in the embedded letters that would trouble the *Notes and Queries* reader in 1863 and that concern critics to this day, the *General Dictionary* biographer expressed the proto-Romantic view that poets and other artists are different from ordinary people, and therefore Behn's life, particularly as related in her amatory letters, could be understood as 'an improvement on romance.'

> It must be confessed, that some of the incidents here related, have very much the air of romance; but then it may be observed on the other side, that the real lives of some persons are even an improvement upon romance. No sett of people furnish us with more or stronger proofs of this assertion, than Poets, Painters and Musicians. (Birch 3:142)

The biographer leaves us with this final assessment: 'Her taste of life was perfectly Anacreontic. She was always for enjoying the present moment . . . ' (Birch 3:149).

These 'improvements upon romance' contributed to the mythmaking that prompted Altick to offer a warning about works like the *General Dictionary*: '[A]long with a certain hard residue of unassailable facts they transmitted a farrago of misinformation and legend that has taken two hundred years to straighten out. Qualifications usually fell by the wayside, and from acorns of hesitant speculation grew the oaks of confident affirmation' (19). We now know that a late seventeenth-century rumor about a cross-cultural, interracial romance between a Restoration writer and her protagonist Prince, as well as other speculations, survived well into the eighteenth century to become the stuff from which an early literary/critical biographer formulated his young art. Both touchstone and amorphous entity, Aphra Behn left a legacy that included her public and published 'self,' the problematic woman writer, the basis for more than one early literary 'life' that reads, at least in part, 'very like a fiction.'

Notes

Early versions of this study were delivered at the 1993 meeting of the Northeast Modern Language Association and the 1997 meeting of the Northeast American Society for Eighteenth-Century Studies. An abbreviated version was read at the International Conference on Aphra Behn in Paris, 1999, and will appear in the proceedings of the conference, *Aphra Behn: Identity, Alterity, Ambiguity*, edited by Bernard Dhuicq, Guyonne Leduc, and Mary Ann O'Donnell (Paris: Edition L'Harmattan, 2000). I am indebted to Mary Ann O'Donnell, Susan Hastings, and the editors of the present collection for invaluable assistance on this essay.

[1] For recent discussions of Behn's post-humous reputation, see Medoff, Goulding, and Spencer's thorough, incisive work, *Aphra Behn's Afterlife*.

[2] Regarding the genres of biography and novel, Stauffer notes that in the first half of the eighteenth century 'neither form can be fully understood without the other' (*Art* 65). While novelists imitated actual memoirs, they in turn showed biographers that 'the record of human life may be an art' and 'interpretation and appraisal' were more important than simply setting down facts (131).

[3] The portion of the 'History' that recounts and refutes this rumor is reprinted in the criticism section of J. Lipking's edition 191-92, from the 1696 text.

[4] In *The Secret Life of Aphra Behn*, Todd notes that 'the letters may be forgeries, used to fill up sheets in the volume and help sell Behn as a Tory wit and libertine,' and, while acknowledging that 'there is no firm evidence either way,' believes them likely to be genuine (467n6). Even if genuine, the question still remains whether or not they are fictional, though most recent critics read the letters as written in Behn's own voice. For recent critical discussions of these love letters, see Cherniak 139-40, Goreau 197-202, Martin 200-02, and Salvaggio 256-60.

[5] Gildon was first posited as the author of the biography by Ernest Bernbaum in 1913. R. A. Day later rejected Gildon as author of the expanded 1698 version of the Behn biography, citing a 'sentimental and superfluous comment on love,' as well as 'feminine flutters' as evidence of female authorship (230-31). Todd (*Works* 1:x), Greer ('Honest Sam. Briscoe' 39), Duffy (17), Cameron (88) and others accept Gildon as the biographer with varying degrees of certainty. Goreau, on the other hand, finds it 'more logical' to assume the biographer is a woman (10).

[6] All quotations from the biographical 'History' of Behn will be taken from this 1705 edition and referred to in the text as the 'History.' For the purposes of this essay, it is important to distinguish between the 1696 version and subsequent versions of the prefatory biography, hence the distinct

designations 'Memoirs' and 'History.' O'Donnell's bibliography records seven editions of the *History and Novels* from 1700 to 1751.

[7] Janet Todd's recent biography, *The Secret Life of Aphra Behn*, makes frequent references to the 'Memoirs.' See also Jones. For a discussion of both the 'Memoirs' and the 'History,' see Todd, *Works* 1:xi-xiii.

[8] Altick notes that until the late seventeenth century, 'the term "literary biography" would have been meaningless, simply because no one as yet conceived of authorship as a distinct, or at least respectable, occupation.' He dates the appearance of separate, non-dictionary literary biographies to the time of Dryden and Pope, when authorship was developing into a profession (10-11).

[9] The most detailed and helpful source for sorting out fact from fiction in this biographical preface is Cameron's monograph, which posits Behn's possible lover, William Scott, as the real-life equivalent of one of the Dutch suitors. See also Mendelson 122-23, Jones 317, and Todd, *Secret Life* 109-110.

[10] Remarking on both the 'mysterious' expansion of the 1696 'Memoirs' to the 1698 'History' and the addition of three hitherto unpublished tales to the 1698 edition of the *Histories and Novels*, Greer asserts, 'Not content with inventing Behn's text (for this should be assumed to be the case until some less questionable provenance can be found) Gildon was also inventing her' ('Honest Sam. Briscoe' 39).

[11] Stauffer attributes the popularity of prefatory literary biographies in the seventeenth century to 'curiosity concerning the authors of popular books' (*English Biography* 267) and remarks that they served a double purpose, as both 'apologies and introductions' (268). Altick dates the proliferation of prefatory biographies to 'shortly after the middle of the seventeenth century.' Though he notes that 'in this form the fragmentary life stories of certain well-regarded authors were transmitted from generation to generation,' he locates the 'principal chain of biographical tradition' in biographical dictionaries (16).

[12] Todd records that this allegation was repeated in an entry on Behn published in the *Biographia Britannica* (1747), but mistakenly considers the entry's author to be 'original in insisting that it derived from jealous women' (*Critical Fortunes* 36). In fact, the author, Thomas Broughton, was merely paraphrasing the biographical 'History.'

[13] Todd notes the 'History's' 'effort to exploit Behn as a generous and free-living woman' (*Critical Fortunes* 27).

[14] Cameron dismisses both the refutation of the Oroonoko rumor and the

refutation of the authorship rumor as 'word-spinning.' He regards the 'main intention' of the last paragraph of the 'History' to be 'to establish the biographer as an intimate friend of Aphra Behn' (87-88) and bemoans the work of 'ill-informed and even malicious contemporaries who purported to write biographies shortly after her death' (100).

[15] The only notices this biography has received to date are in Todd, *The Critical Fortunes* (33-35) and in Henry's dissertation on the *General Dictionary* (185-192). O'Donnell's bibliography notes a 1750 French translation of the biographical entry published in Amsterdam. Two forthcoming works, O'Donnell's revised, second edition of the Behn bibliography and Spencer's *Aphra Behn's Afterlife*, examine this biography. References to this text will be cited by the name of the principal editor of the dictionary in which it appears, Thomas Birch.

[16] Like the 'History' of Behn, there is some question as to the authorship of this *General Dictionary* biographical/critical entry, first published in 1735. James Marshall Osborn claimed the Behn entry for one of the *Dictionary*'s editors, John Lockman (32; 41). More recently, J. Patrick Lee detects strong indications that Lockman is the author, citing numerous self-referential remarks in the *General Dictionary* entry (private correspondence, 10 April 1999). For further discussion of Lockman and the *General Dictionary* Behn entry, see Henry 185-192. On the other hand, one of the contributors to the *General Dictionary*, William Oldys (later general editor of the first edition of the *Biographia Britannica* and co-editor of the *Harleian Miscellany*), appears to claim authorship of the entry in marginal notes to his copy of Langbaine's *An Account of the Dramatick Poets* (1691), now held at the British Library (BL C28.g.1, 17). The same notation is repeated verbatim in some of Oldys's manuscript notes, later published in the nineteenth century (*Notes and Queries* 2nd series, XI, March, 1861,161; rpt. Yeowell 48). As contributors to *The General Dictionary*, Oldys and Lockman were certainly acquainted and may have collaborated. Oldys' diary records a 1737 conversation with Lockman about the latter's *General Dictionary* entry on *Hudibras* (*Notes and Queries*, 2nd Ser., XI, February, 1861, 102). The question awaits resolution through further research; in this essay, the author of the *General Dictionary* Behn entry will be unnnamed.

[17] For interpretations of the competition between the narrator/author and Imoinda based on the text of the novel and not the rumor, see both of Ferguson's essays as well as Sussman 228-30.

[18] It is possible that the *General Dictionary* biographer was influenced in his rewriting of *Oroonoko* by the popularity of Thomas Southerne's dramatic adaptation of Behn's novel, in which Imoinda is a white woman. He neglects to mention that Behn had treated the subject of interracial romance in an earlier work, *Abdelazer, or the Moor's Revenge*, probably because he gave scant attention to her plays, except to list their titles, and to use Steele's *Spectator* castigation of Behn, Pix, and other 'luscious' female playwrights as a platform for his own attack on the 'stupid ribaldry' of the stage in his own time (Birch 3:145). Spencer astutely observes that although eighteenth-century men of letters disdained Behn's works and disparaged her character, her plays, though 'diluted,' remained popular and influential.

[19] In the conclusion of the entry, the biographer recounts a conversation with Mr Bowman, a comedian of the Theatre Royal, who had known Behn. According to the old actor, she was uncommonly sprightly in her conversation, agreeable in her person, and 'of a very graceful stature.' When the biographer expressed doubt as to whether Behn's Oroonoko was a real individual, Bowman assured him that 'she always spoke so tenderly of Oroonoko, that it was impossible for him to have been a fictitious person' and that she 'always represented him as a miracle with regard to the graces both of body and mind' (Birch 3:149). William Oldys' manuscript notes also record information on Behn obtained from Bowman (Yeowell 50).

[20] The most likely candidate for the 'Black' to whom this passage refers would be Ayuba Suleiman Diallo, known as Job ben Solomon, who visited England in 1733 as a guest of the Royal African Company, after two years of slavery in Maryland. Taken up by Sir Hans Sloane's circle, he was elected an honorary member of the Gentleman's Society of Spalding, a distinguished antiquarian group. His 1734 'Memoirs' were written by Thomas Bluett. See Fryer 421-22. I am grateful to Brycchan Carey for this identification.

[21] The *Muses Mercury* editor claimed to be working from a manuscript in Behn's hand (which is no longer extant). Todd notes that it is therefore impossible to know just how the editor revised the poem for publication in his serial. Comparing the *Muses Mercury* text to versions of the poem printed during Behn's lifetime, Todd finds only one variant that could be interpreted as rendering the poem more 'decent,' and suggests that the editor was deliberately 'exaggerating the sexual content' of the poem (*Works* 1:375).

[22] More recently, Behn's lines contrasting 'Strong Manly Verse' with 'Womanish Tenderness' have been read as a 'formulation of the internalized

split involved in being a woman writer' (Saltzman 123). Warren Cherniak correctly warns against 'tak[ing] the modesty *topos* or the conventional hyperbole of commendatory poems literally,' but notes that these lines 'come uncomfortably close to suggesting a hierarchical view by which women fall short of a masculine ideal of perfection' (168).

For a nuanced and sophisticated discussion of 'mixed messages' and 'meditation[s] on the problems of identity' in the poetry of one of Behn's female contemporaries, see Kathryn King's forthcoming book on Jane Barker.

[23] Greer and Hastings note that Dido was a popular subject for late seventeenth-century poets like Denham, Tate, Dryden, and Anne Wharton (311).

[24] This remark from issue number 23 of *The Lover* is not noted in the first edition of O'Donnell's bibliography nor in Todd's *Critical Fortunes*.

[25] The Reverend Andrew Kippis, revising the Behn entry for the second edition of the *Biographia Britannica* in 1780, castigates the *General Dictionary* biographer for relying on 'testimonies from authors whose judgment is of little weight' (apparently overlooking quotations from Dryden, Southerne and others), and points to another aspect of the biographer's ambivalence, '[T]hough he allows her to have been a genius, [he] will not grant that she was of the first or perhaps second rate' (Kippis 146).

[26] At one point the *General Dictionary* biographer does compare Behn to Ovid himself, rather than to his heroines: 'the celebrated Love Letters between a Nobleman and his sister that has been laid under the pillow of many an amorous nymph is perhaps as well calculated to inspire a fond passion, as the more delicate writings of Ovid or Heloise' (Birch 3:148).

Works Cited

Altick, Richard D. *Lives and Letters: A History of Literary Biography in England and America.* New York: Knopf, 1965.

Behn, Aphra. *The Histories and Novels of the Late Ingenious Mrs. Behn: In One Volume.* London: S[amuel] Briscoe, 1696.

_____. *All the Histories and Novels Written by the Late Ingenious Mrs. Behn, Entire in One Volume.* London: Samuel Briscoe, 1698.

_____. *All the Histories and Novels Written by the Late Ingenious Mrs. Behn, Entire in One Volume.* London: R. Wellington, 1705.

_____. *The Younger Brother: Or, The Amorous Jilt.* London: J. Harris, 1696.

Birch, Thomas, et al, eds. *A General Dictionary, Historical and Critical.* 10 vols. London, 1734-41.

Bernbaum, Ernest. 'Mrs. Behn's Biography a Fiction.' *PMLA* 28 (1913): 432-53.

Cameron, W. J. *New Light on Aphra Behn.* Auckland: U of Auckland, 1961.

Chernaik, Warren. *Sexual Freedom in Restoration Literature.* Cambridge: Cambridge UP, 1995.

Dhuicq, Bernard, Guyonne Leduc, and Mary Ann O'Donnell, eds. *Aphra Behn: Identity, Alterity, Ambiguity.* Paris: L'Harmattan. Forthcoming.

Day, Robert Adams. 'Aphra Behn's First Biography.' *Studies in Bibliography* 22 (1969): 227-40.

Duffy, Maureen. *The Passionate Shepherdess.* New York: Avon Books, 1977.

Ferguson, Margaret. 'Juggling the Categories of Race, Class and Gender: Aphra Behn's *Oroonoko*.' *Women's Studies* 19 (1991): 159-81.

_____. 'Miscegenous Romance in Aphra Behn's *Oroonoko* and *The Widow Ranter*.' *The Production of English Renaissance Culture.* eds. David Lee Miller, Sharon O'Dair and Harold Weber. Ithaca: Cornell UP, 1994. 151-89.

Fryer, Peter. *Staying Power: The History of Black People in Britain.* London: Pluto Press, 1984.

Gallagher, Catherine. 'Who Was That Masked Woman? The Prostitute and the Playwright in the Comedies of Aphra Behn.' Hutner 65-85.

Goulding, Susan. 'Publishing the Literary Authority of a Woman Writer: The Case of Astrea and Orinda.' Paper presented at the 1997 meeting of the Modern Language Association.

Goreau, Angeline. *Reconstructing Aphra: A Social Biography of Aphra Behn.* New York: Dial, 1980.

Greer, Germaine. 'Honest Sam. Briscoe.' *A Genius for Letters: Booksellers and Bookselling from the 16th to the 20th Century.* eds. Robin Myers and Michael Harris. New Castle: Oak Knoll Press, 1995. 33-47.

_____. 'How to Invent a Poet.' Rev. of *Poems By Ephelia (c. 1679)*, ed. Maureen E. Mulvihill. *TLS* 25 (1993): 7-8.

Greer, Germaine, Susan Hastings, Jeslyn Medoff and Melinda Sansone, eds. *Kissing the Rod:*

An Anthology of Seventeenth-Century Women's Verse. New York: Farrar, Straus, and Giroux, 1989.

Greer, Germaine and Susan Hastings, eds. *The Surviving Works of Anne Wharton*. Stump Cross: Stump Cross Books, 1997.

Henry, Rolanne. 'A *General Dictionary* (1734-1741).' Diss. Columbia U, 1972.

Hutner, Heidi, ed. *Rereading Aphra Behn: History, Theory, and Criticism*. Charlottesville: U P of Virginia, 1993.

Jones, Jane. 'New Light on the Background and Early Life of Aphra Behn.' *Notes and Queries*, Nov. 1990; rpt. *Aphra Behn Studies*, ed. Todd. 310-20.

King, Kathryn. *Jane Barker*. Oxford: Oxford UP. Forthcoming.

Kippis, Andrew, ed. *Biographia Britannica: or, the Lives of the Most Eminent Persons who have flourished in Great Britain and Ireland*. London: C. Bathurst, et al, 1780.

L., J. A. 'Mrs. Behn.' *Notes and Queries* 3rd ser., 3 (1863): 368.

Langbaine, Gerard. *An Account of the English Dramatick Poets*. Oxford, 1691.

Lipking, Joanna, ed. *Oroonoko*. By Aphra Behn. 1688. New York: W. W. Norton, 1997.

Martin, Roberta C. '"Beauteous Wonder of a Different Kind": Aphra Behn's Destabilization of Sexual Categories.' *College English* 61 (1998): 192-210.

McDowell, Paula. 'Consuming Women: The Life of the "Literary Lady" As Popular Culture In Eighteenth-Century England.' *Genre* 26 (1993): 219-52.

Medoff, Jeslyn. 'The Daughters of Behn and the Problem of Reputation.' *Women, Writing, History, 1640-1740*. eds. Isobel Grundy and Susan Wiseman. Athens: U of Georgia P, 1992. 33-54.

Mendelson, Sara Heller. *The Mental World of Stuart Women: Three Studies*. Amherst: U of Massachusetts P, 1987.

O'Donnell, Mary Ann. *Aphra Behn: An Annotated Bibliography of Primary and Secondary Sources*. New York: Garland, 1986.

_____. *Aphra Behn: An Annotated Bibliography of Primary and Secondary Sources*. 2nd. edn. Burlington, VT: Ashgate. Forthcoming.

Osborn, James Marshall. 'Thomas Birch and the *General Dictionary* (1734-41).' *Modern Philology* 36 (1938): 25-46.

Salvaggio, Ruth. 'Aphra Behn's Love: Fiction, Letters, and Desire.' Hutner 253-70.

Salzman, Paul. 'Aphra Behn: Poetry and Masquerade.' *Aphra Behn Studies*. ed. Todd. 130-153.

Spencer, Jane. *Aphra Behn's Afterlife*. Oxford: Oxford UP. Forthcoming.

Stauffer, Donald. *The Art of Biography in Eighteenth Century England*. 1941. rpt. New York: Russell and Russell, 1970.

_____. *English Biography Before 1700*. 1930. New York: Russell and Russell, 1964.

Summers, Montague, ed. *The Works of Aphra Behn*. 5 vols. 1915. New York: Phaeton Press, 1967.

Sussman, Charlotte. 'The Other Problem with Women: Reproduction and Slave Culture in Aphra Behn's *Oroonoko*.' Hutner 212-33.

Todd, Janet, ed. *Aphra Behn Studies*. Cambridge: Cambridge UP, 1996.

_____. *The Critical Fortunes of Aphra Behn*. Columbia: Camden House, 1998.

_____. *The Secret Life of Aphra Behn.* New Brunswick: Rutgers UP, 1996.
_____. ed. *The Works of Aphra Behn.* 7 vols. Columbus: Ohio State UP, 1992-96.
Yeowell, Thomas. *A Literary Antiquary: Memoir of William Oldys, Esq.* London, 1862.

Notes on Contributors

URSULA APPELT is an Assistant Professor of English literature at the State University of New York, Stony Brook. Her research interests include early modern women writers, as well as economic theory. She is completing a book on the connections between historiography and colonialism in the early modern period.

MARGARET J. M. EZELL is the John Paul Abbott Professor of Liberal Arts at Texas A&M University and the author of *The Patriarch's Wife: Literary Evidence and the History of Family* (1987), *Writing Women's Literary History* (1993), and *Social Authorship and the Advent of Print* (1999). She has edited *The Poetry and Prose of Mary, Lady Chudleigh* (1993), and is co-editor of the forthcoming *English Manuscript Studies 1500-1700* special edition on early modern women and manuscript texts.

PAMELA HAMMONS received her Ph.D. from Cornell University and is currently an Assistant Professor of English literature at the University of Central Florida. Her essays on early modern women poets have appeared in *ELH* and *SEL*. She is completing a book on the relationship between seventeenth-century women's lyrical production and social change.

MARGARET P. HANNAY, Professor of English Literature at Siena College, has edited *The Collected Works of Mary Sidney Herbert, Countess of Pembroke* with Noel J. Kinnamon and Michael G. Brennan (1998). She is the author of *Philip's Phoenix: Mary Sidney, Countess of Pembroke* (1990) and editor of *Silent but for the Word: Tudor Women as Patrons, Translators, and Writers of Religious Works* (1985). With Susanne Woods she has edited *Teaching Tudor and Stuart Women Writers* (forthcoming).

CLARE R. KINNEY is Associate Professor of English at the University of Virginia. Her publications include *Strategies of Poetic Narrative: Chaucer, Spenser, Milton, Eliot* (1992) and articles on the Gawain poet, Sidney, Shakespeare, Marlowe, Anna Weamys, and the Renaissance perception of Chaucer.

JOAN PONG LINTON is Associate Professor of English at Indiana University and the author of *The Romance of the New World: Gender and the Literary Formation of English Colonialism* (1998). She is currently working on the cultural interplay between the stake and the stage as sites for the performance of agency.

JESLYN MEDOFF teaches American and British literature at the University of Massachusetts, Boston. She holds a Ph.D. from Rutgers University and is a co-editor of *Kissing the Rod: An Anthology of 17th Century Women's Verse* (1989). She has published essays on Aphra Behn, Sarah Fyge Egerton, Elizabeth Singer Rowe, Willa Cather, Elizabeth Bowen, and other women writers.

SHANNON MILLER is an Associate Professor of English at Temple University. She is the author of *Invested With Meaning: The Raleigh Circle in the New World* (1998), and of articles on Mary Wroth, Aemilia Lanyer, city comedy, and Shakespeare. Currently, she is working on a book project that examines the relationship between violence and social control in the work of early modern women writers.

JACQUELINE PEARSON is Professor of English Literature at the University of Manchester, England. Her research interests center on women's writing and reading, gender and intertextuality. She is the author of three books, most recently *Women's Reading in Britain 1750-1832: A Dangerous Recreation* (1999), and has published widely on Restoration women dramatists and other seventeenth- and nineteenth-century women writers, including Aemilia Lanyer, Aphra Behn, Mary Pix, Jane Barker, Frances Burney, and Maria Edgeworth. She is currently completing an edition of four plays of Susanna Centlivre.

BRONWEN PRICE is senior lecturer in English at Portsmouth University,

England. She has published widely on seventeenth-century poetry and has particular interests in early modern women's literature. She is editing a volume of new essays on Bacon's *New Atlantis*.

ANNE RUSSELL is Associate Professor of English at Wilfrid Laurier University, Waterloo, Canada. She has edited Aphra Behn's play *The Rover* (1994 and 1999) and is co-editor with Viviana Comensoli of *Enacting Gender on the English Renaissance Stage* (1999).

ANDREW SHIFFLETT holds a Ph.D. from Princeton University and is Assistant Professor of English at the University of South Carolina, where he teaches courses on sixteenth- and seventeenth-century literature. He is the author of *Stoicism, Politics, and Literature in the Age of Milton: War and Peace Reconciled* (1998) and of several essays on Renaissance topics. His current project is a book on the politics of forgiveness in early modern England.

BARBARA SMITH is Associate Professor of English at the College of Mount Saint Vincent in Riverdale, New York. She is the author of *The Women of Ben Jonson's Poetry: Female Representation in the Non-Dramatic Verse* (1995) and has co-edited with Alice Robertson *Teaching in the 21st Century: Adapting Writing Pedagogies to the College Curriculum* (1999). Research interests include women's writing, seventeenth-century literature, and writing theory and pedagogy.

HELEN WILCOX is Professor of English Literature at the University of Groningen, The Netherlands. Her research interests include Shakespeare, devotional poetry, and the works of early modern women writers. Among her publications are *Women and Literature in Britain 1500-1700* (1996) and *Betraying Our Selves: Forms of Self-Representation in Early Modern English Texts* (2000, co-edited with Henk Dragstra and Sheila Ottway).

Index